B+J
5/8/84
22.50

Europe in 1830

By the same author:

Revolution and Red Tape. The French Ministerial Bureaucracy, 1770–1850 (1981)
Practice and Perspective in Validation (editor; forthcoming)

Europe in 1830

Revolution and Political Change

CLIVE H. CHURCH

Senior Lecturer in European Studies
University of Kent at Canterbury

London
GEORGE ALLEN & UNWIN
Boston   Sydney

George Allen & Unwin (Publishers) Ltd,
40 Museum Street, London WC1A 1LU, UK

George Allen & Unwin (Publishers) Ltd,
Park Lane, Hemel Hempstead, Herts HP2 4TE, UK

Allen & Unwin, Inc.,
9 Winchester Terrace, Winchester, Mass. 01890, USA

George Allen & Unwin Australia Pty Ltd,
8 Napier Street, North Sydney, NSW 2060, Australia

First published in 1983.

094248

British Library Cataloguing in Publication Data

Church, Clive H.
  Europe in 1830.
1. Revolutions—Europe—History—1830–1848
I. Title
940.2′83   D385
ISBN 0-04-940067-3

Library of Congress Cataloging in Publication Data

Church, Clive H.
  Europe in 1830.
Bibliography: p.
Includes index.
1. Europe—Politics and government—1815–1848.
I. Title.
D385.C43 1983   940.2′82   83–11917
ISBN 0-04-940067-3

Set in 10 on 11 point Plantin by V & M Graphics Ltd, Aylesbury, Bucks
and printed in Great Britain by
Billing and Sons Ltd, London and Worcester

For Hilary and Joanna, and not forgetting Penny, who all lived through the revolutions in their various ways, in the hope that they may find this a convincing explanation of what it was all about

All these were caught in the net of the Doom of the Noldor; and they did great deeds which the Eldar remember still among the histories of the Kings of old.

J. R. R. Tolkien, *The Silmarillion*, p. 148

Contents

Preface

Some books have very precise origins, but I am no longer wholly certain where this one had its beginnings. And, the more people ask, the more my uncertainty grows. Certainly, a period teaching nineteenth-century European history in Dublin made me aware that there was a large gap in historical knowledge where 1830 was concerned – an awareness reinforced by the chance purchase there of the 'Symphonie funèbre et triomphale' by Berlioz. Then the persistent habit of the University of Lancaster Library of shelving Robert Demoulin's *La Révolution de 1830* under French history made me aware that there was a Belgian dimension to 1830, not to mention that Europe cannot be understood as an enlargement of France. An abortive plan to edit Cobbett's lectures on 1830 in a projected edition of his collected works played some part, too, no doubt. But probably more important than all this was a personal foible – the perverse appeal of something upon which historians have so consistently turned their backs. As R. G. Collingwood says in his *Autobiography*, 'Obscure provinces, like Roman Britain, always rather appeal to me. Their obscurity is a challenge; you have to invent new methods for studying them, and then you will probably find that the cause of the obscurity is in some defect in the methods hitherto used.'

Now, it may not be exactly true to say that methodology lies at the root of a century and a half of neglect, in which no full and comprehensive study of 1830 has apparently been written, unless, that is, professional and political obsessions with mononational history are really a methodological failing. Yet it is true that to try to remedy this neglect requires a pan-European approach. To this extent, the book also has roots in a developing interest in European Studies. However, such disregard can hardly be remedied by, or in, one volume. This book does not claim, therefore, to be more than a starting-point: a first survey in English of an obscure historical province, designed to present to students and teachers alike what has so far been revealed of the national contours, and attempting to place these in a wider context. It would, of course, have been nice to have had the book ready in time for the 150th anniversary of the events, but pressures of everyday academic life conspired against this. My consolation is that it has been at least twice as rapid in its gestation as my first book, on which it follows rather as Brahms's Second Symphony followed on his long-delayed First.

None the less, for such an introductory study it has incurred a vast number of debts over the years, partly because of the disparate nature of the subject itself. To begin with, I must thank my wife and daughters for their willingness to go where the revolution listed, whether the Continent or Canterbury – even when this demanded, in my wife's case, dividing up the remaining clean clothes on the dockside or nursing ailing cars home.

Hilary and Joanna have also had to sacrifice much of their fair share of fatherly attention while the book was being written. Anne Dalton has patiently typed not merely this, but other things as well, so that, as with Janet Howarth, the Secretary of the School of European Studies in Lancaster, I have always received unflagging help and tolerance in matters secretarial. The support of Keith Ashfield, of Allen & Unwin, has been equally appreciated.

A special word of thanks is also due to my former colleagues at Lancaster who have commented so helpfully on my preliminary drafts. Mark Wheeler, an *aficionado* of obscure Balkan provinces, gave unstinting care and attention to the final draft. In the case of Graham Bartram, Dick Geary and especially Jaroslav Krejčí I am equally grateful for the way they translated things for me, as did two undergraduates, Christine Brockwell and Elizabeth Kondur, and a number of Polish neighbours. I can only hope I have not traduced the nations and languages which they hold dear. The same gratitude is due to all the foreign colleagues who have offered their advice and knowledge, not to mention their hospitality. In Italy I received much kindness from Professors Emilia Morelli, Umberto Marcelli and Carlo Poni, just as I did from Robert Demoulin and others in Belgium and Albert Soboul in Paris. In particular the city of Lausanne has become a second home in more ways than one, thanks to François and Marie-Claude Jequier, whose help, interest and hospitality cannot be repaid by mere words. Similarly, in Switzerland I have been grateful for the support of Professors Gérald Arlettaz, Jean-Charles Biaudet and Guiseppe Martinola. In 1980 it was an equal tonic to meet so many foreign colleagues at the conferences on 1830 which took place in Bucharest and Leipzig, and I hope they will find some echoes of what I have learned from them in the pages which follow. Finally, on this personal note, I must not forget either the new generations of students at Lancaster, who not merely listened to lectures on the 'forgotten revolutions' but often shared in the explorations, or the many friends who provided me with hospitality while I was on my travels whether abroad, notably with Mike and Melanie Kirkwood, Gianni and Costanza Romano, and the Hulls, or in Lancaster *chez* Keith Wren.

Where more formal support is involved, the Nuffield Foundation, the Twenty-Seven Foundation and the Belgian and Italian governments, through the good offices of the British Council, provided funds for a first trip to Italy, Switzerland and Belgium in 1971. Then, in 1975, the British Academy and the Fondation Pro-Helvetia financed a further trip to France and Switzerland. Finally, the Academy again made funds available, this time thanks to that underrated and surprisingly co-operative body, the University Grants Committee, to support a last trip to all four countries in the autumn of 1978. I would like to thank them not just for the monies themselves, but also for the intellectual excitement of getting to know new places and historical problems which they made possible. I must acknowledge the way the Departments of French and History, and especially the School of European Studies, provided the leave and other facilities necessary.

Lastly, it has to be said that the whole thing would not have been possible. I must also acknowledge the way the Departments of French and Continent. In Bologna, the fact that the Archinginnasio Library and the Museo Civico del Primo e Secondo Risorgimento did not close their doors during a wave of academic strikes, and even, in the case of the latter under Dottoressa Lucetta Franzoni Gamberini and her charming staff, provided a home from home, was an immense relief. Access to the Archivio di Stato in Bologna, Modena and Parma, along with libraries like the Biblioteca Malatestiana in Cesena, the Biblioteca Communale in Forli and those of the University of Rome, was also much appreciated. In Belgium the Bibliothèque Royale in Brussels proved a marvellous place in which to work and make friends, while the Archives Générales du Royaume, the Archives de l'Etat à Namur and particularly the Archives de la Ville de Bruxelles all proved helpful. In Switzerland the Bibliothèque Cantonale et Universitaire and especially the Archives Cantonales Vaudoises under Mademoiselle Laurette Wettstein made working in Lausanne pleasant and rewarding. In the Ticino the same was true of the Archivio Cantonale in Bellinzona and the Biblioteca Cantonale in Lugano. Assistance was also provided by the Officio delle Ricerche Economiche in Bellinzona and the Bundesarchiv in Berne. In France the resources of the Bibliothèque Nationale and the Bibliothèque Cujas, amongst others, were appreciated as always. In this country access to the British Library, the University of London Library, the Institute of Historical Research, the Bodleian and, by no means least, the University of Lancaster Library was a *sine qua non* for completing the project.

Needless to say, none of these institutions or colleagues is in any way responsible for the imperfections in these pages. These are due solely to myself and my temerity in tackling a subject which most others have, understandably if wrongly, been willing to pass by and leave on the other side. The translations and maps are also very much my own. I hope that the latter will do something to remedy the failings in graphicacy which beset many writers on 1830 who assume a knowledge of European geography on the part of their readers which is far beyond their own.

Lancaster
Winter 1981–2   CLIVE H. CHURCH

List of Maps

The cover illustration is of a lithograph by the Füssli brothers of Zurich and is reproduced by kind permission of the Graphical Collection of the Zurich Central Library. It depicts an incident, referred to on page 68, during the conflict between the City of Basle and its rural subjects. The latter were protesting against the lack of real political change in the old canton after 1830. Hence, as is shown, on 21 August 1831, troops from the city stormed through the Lower Gate of Liestal, the centre of rural opposition (see page 59). Almost at once they were ignominiously routed and Liestal went on to become the capital of the half canton of Rural Basle.

1 Introduction: The Forgotten Revolutions

If we were to judge by the number of times paintings of the events of 1830 have appeared, we would be justified in thinking them amongst the best-known and appreciated of revolutions. For not merely has the famous picture of 'Liberty Leading the People' by Delacroix been used repeatedly to illustrate historical works, but it has now graduated to the august heights of decorating France's hundred-franc note. Yet neither this visual familiarity nor the fact that the revolutions inspired at least two famous pieces of music – by Berlioz and Chopin – is a true guide to the general standing of 1830 in the historical hall of fame. If we peruse some of the books which make use of the image of 1830, it soon becomes apparent that the position of the revolutions of that year is really a very lowly one. In fact the events of 1830 have largely been ignored by historians, so that such accounts as are available are often extremely flawed, and usually leave an impression of slightness and insignificance. So neglected and misconceived has been their historical image that the revolutions of 1830 are very much the forgotten men of the fraternity of European revolutions.

A quick inspection of the shelves of the average academic library will usually yield a dozen general studies of the revolutions of 1848 but none of 1830. This is because there has never been a detailed study of the events of 1830 as a whole, whether in English or in any other major European language. Furthermore, research into 1830 has been far less common than for comparable events. Hence, although there have been many luminous discussions in general works, these have often lacked something in detail, especially when such accounts appear in textbooks. Where detailed studies do exist these are usually devoted to a single country.

The resulting picture of 1830 is therefore seriously deficient. Many writers fail to notice the events of that year at all. Others offer incomplete and often quite inexact accounts. Whole countries and their experiences can be overlooked or, which is obviously worse, reported in quite erroneous ways. One reputable authority thus has the French army expelling the Dutch from Belgium before ever the revolution broke out there; another claims that the Polish revolt was crushed four months before it actually began – which at least is better than attributing the main battle of the Polish war of liberation to the Crimean War (as has been done)! – and yet another attributes the Italian troubles to the wrong city and the wrong year.

To add to these errors of omission there is another sin, this time one of commission. Even authors who treat 1830 more fully and carefully are inclined to minimise its importance. Because 1830 does not seem to compare with 1848 or 1789 in terms of depth, colour and impact, judgements on its nature have been very slighting. It is often described as an insignificant wayside halt on the road to 1848: as simply a hiccup induced by secret societies or foreign agitators; as a preliminary assault on power by the capitalist bourgeoisie, the almost mechanical result of the burgeoning Industrial Revolution; or merely as the Parisian July Days writ large, and thus explaining the over-use of Delacroix's picture.

In other words, despite – or perhaps because of – the lack of research and publication on 1830, there seems to be a clear and firmly held consensus about the nature of the events of that year. Certainly a good many textbooks are written as if our understanding were a great deal more certain than it actually is. Very often the vision of 1830 is of a movement which both centred on and originated in France. It was the July Days and the secret societies which produced a wave of revolution in Europe 'as though by a pre-arranged signal' (although there is, however, an alternative orthodoxy which views the various outbreaks as having had nothing at all in common). It is generally agreed, though, that the outcome of the revolutions was limited to a few constitutional refinements and, more importantly, to a measure of diplomatic change. In so far as a social dimension is recognised, it tends to be the idea of the progress of trade and industry producing a rising bourgeoisie which adopted liberalism as a tool and came to triumph after the July Days. Hence Soldani can say that 'the European crisis of 1830 [was] the decisive affirmation, the point of no return of the Industrial Revolution and of bourgeois strength in the European countries of prime importance'. Where other forms of social protest are noticed they tend to be seen as largely related to the essential contest between an industrial bourgeoisie and an aristocratic establishment for constitutional and international freedom. Thus 1830 is viewed as essentially different from 1789, being clearly bourgeois and capitalist, and lacking the general participation visible a genereation before. As such the revolutions were too easy – all the stress is laid on causes rather than on development – as well as too colourless to merit much attention.

Obviously, there is much that is true in this picture. The stress on political and especially on constitutional change and freedom is thus justified, but overall it does not give a fair impression of what happened. In the first place, the events of 1830 were not restricted to France or even to the major countries of Europe. They were far more widespread. Similarly, they were not produced by secret societies and French agents, but by spontaneous response to government action. Nor were they simply the work of a new class of factory owners. Not only were they led and exploited by a much more old-fashioned professional middle-class, but they were also really made possible by the intervention of the lower classes, much as in 1789. The revolutions of 1820 may have lacked this kind of *sans-culotte* element, but those of 1830 did not. They therefore involved a greater proportion of society than has often been appreciated. Finally, the upheavals of 1830 were neither mirror-images of the July Days in France nor something quite separate; for, while they drew their inspiration from what was happening in Europe at large, they also owed their ultimate origin to a whole series of domestic problems.

Any effort to remedy such misconceptions usually calls for an appeal to new sources. Yet because of the neglect and errors which dog the historiography of 1830 this is not really possible, as it assumes firm foundations which do not exist. There is just not enough acquaintance with the events of 1830 to warrant highly sophisticated examinations of specific aspects. Something more basic is called for: an examination of exactly why so many upheavals did take place in 1830 and to what extent they derived from the promptings of conspirators or the French; a detailed exposition of what actually happened, both in Europe as a whole and in the various centres of disturbance, in order to see the mixture of similarities and differences between them; and, finally, an attempt to establish both the dynamics of revolution and their place in the development of European politics and society in the early nineteenth century – a place which represents less the beginning of a new style of revolt than the end of the cycle of revolutions which had begun in 1789, yet which was, as Emilia Morelli has said, Janus-faced. In other words, we are concerned to answer three simple questions: why, what and wherefore.

Such an undertaking is less simple than it sounds. This is because the information available to us is not merely limited, but often also, a little flawed and certainly variegated. To begin with, there has not been a great deal of research and writing on the subject. What there has been tends to centre on diplomatic rather than domestic concerns. In particular, there has been little investigation of the social histories of many of the smaller countries of Europe. As a result, it is not easy to establish exactly what happened or who took part. Moreover, whereas in countries like Britain and France sources are relatively centralised, in other areas they can be very scattered. Furthermore, because so many countries were involved there is a very large number of sources to explore, most of them only available in the original places and tongues. So there can be no question of basing such an introductory study as this on intensive archival research in every country, nor even of indicating often unreachable secondary sources in voluminous notes.

Not only, then, is the information available sparse and scattered, but also, where secondary works are concerned, it is not always wholly reliable. In addition, to concentrate on one relatively short period – even though we are not aiming at simply 'the story of a year' – can be dangerous if it encourages what has been called 'source mining', that is, burrowing through books looking for all the references to 1830 but in the process losing sight of the backgrounds out of which the events actually grew. Even if we can establish the context properly, there are other pitfalls. Perhaps the major methodological obstacle to a rounded understanding of 1830, as Collingwood might have seen it, is the fact that virtually everything has been written in national blinkers. Many studies both concentrate on one country in isolation and partake of polemical debates the intricacies of which are hard to grasp today. Thus, there can be a plethora of information on individual countries, all of which the foreign historian is encouraged to dwell upon to the exclusion of other stories and other states. Moreover, since there was a pronounced national element to 1830, historical writing about it can be very sensitive. Much of what has been written has been blighted by an excess of patriotic fervour as civic-minded historians have sung the praises or blame, if not of kings, then certainly of patriots who figured in the great deeds of national liberation. Even today mild criticism of such patriotic views can bring down wrath upon the head of the unwary outsider.

A further flaw in the historiography of 1830 is that, besides being resolutely mononational, it developed in a rather unhelpful series of fits and starts. Thus, while contemporaries paid a great deal of attention to 1830, often again polemically as participants tried to justify themselves, the whole affair was soon overshadowed by 1848. Not until the 1860s and 1870s were the foundations of a cooler appraisal laid. Yet no sooner had documents started to emerge and more sober evaluations begun to appear than a series of anniversaries reinforced the nationalistic interpretation. When it came to the centennial, a whole crop of new studies blossomed, but all written at the same time and in isolation so that no cumulative picture emerged. And, even though the worst of the old nationalism has faded since 1945, the period has not been a prime object of study, so that the techniques of modern historiography have rarely been applied to 1830, forcing us to continue to rely on work which is now old both in time and style.

Finally, not merely is the information available to us limited and flawed, it is also highly variegated. For, although the conventional image of 1830 is often of a series of risings which were much the same as the mother outbreak in Paris, and indeed may have been directly induced by it, the reality is that the movements usually varied significantly in nature and were essentially unco-ordinated, despite the arguments of such as Hobsbawm, who sees 1830 as one of the rare occasions when Britain and the Continent marched in step. Indeed, the variegation was frequently marked within nations or other political groupings, which causes problems when we try to sum up what happened in largely decentralised political systems like Italy and Germany. So, while the experience of the east of Europe may have been relatively homogenous, that of the west was not. As Bismarck observed, 'Anyone who speaks of Europe is wrong – it is nothing but a set of national expressions'. This may be going too far; for, although we cannot fairly speak of European integration in the way that modern political scientists do, there was an international community of a kind and one to which all the countries involved in 1830 belonged, not to mention a certain degree of unofficial integration in which states as such were not involved. After all, one English observer castigated the Belgian revolt for being anti-European precisely because it destroyed the system of checks and balances by which this wider community was held together.

So the problem is, in part, to achieve a balance between treating Europe as a uniform whole and treating it as a set of quite unrelated upheavals, reflecting the fact that the revolutions of 1830 were at one and the same time both parts of a general crisis and products of distinctive local situations. Hence they could sometimes be self-evidently revolutionary – however we wish to define this – and elsewhere the product of accommodation to demands which were no more than latent. The various countries of Europe thus sought similar goals in differing ways. Political change was the outcome of the crisis as a whole, but it was not always achieved through classic revolutionary violence; and this, too, makes understanding of 1830 difficult because of the tendency of scholars and militants to insist on rigid views of what constitutes revolution.

To try to overcome all these obstacles and to answer the three basic questions which face us demands, first, an approach which focuses not just on the critical events of July 1830, but also on the whole period of crisis in Europe which embraced a period of some fifty months from late 1829 into the winter of 1832–3. In other words, 1830 is really a conventional term for a wider and longer process towards political change in Europe. Secondly, the approach must be narrative rather than analytical, although some attempt to carry the investigation deeper must of course be made. Hence a narrative history restricted simply to biographical politics will not suffice, nor can over-sophisticated methods of social analysis be applied in the absence of archival sources (and given the fact that even printed and secondary sources are not easily available in this country for such claims to be tested by others). Some comparative and conceptual framework is necessary to supplement the main narrative attempt to set out what did actually happen in 1830. The narrative must also be both comparative and respectful of national – and, indeed, regional – identities.

In other words, a third requirement is that the whole of Europe must be considered, not just the great powers. To this end maps are provided to help locate some of the less well-known revolutionary centres, especially those of Belgium, Italy and Switzerland which have been singled out for special attention because they are less well known than France, or even Poland, at this time. However, they are all part of what Pollard and others have called 'the heartland of Europe', that is to say, the relatively advanced urbanised areas where the French Revolution had helped to establish some degree of political awareness amidst similar social structures. This heartland was centred on the Rhineland, from Brussels and Antwerp in the north down through the border areas of France and Germany to western Switzerland and over the Alps to northern Italy – an area once called Lotharingia. Outside this heartland lay two peripheries, one along the North Sea which was perhaps more advanced politically and socially, and another to the south and east which was rather less so, though in all three areas there was enough of a civil society to enable political change to be considered. This was not, of course, the case in the far east of Europe apart from Poland.

While the achievements of these fifty months in the heartland zone were less extensive, and certainly less enduring, than those involved in them hoped or feared, the European political system was much altered by them; and its rate of change was both speeded up and reorientated towards more social questions thereafter. In Spain, for instance, 1830 took the form of a crop of liberal invasions aimed at overthrowing the reactionary Ferdinand VII which, if they were wholly unsuccessful at the time, did play a part in dividing Spain into two bitterly warring camps. In France and, ultimately, in Portugal the revolts brought to power new rulers more committed to constitutional monarchy – thanks, on the one hand, to three days of fighting in Paris in late July which resulted in the unexpected replacement of Charles X by Louis-Philippe of Orléans and, on the other, to a civil war between the forces of liberalism and obscurantism in Portugal in 1832-3. Similarly, a revolution and two brief wars of independence led to the Dutch and their king being ejected from their erstwhile sister-region of Belgium, which was then reconstituted as an independent kingdom guaranteed by Europe and ably defended, within the terms of a very influential liberal constitution, by Queen Victoria's favourite uncle, Leopold of Saxe-Coburg.

Elsewhere violence was less crucial to the changes. In Britain the beginning of the end of.the old political system was ushered in by the apparently tumultuous but eventually pacific Reform Bill crisis leading to the passage of the Act in 1832. Equally, in Switzerland a majority of cantons renewed their constitutions in a strikingly liberal, not to say democratic, direction despite resistance at the federal level, notably from the forces of conservatism. There were echoes of such political change in Scandinavia, especially in Denmark, although these were totally non-violent, and even more faintly, if less peaceably, in parts of the Balkans, where the independence of the new kingdom of Greece and the autonomy of a Serbian principality were confirmed and the ambitions of the Danubian principalities were at least recognised. With the exception of Spain, most of these movements were successful to some extent, but the relatively non-violent and constitutional experiments in such German states as Brunswick, Hanover, Hesse-Kassel and Saxony proved to be rather more ephemeral and insubstantial. And in the two cases where revolts turned into military confrontations with the great powers – with Austria in the case of the Duchies of Parma, and Modena and the northern Papal States and, more dramatically, with Russia in the case of Poland – the movements were snuffed out even more emphatically. Yet even where the events of 1830 were least successful their influence was to be felt for many years after.

The examination of these events which follows falls obviously and naturally into three broad sections. The first tries to show why there was so much political turmoil in the early 1830s by looking at the medium- and long-term causes provided by political disaffection and social strain throughout Europe, at the short-term causes of the political and economic crisis of the late 1820s and, finally, at the way in which the July Days and other initial outbreaks actually ignited the smouldering resentments of many countries. Having tried to explain why there was revolution in 1830, we must then turn to the question of what actually happened as the revolutions developed – first, as a general European social, political and diplomatic crisis and, secondly, as a series of individual outbreaks. The crisis can only really be appreciated by not only treating it on a transnational level but also remembering the peculiar problems of individual countries on a case-history basis. Finally, the third section tries to assess some of the hows and wherefores of the revolutions, reverting to comparative study. The dynamics, the participants and the effects of revolution are examined in turn, so as to arrive at some kind of estimate of the significance and nature of the experiences of 1830.

These experiences, collectively and severally, and whether revolutionary or evolutionary, amounted to the most significant attempt to reverse the Restoration and return to the kind of political life which the Revolutionary and Napoleonic upheavals had previously brought to the peoples of Europe. Even though they were not wholly successful, they still did something to help move Europe away from being a continent of subjects towards being one of citizens. Of course, this did not mean any real democratisation, nor yet any increase in harmony, since the outcome of the crises brought to light deep social divisions in Europe and ushered in an age of class conflict – even though this was little appreciated at the time. In fact 1830 was a paradoxical stage in the education not merely of oppositions, but also of governments, which were just as much initiators and contenders in 1830 as the revolutionaries themselves.

In what was essentially a pre-industrial world political questions remained much more important than social ones, and 1830 was in no wise a clear and decisive uprising of a new industrial bourgeoisie. Its roots lay in an older world formed partly by the French Revolution and its legacy, which meant that questions of representation and participation mattered deeply, not only to landowners, professional men and intellectuals, but also to many of the lower classes, notably the artisans. Their world, too, was traditionalist, although coming under acute strain from population growth and its effects. As a result, social protest was absolutely central and vital to the movements of 1830, and deserves infinitely more attention than do the almost non-existent secret societies of the time, which have so besotted generations of historians.

It is perhaps a measure of the actual irrelevance of professional revolutionaries to the experiences of 1830 that the latter have so often been denigrated as not being effective revolutions, perhaps as not being really revolutions at all. In fact the events of 1830 were not namby-pamby revolts, but affairs of considerable import and significance. Things did not happen despite them, but because of them, although this was as much the result of their inherent limitations as it was of some quintessential revolutionariness. In other words, change can come about for negative as well as for positive reasons.

Sometimes the social and political forces coincided and revolutionary change resulted; at other times things happened more peacefully. But the outcome was the same kind of political change. Not merely were the movements related, as well as opposed, in their origins and development, but their effects were also similar. A single revolutionary crisis could thus issue in either revolution or pacific political change. We must not, therefore, consider revolutions as some kind of metaphysical 'super-event' symbolising human liberation in the abstract, a kind of secularised transfiguration leading to a brave new world, but basically unconnected with the base clay of normal political life. They were – and perhaps still are – a form of ordinary social and political change: 'politics continued at the level of a violent showdown' as two American writers have called them. Conflict being endemic in society, there are always demands for change, but normally these are kept within tight bounds or are settled through normal channels. It is only when governments fail both to repress and to concede that revolutionary situations emerge.

Particularly in pre-industrial societies, revolutionaries merely arrive on the scene to exploit the situation, rather than to create it. And, where governments do concede in time, peaceful political change can emerge as well as revolution. Obviously all this is only the barest beginning of a possible reinterpretation of the events of 1830. Much more research and debate will be needed to test and refine what is suggested here. Yet for the moment it can serve to guide us in our attempt to resolve the why, what and wherefore of 1830. Thus, if both revolution and political change grow out of normal political and social processes, we must start to answer our first question by looking back to the underlying causes of dissent in the Europe of the 1820s, and notably to the effects of the Great Revolution of 1789 on continental Europe.

2 Causes: Preconditions and Precipitants

The question of why there were revolutions and political changes in Europe in 1830 has all too often been answered in terms of the effects of the July crisis in Paris. One reputable textbook speaks for many when it says that 'the immediate effect of the three-day Parisian revolution of 1830 was to set off a series of similar explosions throughout Europe'. Some observers have made the same claim in even more extreme terms, arguing that the moments of 1830 were quite deliberately caused by the French to advance their own interests. This is far too simplistic to be convincing: on the one hand, evidence for French involvement is lacking; while, on the other, it is hardly likely that people would revolt simply because the Parisians had done so. In fact their willingness to revolt can only really be explained by the situations in which they found themselves, which were in turn the products of earlier events and problems. The causes of 1830, indeed, lie deep in the development of Europe over preceding generations, and not in the work of a few French or other conspirators.

Seeking for such causes is, of course, rather an anachronistic thing to do, because it implies that revolution was expected. In reality very few people seem to have believed that there would be any new uprisings, and no one anticipated the precise course of events. What we have to do is look for the factors which caused dissent, the developments which allowed it to fester, and the reasons why the boil burst. Such causal factors operate, then, as Lawrence Stone and others have suggested, on the three levels of preconditions, precipitants and triggers. Preconditions are the background factors which produce the basic conflicts in society, that is to say, the underlying causes. Precipitants are the factors which help to bring conflicts not to resolution, but into open crisis. Yet, while many societies experience conflicts and crises, they do not always lead to political and other changes, let alone to revolution. The development of conflict into confrontation is the result not only of the way the precipitants are handled, but also of the appearance of some trigger event, some action – like the former, due as much to government as to opposition – which throws a lighted match into the powder-kegs filled and then piled on top of each other in the earlier phases.

Such a model of the causes of revolution is obviously inexact, and cannot be taken too far. None the less, it offers a useful way of thinking about the reasons why there was a sudden outbreak of revolution and political change in 1830. It reminds us that these revolutions were not events unrelated to what had gone before, brought about by self-conscious revolutionaries, but things which grew out of the stuff of normal political and social life. And while the triggers of 1830 were very closely interrelated – with the July Days playing a crucial role here – the preconditions were much more marked by local peculiarities and differences. Naturally, there were some common themes in the reasons why Europe prior to 1830 was so riven by conflict and why these conflicts were not contained, but the actual experiences of countries varied. Thus it makes sense to look at these experiences here, leaving the critical phase to the next chapter.

The preconditions of 1830 are to be found in two areas. The first was the new social and economic pressures which unsettled many social groups and offered the possibility of popular participation. These pressures came less from industrialisation as such than from the effects of population growth and commercialisation on what was still a traditional society. The second, and probably the more important, area was the political impact on Europe of the French Revolution of 1789, which operated not so much on the diplomatic level but internally, producing a thwarted desire for political participation. After an initial explosion amongst those most directly and personally affected by the new world of the Restoration in 1820–1, a period of prosperity damped down dissent and encouraged governments to ignore the problems. Then a new phase of economic depression and political tension turned the conflict into open and increasingly damaging confrontation. By 1829–30 Europe was in deep crisis.

Social and economic factors played a significant part in the underlying conflicts of post-Revolutionary Europe. However, it was rarely the case that revolt could be directly ascribed to such factors. Rather, the economic strains and the social conflicts which flowed from them were responsible for a deep-seated malaise on which the more salient political issues could feed, thereby giving the men of 1830 advantages not open to the revolutionaries of 1820. Hence, on the one hand, the endemic peasant dissidence of the Russian Empire never dented the *status quo* because it was unconnected to broader political and social strata and, on the other, there was no simple pattern of class conflict which can satisfactorily explain the outbreaks of 1830. Vertical divisions were in fact just as important as horizontal ones and, in any case, such divisions varied quite considerably from country to country.

European society after 1815 is often described as being in the process of industrialisation, but this is an exaggerated view when applied to the situation of the 1820s. Early nineteenth-century society remained highly traditional; but it was severely pressed by massive population growth and, partly as a result of this, by a significant shift towards larger-scale and more capitalistic organisation of the economy. These changes did much to unsettle both urban artisans, who were to play such a large part in

1830 (especially when they were politicised), and the middle peasantry of the heartland zones. The threat of downward mobility was to make the artisans in particular highly inflammable by 1830. At the same time, the general expansion of social organisation led to the emergence of more professional and intellectual groups amongst the middle class, who found that the reimposition of a property-owning élite in 1815 barred their way both to political influence in general and office-holding in particular. There were, of course, many other social forces at work, but the way the expanding society of the 1820s pressed these three groups was undoubtedly the key issue.

Society was still dominated by land; indeed, the importance of land may well have been increased by the confiscations and sales of the Revolutionary era. But large estates, farms and smallholdings were closely involved with a myriad of small towns which provided the agricultural hinterland with crafts and commercial and professional services. The towns of the time, therefore, were full of tailors, carpenters, cabinet makers, blacksmiths, weavers, spinners and the like, not to mention innkeepers, café proprietors and shopkeepers. Some were masters, owning small workshops in their own right, some were journeymen, aspiring to independence, some were apprentices, and many were not really employed at all. For, though their incomes generally rose over the Revolutionary period, they were poised on a knife edge as their guild organisations decayed or were destroyed, as new men came in from the country to try their luck in already overcrowded crafts, and as entrepreneurs sought to undercut them, whether by reorganising manufacturing on a commercial basis or by using cheaper labour in rural areas or distant small towns. Thus, they sought unskilled labour to carry out specific parts of the manufacturing process – making just sleeves, for instance, rather than whole suits, which required more expensive craftsmen.

Artisan numbers tended to rise right up till the 1870s by which time they made up at least half the population of most towns. And, as numbers rose, so social status and incomes dropped. Home-loom weavers in England, for example, saw their wages fall by 60 per cent between 1830 and 1840. Although such people did not have modern class-consciousness, they were traditionally bound together by custom, organisation and a shared concern for a reliable and cheap supply of food. They were therefore very likely to respond to calls to political action or to take matters into their own hands if they felt their livelihoods or traditional rights were threatened by the way society was changing.

Sometimes their exclusiveness could be directed not against entrepreneurs or state officials, all of whom tended to add to their burdens, but against new, young and unskilled workers. These people found it hard to gain acceptance into the ranks of skilled artisans, and their exclusion could mean that they became a threat to law and order.

Towns, of course, were not composed of such workers alone. There was also a whole lower class of servants, street vendors and service employees like sempstresses, laundresses and water carriers, not to mention students, soldiers and the many members of the upper and middle classes who lived there. Together they helped to swell the size of capital cities and provincial towns alike, so that by 1830 perhaps 15 per cent of the population may have been urban. And it was in such towns, swollen by new immigrants and unable to provide the necessary facilities, that social discontent was at its greatest.

Such discontent also touched the middle classes; for, although the post-Revolutionary élite was perhaps more open and less flamboyant than the nobility of the *ancien régime*, it was still exclusive and did not warm to the old mercantile and banking strata any more than it had before 1789. In any case, the vote and political influence in general were usually restricted to those with landed property, and this tended to hit the intelligentsia and the professional elements of the middle classes who were a fundamental element of the towns of pre-industrial Europe. Many of them, of course, had been excluded from office after 1815, which they naturally much resented, especially as there was a marked trend towards more technical education and expertise as training schools modelled on the Ecole Polytechnique sprang up in towns from Prague to Copenhagen. Again, there was probably some overcrowding in professions like administration, the law, the ministry, medicine and the arts, and it is certain that such people made up the bulk of the liberal movements of the 1820s.

The middle classes thus reflected the professional and commercial nature of the towns from which they came. Teachers, clerks and journalists often lacked the security of the other professionals, as did many of the small shopkeepers, traders and manufacturers who were often hard to distinguish from the artisans, and equally prone to engage in political activity. Factory owners, on the other hand, were few and far between and often counted for little in public affairs because of the demands made on their time and energy by nascent industries. And, as in Belgium under the progressive-minded William I, industrialists tended to be supporters of the *status quo*, so that it was the landed nobility who were the most disgruntled.

Nobles could turn to liberalism in other places, too, since it often appealed to men who had lost rights and land during the Revolution and found that the new conditions demanded more skill and capital than they possessed. And, although large-scale noble land-owning remained dominant in places like Britain, the Po valley and Spain, the sale of noble land was quite common elsewhere. A third of all noble estates changed hands in Prussia between 1815 and 1848, for example. Much of the cost of this could be passed on through increased rents and, in some places, dues on the peasantry, who were even more hard pressed by the economic changes of the times. The birth rate was always highest in the countryside, so that the population pressure was increasingly forbidding, as was land hunger. Added to this was the way more commercial and rational farming was making itself felt – through enclosure and reclamation, for example. Moreover, while emancipation of the peasantry was increasingly common, it had often been conceded on very harsh terms, so that, although the peasant got his land, he was still bereft of status and self-sufficiency. Outside Scandinavia and Britain the pressures led to plots getting smaller and smaller. All too often smallholders could not manage, especially where the wages of domestic industry fell or vanished altogether.

A few peasants succeeded in enlarging their holdings, but many more failed and left for the towns or were increasingly downgraded to landless labourers ever more exposed to rising food-prices in an age of particularly bad harvests. The immediate postwar period of 1816–17 had thus seen the last great subsistence crisis in western history, which did immense harm to the peasantry. Agricultural distress was thus very common in the 1820s, and in Germany especially the middle peasants came under immense pressure. A hundred thousand were driven from their farms in Prussia alone. As a result, rural violence became common, and was often directed against the remaining feudal landlords. However, risings were also usually directed against specific grievances, including the loss of old rights; and, as in Russia, the establishment was rarely seriously threatened.

Obviously, the precise pattern of social distress and bitterness varied from place to place. In the east and south, of course, society was polarised between large magnates and poor but proud gentry on the one hand, and a mass of serfs on the other. But to the west society was more complex, and the problems were acute and dangerous. In the heartland zone society was more urbanised, flexible and diverse. Such societies had responded to the French Revolution and enjoyed some kind of political life. Down the gradients from this heartland in the two peripheries problems in both town and country were still equally capable of producing damaging outbursts which were very difficult for not particularly ruthless regimes to contend with.

So in these key parts of Europe society remained largely static and traditional, still clinging to a hierarchical social structure with a sense of reciprocity and a belief that the working class embraced all active elements of society, whatever their status. All these, and not just the artisans, peasants and professional middle classes, came under great pressure. This was, as we have seen, much less because of industrial-isation – at least, outside parts of Britain, eastern Switzerland and southern Belgium – than because of the burgeoning growth of population. The traditionalism of the old society, its internecine conflicts and its lack of influence on the environment made it very hard for it to respond to the new stresses. The Revolution had, amongst other things, changed the legal framework of many societies by abolishing entrenched privilege and feudal rights. It had also stimulated new activities and products – more cafés, more shops, and new consumer goods like cotton – as well as better communications. Population growth had continued unabated despite the wars, rising from about 187 million in 1800 to 210 million in 1820 and 230 million in 1830. The greatest rise was not in Ireland, whose population rose by some 15 per cent from 6.8 million in 1821 to 7.7 million by 1831, but in the Netherlands, where the 2.0 million souls of the early nineteenth century rose by nearly a half by 1830. Since the Restoration also led to the redivision of the European market by revived obstructions like tolls, tariffs and the exactions of regimes burdened both with immense debts and with no possibility of, or interest in, providing economic stimulus, the pressures for change continued unabated.

Yet, because these pressures affected mainly the so-called 'black masses', it is unlikely that they would have led to major outbursts, let alone to political change. However, at the same time there were deeply-lying political issues affecting many parts of Europe. Most of these sprang ultimately from the effects of the French Revolution. Even though historians tend to make 1815 an absolute dividing-line, the truth is that the Revolution continued to mark the political life of Europe for years. Indeed, the Revolutionary era more or less invented politics for many people, for in the course of a quarter-century of upheavals the whole of Europe came face to face with France and its revolution in one way or another. This could be through invasion, peaceful incorporation, internal subversion, wars of resistance or merely by hearing echoes from afar. But in every case people had to think about basic questions of who they wanted to govern them, how, at what cost, and in whose name. One way or another a vast array of people were mobilised into political action, whether for or against the Revolution, and things could never be the same again.

Together with all the changes in social and economic organisation brought about by the Revolution this meant that the unchallenged acceptance of the establishment – monarchy, church and aristocracy – which had prevailed before 1789 could no longer be relied on. In so far as these bulwarks of the old order were restored, in 1815, it was because they fulfilled a particular need. But they had lost their pristine innocence. Institutions now had to justify themselves by what they did, not by the mere fact of their centuries of existence. In other words, the Restoration could only really work if it came to terms with the new forces and expectations. And, in the early period of 1814–16, many regimes, aware of their insecurity, did offer their subjects some kind of participation, thereby recognising the necessity for good administration and the people's right to some kind of political life. Even Metternich was aware that repression alone was no answer.

Thus, in France, Louis XVIII granted the Charter, and sustained it even after the shocks of the Hundred Days. There were also new constitutions in Switzerland, Poland and the Joint Kingdom of the Netherlands. There was even a half-promise of some representative element in the constitution of the new German Confederation, and a few of the south-western states, like Baden and Bavaria, did actually enact constitutional laws. In Scandinavia the Russian and Swedish rulers also thought it wise to recognise the existing constitutional arrangements of Finland and Norway, even though, in the latter, the Eidsvoll constitution was the work of an independence party. If, by and large, southern and eastern Europe were less fortunate in this respect, at least in the Papal States under Cardinal Consalvi, the new Secretary of State, an attempt at administrative reform was made. For those who had been most involved in the political life of the Revolutionary and Napoleonic era, authoritarian though it had often been, constitutions had become symbols of what they wanted. Unfortunately, the rulers' concessions to such feelings proved to be purely tactical and, as time passed and the necessity for such gestures seemed less pressing, especially in the eyes of complaisant new theorists like Haller in his *Restoration der Staatswissenschaft*, constitutions were less and less used, and reform gave way to repression and authoritarianism. Basically, the returned rulers did not accept that others had any right to participate in the political process, and arguments about the terms and details of constitutions were carried on in a language which the establishment neither spoke nor accepted.

To many people in Europe, albeit never to a majority, this was the great issue of the day. It was involved in all the different issues bequeathed by the Revolutionary era to the countries of Restoration Europe. In the case of Portugal it was bound up with resentment of the political and economic protectorate which had been the British price for assistance in liberating the country from Napoleon; and in Spain with the colonial and internal conflicts which led the army to aid the returning king, Ferdinand VII, in setting aside the 1812 constitution in the first *pronunciamento* in 1814. In France the Hundred Days produced a new breach between those who had gained from, or even tolerated, the Revolution and Empire and those who had for so long opposed it, often from exile. It was also a major element in the reservations felt by the peoples of what is now Belgium about the way the Congress of Vienna, for strategic reasons, subjected them to incorporation in a Joint kingdom with the Calvinist Dutch, ruled effectively but very high-handedly by William I of the Netherlands. Similarly, although the Swiss were granted their independence at Vienna, this was at the cost of conservative rule at both federal and cantonal level, often involving the return of the pre-1798 élites. This meant backtracking on the unification and liberation achieved under Napoleon's Mediation settlement. Patriotic aspirations in Germany were similarly unsatisfied by the new German Confederation, dominated as it was by Austria.

The problem of foreign domination was crucial in southern and eastern Europe, too. As Map 1 shows, Restoration Italy lost any sense of unity with the return of the old small states, which, as in the case of Piedmont, sought to re-apply all laws operative in 1796, before the French invaded, and either re-appointed those who had been in office then or, failing this, their heirs. Behind the small states stood Austria, strongly entrenched in Lombardy, and operating elsewhere through dynastic links and the threat of military intervention. The Greeks and the other peoples of the Balkan peninsula still had to face the deadening hand of the Ottoman Empire, whose one-time military and administrative efficiency had given way before a new and disruptive feudalism and violent self-serving warlords. Although the Poles may have felt they had achieved a better deal in the construction of a semi-independent constitutional kingdom under the Tsar, this was only because they failed to appreciate the narrow interpretation that the Russians would place on their rights to autonomy and national integrity. Nor for the Poles was there the solace of new openings in Russia with which the Finns could console themselves for amalgamation. National conflict was also visible in Norway, which submitted to the Swedish union decreed by Vienna with a bad grace, just as the Irish did to the Union of 1800. And in much of northern Europe the loss of old political rights went hand in hand with severe economic dislocation, which was also experienced in victorious Britain.

Such political elements were probably more significant than the purely geographical and diplomatic changes brought about by the 1815 settlements. Hence, even though the promises made by rulers and the general desire for peace meant that the Restoration began smoothly enough, it was not long before protests and opposition developed. While the mass of the population was still exhausted by the experience of revolution and war, small groups began to make their dissent known. Even in France there were military and other disturbances in Grenoble and Lyons in 1816, while the next year saw a rash of conspiracies in the Portuguese and Russian armies, not to mention a small rising in Macerata in the Papal States. In 1818 there was an abortive march on Trondheim at the time of the coronation of Bernadotte, and the following year the beginnings of dissidence in both the universities of Germany and the parliament and army of Congress Poland. Then, almost too neatly, on 1 January 1820 such protests took on a larger and more revolutionary form with the liberal army *pronunciamento* in Cadiz. After a period of ominous quiescence, the revolt began to spread throughout the country. It was paralleled by a military rising in Portugal against the English overlord, Marshal Beresford, by an anti-Austrian rising in Naples and, after assassinations and similar troubles in France and Germany, by a further military *putsch* in Piedmont. A little later there was even to be an attempt at a military installation of a liberal regime in Russia in the shape of the Decembrist *coup* of 1825.

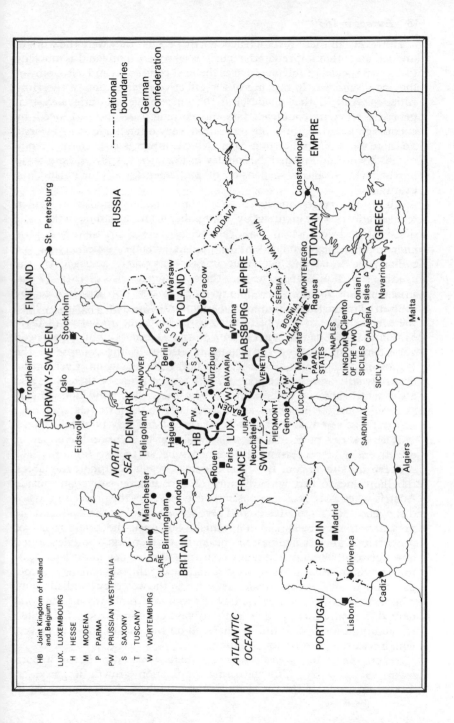

However, all these revolts failed, partly because they were the work of divided and often unprepared minorities who were motivated as much by their own special problems, such as the pay, conditions and autonomy of the army, and partly because of the effective intervention of the Holy Alliance. And, if they made clear the sense of general grievance that pervaded so many countries, they did nothing to resolve it. Indeed, by encouraging and legitimising repression, they often made things worse. So there was a White Terror in Spain which embarrassed even the French royalists who had invaded the country in 1823, show-trials and purges in northern Italy, and a suspension of parliamentary life in Poland, for example.

All this tended to hold back the broader opposition which lexicographers were increasingly calling liberalism. So, although the basic divisions and conflicts in political society were clear, there was little chance that they would lead to political change, especially as the underlying social and economic unease was partly assuaged by the gradual return of prosperity, once the subsistence crisis of 1816–17 was over and manufacturing began to revive in Britain, northern France, the southern Netherlands, Switzerland and parts of Germany. Thus by 1815 the coal industry in Berg had passed its previous record output of 1812. Similarly, the Scandinavian countries and Denmark, which had been very badly affected by the economic effects of the collapse of the Napoleonic imperium, also began to find their feet again. Even in the generally still depressed regions of south and east Europe there were also areas which showed some signs of new life. All this no doubt made political questions less pressing, particularly to the lower classes whose support was essential to the likely success of any new political protest.

With a series of good harvests as well, not to mention the apparent effectiveness of repression, governments began to lose some of their concern for subversion. Even the Russians began to support the Greek rebellion and to flirt with the idea of encouraging subversion inside Austria when Metternich opposed their policy. Yet the problems did not disappear; they merely festered. There was no relief on the land, and the pressure in the towns did not vanish. So, once the brief period of prosperity and calm had passed, the conflicts re-emerged and developed into ugly confrontations in many countries. And, when in the late 1820s the economic situation deteriorated and new political challenges arose, governments were careless and disunited in the way they handled them. The fact that they had not used more propitious times to lance the boil helped to ensure that by 1829–30 there was a crisis in Europe. This called for an application of flexibility and skill on the part of those in power, which was rarely to be forthcoming.

Where the economy was concerned, there were new problems in both town and country. The gathering population growth imposed an increasing strain on the social and economic fabric, depressing wages in the towns, and further undermining the ordinary peasant farmer, threatening both food-supplies and employment prospects. At the same time the effects of the English bank crash of 1825 were felt on the Continent as a result of the growing interrelationship of the European economies. Sales and profits fell, investment was hard to sustain, and new industries often found the task of survival beyond them. Thus, the infant iron industry of the Haute Marne in eastern France literally collapsed after 1828 because it was no longer competitive in the new hard times. The building trades in France also suffered badly, notably in Paris where wages fell by 6 per cent between 1810 and 1830 while prices rose by twice as much. The net result was that by the end of the decade nearly half the population was dependent on poor relief. By 1829 the crisis had also reached western Switzerland. Artisans there and elsewhere in Europe suffered acutely as the market shrank, competition increased, and a general feeling of despair overtook the manufacturing sector.

On the land the basic problems were now compounded by a series of bad harvests. So the extension of commercial farming and development, coupled with the growing burden of taxation, led to an increasing amount of rural distress and disturbance. In the mountainous region of the Ariège in south-west France peasant resistance to large-scale exploitation of the forests on which they depended for their livelihood led to attacks on the entrepreneurs' installations in which the peasants dressed up as women in order to prevent their recognition. In south Wales there was a similar phenomenon, known as the Scotch Cattle attacks, in which colliers dressed up as beasts or women to enforce union solidarity during strikes. Many places also endured regular grain riots, which were common in parts of Ireland, Wallonia and the Rhineland, where land hunger was acute. Thus, in the Namurois by the spring of 1829 there were frequent riots which could easily take on a political colouring.

Not everywhere, of course, suffered to the same degree from the depression. The peripheral regions seem to have suffered less than the heartland zones. Generally speaking, Britain was able to maintain her prosperity, albeit with some difficulty, in a time which was less a slump than a confused pause between two periods of major growth. On the other hand, there was a marked deterioration in rural conditions, again partly because of the string of poor harvests. In Scandinavia the recovery from the postwar slump seems to have continued. The Danish *riksdaler*, which had been falling in value since the Late Empire, began to rise in value after 1828, for instance. The economic development of Poland also appears to have gathered pace – though there were growing problems for the gentry. In the south, the late 1820s also saw the beginnings of recovery in Spain, although Portugal, the Balkan lands and particularly Italy were depressed throughout the decade.

Such economic problems, which obviously increased social friction and unease, were all the more significant because of the way the political climate was changing. By the end of the decade, the unity of the great powers had been severely shaken by the way in which, following their disagreements over the suppression of the revolutions of 1820-1, Britain, France and Russia chose to support the Greek struggle for independence against the Turks, to the point of using their fleets against the Porte's Egyptian allies at Navarino in 1827. This greatly alarmed the Prussians and, even more, the Austrians, who reacted particularly to the Russian invasion of the Danubian principalities in 1828-9, which won for the principalities major concessions in the Treaty of Adrianople, and widened the latitude for new liberation movements in the Balkans. All this threatened Austrian interests and led Metternich to reiterate his warnings against the dangers of revolution. However, even in southern Germany his warnings went unheeded. And, although the appointment of the Prince of Polignac to the French government in August 1829 was seen as clear evidence of reactionary intent on the part of the French king at home, in diplomatic terms it brought a new element of uncertainty to the international scene. Polignac nursed wild ambitions of redrawing the map of Europe which annoyed the eastern powers, while Britain was made uneasy by French designs on Algeria. The concert of Europe thus gave way to an atmosphere of mutual suspicion and non co-operation.

Internally, the Restoration regimes also lost something of their earlier cohesiveness and efficiency. In Iberia the returned monarchy of Portugal and the enlightened absolutism of Ferdinand VII in Spain both came under increasing pressure from the right. The latter had been able to deal with new liberal landings in 1824 and 1826, but his style of rule was not to the taste of the extreme *apostolicos*, who after 1824 began to gather round his younger brother Don Carlos. Ferdinand therefore found himself forced to make discreet overtures to the liberals by encouraging the more moderate policies of Ballasteros after 1827, only to drive some of the extremists into open insurrection. In France, the accession of the dogmatic Charles X in 1825 had apparently led to the final triumph of the ultra-royalists, but no sooner had they gained a vast majority in Parliament than they began to quarrel amongst themselves, so that their electoral strength began to ebb away just as dramatically. In the Joint Kingdom of the Netherlands it also proved increasingly difficult for William I to divide and rule his Belgian subjects, since both Catholics and liberals came to see him as the major obstacle to the remedying of their grievances. Similarly, in many areas of Germany and Switzerland, the eccentricities and bloody-mindedness of princes and élites began to cost them support in society at large. Even in Britain the old conservative majority which had ruled the country since the 1780, began to break up at last.

This growing domestic destabilisation also made itself felt on Europe's eastern fringe; for, while the Poles were kept on a tight leash, in the Ottoman Empire the successes of the Greeks and the internal resistance to the reforms initiated after the quelling of the Janissaries in 1826 caused growing dissidence, notably in Bosnia. Metternich, too, had his own problems with internal rivals, a restive Hungarian Diet and Russian sponsorship of conspiracy in Italy. Within that peninsula there were also uncertainties over the succession in Sardinia, where Charles Felix apparently had thoughts of partly disinheriting the soft-centred Charles Albert in favour of the resolutely conservative Francesco IV of Modena. Farther south, resentment over the way Pope Leo XII had systematically undone all the reforms of Consalvi helped to widen the breach between the Pope and his subjects. Therefore, if it is perhaps an exaggeration to view all this as the disintegration of the Restoration, it certainly is true that governments were less stable than they had been, and as a consequence less able to cope either with the growing economic problems or with the conflicting demands being made on them from both right and left.

Awareness of this weakness, coupled with the continuation of abrasive policies, not surprisingly led to a recrudescence of opposition. To some extent this was the result of intellectual change, especially through the crystallisation of liberalism and, even more significantly, through the growth of Romanticism. Whatever its lack of practical success, by the end of the 1820s liberalism had developed as a doctrine, thanks to the utilitarianism of men like Bentham, the political economy of people like Say and Sismondi, and the constitutionalism of such 'doctrinaires' as Royer-Collard and Cousin. Much more accessible than these, however, was the spreading spirit of Romanticism which, at least on the Continent, began to become the property of the left. Hence Victor Hugo, who had welcomed the coronation of Charles X, soon broke with the Crown. Through his plays, the novels of Scott, the poetry of Byron and Mickiewicz, and the historical writings of Lelewel and Zschokke in Poland and Switzerland respectively, the Romantics offered a vision of societies which would return to their national and libertarian roots if only the Restoration establishment would let them. Such ideas, spread by an expanding press and educational network, offered an attractive image of the future which affected all classes of society.

However, it was in the web of politics that the main roots of renewed opposition lay. In Portugal, Don Miguel and his right-wing supporters had set the constitution aside and begun a reign of terror which drove many into opposition; while in France the accession of Charles X caused the liberals to redouble their efforts and, with the help of Chateaubriand and other dissident royalists, to achieve a major swing to the left in the autumn elections of 1827. News of the liberal gains helped to spark off a massive political riot in Paris that October which showed that the liberals had propagandised the lower classes to an extent where they seemed to have the capacity to deny control of the capital to the government. Then, aided by new issues like the reimposition of censorship, the liberals were able to make further gains in a series of by-elections, with the result that by the end of 1829 all of the 221 deputies who were to throw down the gauntlet to Charles in the spring of 1830 were already in the Chamber.

In a way, the development of opposition to government was even more striking in the southern provinces of the Joint Kingdom of the Netherlands. There resentment of the way William I disregarded Belgian interests and rights, not to mention the political implications of their growing economic strength, led many French-educated liberals, who had previously supported the king, to throw in their lot with Catholics who were already opposing William's religious, educational and language policies. The idea of a 'Union' of such opposition forces had first been floated by Catholic leaders in December 1825, when they became convinced that only by changing the political system could they safeguard their religious beliefs and institutions. Discontented liberals in Liège and elsewhere, whose careers were thwarted by Dutch language requirements and political suspicions, came round to accepting the idea of union early in 1827 and, by the end of 1828, it carried all before it as tens of thousands signed petitions in favour of the freedom of the press. In the German state of Brunswick the antics of Duke Karl after he came of age in 1827 similarly united virtually the whole of society against him, to the extent that the Federal Diet was petitioned to restrain him.

To the south-west the Swiss Confederation felt it unnecessary after 1829 to maintain the curbs on exiles and the press which the great powers had imposed in 1823, while the tercentenary of the Reformation, the influence of philhellenism and the impact of Romanticism led to the emergence of a number of pressure-groups demanding an end to the decentralised impotence forced on the country in 1815. At the cantonal level there were parallel pressures for constitutional ameliorations which, if they were indignantly rejected in the Vaud and the Ticino, did achieve a number of minor victories elsewhere, notably in 1829. Similar radical movements were also visible in Germany and especially in Scandinavia. Thus in Sweden in the late 1820s peasants joined in protests against the burdens of the 1809 regime, and in Norway the so-called 'Battle of the Market-Place' in Oslo on 17 May 1829 testified to continuing regrets for the loss of political independence in 1814. In Britain a similar restiveness was visible, first in the formation of the Catholic Association in Ireland in 1824, then with the emergence of political unions in 1827-9, and ultimately in the surge of trade unionism during the following winter. Finally, liberalism took on a more aggressive and military form in Portugal, where the resistance to Don Miguel emerged into the open in May 1828 and eventually and with difficulty succeeded in gaining a military foothold in the Azores by the following year.

Not every country, of course, was affected to the same extent, let alone in the same way. In Spain and Italy the weight of apathy and repression inhibited opposition, although the continuous series of punitive commissions of inquiry in the Romagna showed that hostility to the Papacy still continued. And, as soon as the Austrian army was withdrawn from Naples in 1827, there was a new outbreak of revolt in Cilento. Troubles were also reported in Pavia and Pesaro. Similarly, the Poles' resentment at the failure of Tsar Nicholas to accept what they believed were their constitutional rights and his insistence on the trial of freemasons and sympathisers with the Decembrists led some hotheads to talk of action as early as 1828. They even considered assassinating Nicholas when he made his annual visit to Warsaw the following year. There was also some dissidence in 1825 both in Serbia, where there was resistance to the personal dictatorship exercised by Miloš Obrenović, and in the Hungarian Diet which had to be recalled after being allowed to lapse for a dozen years and more. Even in Moldavia and Wallachia there were signs of intellectual awakening at least.

By about 1829, then, there was a good deal of combustible social distress, in both town and country, and growing intellectual and practical criticism of the existing European order. This criticism was not revolutionary in either nature or intent. Springing as it did from well-established grievances, it owed as much to frustration as to a positive desire to turn the world upside down. There were, in other words, few eschatological hopes of revolution in the air and, had the establishment been more effective, the frustrations could have been relieved, and their precipitating role diminished. In fact, the rulers of the time were not sufficiently restrained or well enough organised internally, nor yet adequately united internationally, to be able to face the prospect of further pressures with great confidence. In France, Austria and some of the Italian states the governments were very disunited, while in places like Brunswick, Portugal and the Papal States it was their own activities which helped to produce the liberal movements they feared. Although few regimes were really aware of it, the Restoration was very insecure by the end of the decade. Fortunately for them, the emerging liberal movements of the heartland and the northern peripheries were almost equally unaware of their own potential.

Given all this, the invocation of secret societies as the cause of the unrest visible in Europe is merely a resort to over-determination. In any case, such evidence as there is suggests that those secret societies which actually did exist were usually small, mostly bitterly divided, sometimes penetrated by the police, and often rejected by the mass of the population, as was illustrated by the case of the peasantry's reaction to the anti-clerical and middle-class Carbonari in southern Italy. Moreover, it seems that the secret societies were really associations of people who wanted to enjoy the political life and free discussion which were not available to them openly. They were often less conspiratorial vanguards than reflections of the frustrated desire for political participation so common under the Restoration. Significantly, they were most common in places like Iberia, Italy and Poland, where public political activity was more than discouraged. They were much less frequent and substantial in France, Britain, Belgium, Scandinavia and Switzerland, where there was a tradition of civic politics. And, if the myths make secret societies out to have been both more numerous and more influential than they were in reality, this was the result of their own inclination to whistle in the dark, so as to keep up their courage, as well as of the desire of governments to justify their repression and to frighten society into obedience.

On the other hand, it should be remembered that the new political climate did not go unchallenged. Both governments and the forces of conservatism did respond to the rise of opposition, thereby helping to enhance the developing confrontation. In Spain the emergence of Carlism proceeded unabated, producing a *pronunciamento* and then, more significantly, the Catalonian 'Revolt of the Discontented' against Ferdinand in 1827. These moves were to some extent encouraged by the Portuguese Miguelists and, later, by the news of the accession of the Prince of Polignac to power in France in August 1829. Polignac's preferment caused an immense wave of enthusiasm in right-wing circles in Europe, though in France it was extremely provocative, since many royalists imagined that the day of reckoning with the forces of revolution was now – or at least should be – at hand. Liberals accepted the challenge, as their rapturous reception of Lafayette on his tour of the eastern provinces shows. In Italy some governments went so far as to make use of extreme Catholic vigilantes known as 'Sanfedisti' to harass liberals. But, like the secret societies, the importance of these has been somewhat exaggerated. Very real, however, was the reaction in Russia, where the Tsar strengthened his control over government and, in Finland, began to replace native officials and practices by Russian ones.

Elsewhere, some governments were more flexible. Although the British government banned the Orange Order in 1828 and tried to dragoon agrarian and religious defence-groups like the Whiteboys, the Ribbonmen and other Catholic political organisations into submission, the success of the Catholic Rent, reinforced by O'Connell's victory in the County Clare by-election, persuaded Wellington that anarchy could only be averted by emancipation and, despite Protestant resistance in Ulster and elsewhere, this went through in early 1829. At about the same time William I of the Netherlands, finding counterproductive his attempts to punish leading Belgian critics of his regime, decided to drop controls on the press and the highly unpopular tax on the slaughtering of animals. However, when faced with a second wave of petitions from November 1829, which rallied even more support for the ideas of the freedom of association and the reform of the States-General, he rejected both out of hand. Evidence of greater awareness and flexibility can, however, be found in Hungary, Serbia and Switzerland.

Yet even such concessions as there were were often made only reluctantly, or against a background of vituperative complaint from the right. Governments thus did little to lance or cauterise the boil of grievances, and allowed political opinion to become a great deal more extreme and polarised than had been the case a few years before. And, in comparison to 1820–1, the opposition was larger, more representative, better organised and more able to draw on growing social and economic difficulties. The developments of the later 1820s had thus precipitated the prospects of political breakdown. By the winter of 1829–30 Europe was uneasily and insecurely poised for change. Conflict had, in many cases, already developed into open confrontation. Even so, there was no certainty that this would lead to an explosion, let alone to the kind of breakdown which actually took place. That there was to be such a breakdown was to be due to the events of 1830 itself.

3 The July Days and the Triggers of Revolution

'By 1830', in the words of Frederick Artz, 'the whole political order was so unstable that a serious disturbance in any of the capitals of Western Europe would almost certainly lead to outbreaks in a number of other states.' That year was to see a number of events which were to trigger off just such a series of upheavals. And, though some of them were to take place outside France and before the end of July, they were really only premonitions. The event which lanced the boil took place in Paris. Yet, despite the long-standing confrontation between the Crown and its supporters on the one hand and the liberal opposition on the other, the July Days were neither planned nor really expected. None the less, the Parisian crisis was to trigger revolutionary outbreaks in ten states in the course of the next few months. At the same time other countries moved more peaceably towards political changes similar to those sought by the revolutions, and the resultant crisis seemed to many to threaten the Continent with a new revolutionary war.

Actually, the situation was very different from that in the 1790s, so that the revolutions of 1830 were not brought about by military action as had been the case then. Indeed, they were not even the result of direct political action by the French, or even of deliberate emulation. It may be a slight exaggeration to say, as Riballier does, that the 'repercussions of the July Days abroad were purely accidental, rather than being even repercussions, they were simple coincidences', but it is equally wrong to think that French agents caused the August troubles in Brussels or that the Swing rioters in south-east England sought to copy the French. The July Days served basically as a symbol to a tense Europe. They created a European-wide crisis by what they did to France and also by the fears and expectations they produced elsewhere. Reacting to them called for more skill and flexibility than many governments had previously shown and, not surprisingly, there followed a whole series of errors and omissions by governments which played a larger part in triggering off revolution than did conscious efforts by oppositions. Often these errors were political in nature but, as in Warsaw, they could also be social and economic. All of them, though, were psychologically significant and drew on political weaknesses or blunders. Together they created a movement which fused a series of outbreaks which, while they shared common roots, developed in different ways and emerged from varied responses to the July Days.

The year 1830 began with a glacial winter, compared by one Swiss to those more normal in Spitzbergen, and this did nothing to ease popular distress, which continued to trouble parts of southern England, Ireland, Wallonia, northern France and Hesse-Kassel, often leading to further protests and violence. In France food-prices rose by some 75 per cent, and in Belgium the slump had a dire effect on manufacturing, leading to bankruptcies, wage-cuts and unemployment, not to mention a rise in the crime rate. The winter meant that the prospects for the harvest of 1830 were poor, so that no relief was visible. Politically the winter was equally troubled, with O'Connell in Ireland calling for the repeal of the Union and encouraging electoral violence in Waterford, the nobility of Brunswick, Hesse and Saxony quarrelling with their unreasonable rulers, and the Pragmatic Sanction of 27 March – transferring the succession away from Don Carlos – opening the way to a new period of trouble in Spain. And, had his Brazilian subjects not prevented it, Don Pedro might well have joined the continuing liberal opposition in Portugal.

Over and above all this was the fact that, since August 1829, France had had a government headed by Prince Jules of Polignac which was regarded by friends and enemies alike as having been installed simply to stage a *coup* against the liberals. The latter, egged on by the royalist press, prophesied a coming crisis, while the ultras derided the government's slowness to act on its alleged mandate as it remained passive through the winter. Small wonder, then, that one Belgian politician observed late in February that 'it is notorious that Europe is in the grip of a new crisis. It is more difficult to grasp what its nature and effects will be than to know the theatre in which it will be played. Each of us feels within himself that this theatre must be France.'

This feeling of expectancy was widely shared. On the last days of May an inflammatory pamphlet circulated in Brussels calling for resistance to the king, while a leading Swiss wrote to his former pupil, the Grand Duke Constantine, in Warsaw that constitutions were in the air, even if Europe still lacked the men and institutions to make them work. The Tsar, moreover, was grievously worried by the state of affairs in France, since the follies of Charles made him fearful of the future. The papal nuncio in Paris similarly feared some kind of catastrophe and, at a ball held in late May by the Duke of Orléans for the visiting Neapolitan royal family, one of the former's advisers, noting that the arrival of Charles caused a hostile demonstration, remarked that they were all walking on the edge of a volcano. Metternich thus had some cause to believe that revolution was nearer that summer than it had been for years past. Yet he had no idea what to do about it, and could only wait on events.

Then, at the very time that William IV was telling the House of Commons on 23 July that 'it is with the utmost satisfaction that I find myself enabled to congratulate you on the general tranquillity of Europe', the first breaches were made in the increasingly fragile fabric of the Restoration. These came not in France but in Switzerland. There, in the French-speaking canton of the Vaud, the government had become uncomfortably aware of growing support for constitutional revision and, despite its earlier opposition to the idea, had worked secretly through the winter to draft a pre-emptive and somewhat restrictive reform of its own, which was rushed through a somewhat startled legislature in May. Even more significant were the events in the Ticino, where the old governing élite had found itself facing a canton-wide newspaper and pamphlet campaign against its corrpution, authoritarianism and lack of representativeness. Though the government at first fought back, the extreme measures adopted to this end by its head, G. B. Quadri, cost him the support not only of the capital but also of his own colleagues in the Council of State. The latter therefore decided to adopt the idea of constitutional reform themselves and, with Quadri shouldered aside, this was agreed and publicly ratified by 4 July 1830. A virtual revolution had thus taken place in a state which, although small and backward, was none the less a pillar of the Restoration order.

There were premonitions of the shape of things to come elsewhere. Bosnia and Albania experienced continuing disturbances, while in February 1830 the Serbs finally learned that the Turks would grant them autonomy. In the Danubian principalities the reform commissions created by the Russians after the Treaty of Adrianople were still at work, and in Greece the deteriorating political situation showed itself by a crop of tax revolts early in the year. Even Vienna experienced social disorder on 5 March. Later the royal ban on celebrations of the centenary of the Confession of Augsburg led to riots in the main Saxon cities on 25-7 June. At the same time the death of George IV opened the way for the reviving Whig party to exploit the consequent general election. Finally, liberal activities continued in Iberia. A group of London-based Spanish exiles had to be stopped from attempting a new invasion in early July, while Portuguese rebels in the Azores drove off the Miguelist fleet which descended on them during the summer.

However, if all these events testify to the continuing political tension in Europe – tension squarely based on local problems – they were not sufficient to move Europe. It was to be France which gave the warning signal to governments and governed alike, even though the actual situation in France was rather different from what many of them imagined it to be. Because France had been keyed up ever since 8 August 1829, people read more into the situation than it merited. Thus, to begin with, the threat of Armageddon was more apparent than real. Events show that the government at least was not really set on conflict. There were considerable divisions and uncertainties in the cabinet on domestic matters and, in any case, it was more concerned with foreign ventures. So no domestic initiative was taken until March 1830 when a warning to the opposition was inserted in the speech from the throne at the opening of Parliament. Even when the opposition carried an aggressively hostile reply the government still hesitated. Only in April was a dissolution agreed, and reluctantly at that. Not surprisingly, the government was to fare but badly in the elections, despite both the way the king nailed his own colours to its mast and its own desperate expedients to try to influence the results.

Regardless of the increasing likelihood of defeat, the government still havered, partly because of a last-minute reshuffle in May. Some elements wanted to let the new Chamber meet and, it was hoped, damn itself by extremism and inefficiency. But in the end, after protracted discussions amazingly lacking in urgency, it was decided in July to make use of a clause in the constitution which supposedly allowed the king to set aside normal constitutional procedures in an emergency. Hence on Monday, 27 July, Four Ordinances appeared, effectively annulling the elections and calling new ones under a restricted franchise which was expected to provide a conservative majority. At the same time the press was muzzled. Although these inflammatory acts were exactly what the liberals had been preophesying for months, the government was so silly – or so oblivious to the situation – as not to back them up by adequate military preparations. Thus an apparently deliberate onslaught on popular liberties was really an unconsidered act of panic.

Secondly, although the government was somewhat surprised to find that the publication of the Ordinances was provoking large-scale opposition, this did not really come from the liberals. Despite all their previous fighting talk, the politicians were too shocked and alarmed to take decisive action. This was left to the journalists and printers who had been most immediately affected by the Ordinances. Their protests were followed by clashes with the security forces which were at first suppressed easily enough; but on Tuesday, by which time many businessmen had closed their shops and factories and thereby driven their workers on to the streets at the very time the police were trying to close down the newspapers, things rapidly got much worse. The disturbances were only mastered with difficulty. By Wednesday barricades had gone up everywhere, and it was understandable, though unexpected, that an attempt by the army to clear the obstructions away by a threefold offensive on the centre of the city should fail abysmally. The royal forces suffered heavy losses and even worse desertions, so that the heart of its own capital was lost to a government which still seemed unaware of its predicament.

Only when the remaining defence-line crumbled and the army fell back in disorder on the suburbs on the Thursday did the government drop its refusal to negotiate or concede. By then, after almost equal hesitation, the parliamentary liberals had created a makeshift counter-adminstration in Paris. None the less, only grudgingly were the Polignac ministry and its policies abandoned. By then it was too late, particularly as the installation of a more acceptable cabinet was handled with the now typical ineptitude and lack of vigour. Before the crowds in Paris, let alone the Crown, could take an alternative action, Louis-Philippe was brought in to rule France, first, on 30–1 July, as lieutenant-general and later as king under a charter rapidly if slightly revised in a mere ten days. Any hopes of a royalist riposte soon evaporated, and the political revolution was soon consummated at the centre.

Viewed up close all this was very surprising. Despite the apocalyptic mood of the country the Crown had acted with total lack of energy and foresight, only proving resolute when it was suicidal to do so. The liberals had not been a great deal better, and the general impression was of two blind men struggling back to back. Whatever the popular feelings about Polignac, the clash need not have come, nor need it have been so mishandled. Strategically and tactically the July Days were a revolution which might never have been. Like 1789, it was a revolt which sprang more from the weakness imposed on the monarchy by a relatively advanced political system than from reaction to a ruthless autocracy. But, of course, similar conditions did not pertain in many other countries, and attempts to follow the Parisian lead were built on different foundations. Little of this was known or understood outside Paris, not to mention outside France. The July Days were seen in the deliberate terms of 1792, and as a deep-seated general movement, and therefore as a prelude both to a drastic restructuring of social institutions and to a new war of conquest and international liberation. All this was to prove highly mistaken.

Perhaps it was understandable, however, since the first responses to the July Days came as much from the rural masses in France and elsewhere as from the politically aware. Inside France not merely was there an immediate collapse of authority in the towns, but even more in the countryside there was a spontaneous, almost anarchic outburst of violence directed not so much against Charles X himself as against the traditional enemies of the French peasantry: grain merchants in the northern half of the country and the *fisc* in the south. Apocalyptic hopes of a social and economic nature were released by the July Days. People seemed to believe that their lives would be transformed and all their earthly burdens removed. Such eschatological beliefs led the inhabitants of the small manufacturing town of Issodun in the Indre to eject all authority from the town as a sign of the new age.

Such places had often had a tradition of conflict over taxation and food. In November 1828 in Issodun there had been shouts of 'Long live the king, and down with the tax collector', and the fact that the harvest of 1830 was one of the worst since 1815, especially for wine growers, simply made things worse. As early as 30 July there were stories of mysterious commands to cease paying taxes in the Dordogne, and generally trouble started during the second week of August. Attacks on markets – as by the 300 women of Château Chinon in the Nièvre who, on 15 August, seized grain from the merchants and put it under lock and key in the town hall –

and interference with the movement of grain were accompanied by onslaughts on the tax services. The direct-tax office in Clermont-Ferrand was burned down, the restoration of *octrois* and *droits d'entrée* was bitterly resisted in many places and, again in Château Chinon, an unauthorised wine-seller resisted the security forces with a sabre when they came to tax him. In forest areas like the Ariège and the Rhineland departments the landowners' selfish exploitation of trees and workers made them frequent targets. Attention could also be turned to landowners and their mansions, to farmers, whose barns might be burned, to entrepreneurs whose mills were threatened – as was the case in Issodun – and against the church. There was, in fact, a distinct anti-clerical element in all the troubles.

Very often such outbursts were supported by workers in the towns and elsewhere. Wood cutters employed by some eastern ironmasters refused to accept wage-cuts, shoemakers in Dijon demanded higher pay, and other workers, like the typographers of Blois and the wallpaper makers of Vizille, were also active. In major centres like Paris and Rouen the protests were nearly always for better pay and conditions. Cotton-spinning in the latter city was almost brought to a halt on 27 August when the town was taken over by indignant workers. Such popular violence, though it took on an apocalyptic tone because of the July Days, really reflected the basic social problems of the time, and was to last as long as the slump did. It could often make the depression worse, as happened at La Souterraine in the Creuse when the merchants at the market there on 12 August were forced to sell their grain at prices well below the economic rate. This led them to desert the market, thereby causing a grave food crisis. The early 1830s proved to be one of the peaks of early nineteenth-century popular unrest and, although the news of the July Days was largely symbolic, the popular reaction helped to prevent the Bourbons from making a fight of it and later forced the new monarchy of Louis-Philippe to make concessions which would never have been considered in other circumstances.

The same chiliastic social and economic hopes were also present in neighbouring Belgium. There the tricolour was flown in Givet as early as 7 August; news from Paris dominated the press throughout the month; and the continuing food troubles round Namur quickly took an anti-Orangist turn. In Germany, not merely was there student enthusiasm for the news from Paris, but there were also Luddite riots in Bremen, Breslau, Aachen, Chemnitz, Cologne, Krefeldt, Nuremberg, Schwerin and several Silesian towns. In Warsaw there were labour disturbances at the Fraenkel factory by October, too. But it was not just the towns which perceived the news from Paris as a sign of coming liberation. In the Rhenish countryside there were tax strikes and stories of mysterious bands of travellers appearing from nowhere to offer deliverance to hard-pressed and demonstrative villagers. There was also to be a rural element in the political troubles in Hesse and Hanover; while one underlying cause of the crisis in Brunswick was the way in which the Duke had interfered with long-established settlement and social policies to the detriment of the rural population. Significantly, one of the longer-term effects of the July Days and the subsequent revolutions was to be the revival of political consciousness amongst the Scandinavian peasantry. The Channel and the Irish Sea proved to be poor insulators. Not only was there great political enthusiasm in Britain, with the tricolour being flown in Armagh city and by union organisers, and large-scale political rallies taking place on Glasgow Green and in other Scots towns, but there was also an immense wave of rural protest which some observers wrongly attributed to French agitators. On 28 August in Lower Hardres, just south-west of Canterbury, threshing machines were burned and Irish labourers were attacked. Within a few days the movement spread throughout Kent and began to affect Surrey. By October arson and menaces to landlords had made their appearance in Sussex, and by December the whole of south-east and central England was affected. Hopes of greater change to come played a part in this as they did on the Continent.

One example occurred in the desolate fen-like region of Otmoor in Oxfordshire, where small farmers had been able to resist the encroachments of enclosures and reclamations thanks to the common grazing, fuel, game and osiers provided by the moor. When these came under renewed pressure in 1830 attacks on hedges and stakes took place in August and, on 6 September, there was an occupation of the moor by the local population. Although the militia arrested many, they were freed by crowds in Oxford. Then, despite the strengthening of the militia's presence in the aftermath of the Swing riots, the disturbances resumed once it was removed in the winter. If such movements rarely involved violence to persons, the same cannot be said for the Irish Tithe War, which also began in the summer of 1830 as tithes were extended to grazing-land and commutation dues became payable by peasants. A third of all violent deaths in Ireland before the Famine were due to these troubles in Munster and Leinster between 1830 and 1833, the massacre at Carrickshock Hill outside Killmegarry in west Kilkenny on 14 December 1831 being the worst example. Ireland, however, did not see the surge of militant unionism which spread from north-west England into Wales at this time, leading to miners' strikes in Denbigh and Flint.

Thus, notwithstanding their urban and political nature, the early revolutions did strike a responsive chord in many peasants in the heartland zone, even if they rarely saw fit to act in defence of the revolutions. Their problems were part of the whole nexus of social grievances, remedy of which suddenly seemed possible to the excited artisans and the populace in general with the inauguration of the new age in Paris. Inflation, fiscality, the price and supply of bread, the guilds, factory and foreign competition, unemployment, lack of representation, police brutality, customs policies and the doings of incoherent and inept governments were issues which played a large part in mobilising such people. This was the case in Germany, for instance. This dimension of the events of 1830 has rarely been appreciated – at least, outside France. Yet it was present and it helps to explain why the news from Paris and Brussels had such an immediate impact. Revolution was thus a symbol of unexpected hope in the midst of increasing misery and oppression, and provided a vital impetus to the general movement for change unleashed in July and August 1830.

This sense of liberation was some way removed from the more political concerns which animated radical activists and middle-class liberals alike. The former saw in the July Days not so much release from old social burdens as the chance for a wholesale restructuring of society. It was not a chance they had really expected, since many radicals, like the indefatigable organiser of secret societies, Filippo Buonarotti, were taken by surprise by the July Days. It was only afterwards that they began to organise themselves, as they did in Paris in the Café Lointier, in order to try to lead the revolutions into more democratic and outward-looking paths. Even so, where other countries were concerned, they were uncertain whether to plan something or to wait for spontaneous uprisings.

Hence, though there was some talk of action inside Belgium and pamphlets were printed at the Café Belge in the Galerie Vero Dodat behind the Louvre, this does not seem to have amounted to very much. In Switzerland, where there was no real radical movement, some of the liberal leaders who were holidaying together on the Righi took the July Days as the sign that the time had come to act. Yet, in the event, the people who actually set the process of change in motion later in September tended to be local notables. None the less, the enthusiasm provoked by the July Days counted for a good deal in Belgium and Switzerland. As one Swiss historian later noted, it was the gale which blew the clouds together and made possible the storm to come.

Even in England many radicals, and not a few Whigs, responded electrically to the news from Paris – news which seemed to offer the former the encouragement to advance into a new era of democracy and the latter the possibility of limited but necessary reforms. 'France is making rapid strides,' declared the Manchester MP, Mark Philips, whereas 'England is standing still'. Radicals therefore tried to capitalise on the July Days by positive action: sending delegations to Paris and calling celebratory public meetings. The liberal middle classes, believing as Palmerston did that 'the event is decisive of the ascendancy of liberal principles throughout Europe', were flattered to find France following England for once. So, even if the news from Paris did not influence the outcome of the election than being held, it did influence the way the new House of Commons behaved thereafter. Butler may be right to speak of a sense of 'boundless exultation' amongst reformers, although they did not always know very much about what had actually happened on the Continent, and in the case of Belgium they did not always like what they did know. Radicals like Cobbett may have warmed to the new encouragement from Brussels, but much liberal opinion took a dim view of a revolution which destroyed a deliberately created bulwark of British interests on the one hand, and encouraged Catholic dissidence in Ireland on the other. The kings of Denmark and Sweden, who also enjoyed suzerainty over joint kingdoms, were also inclined to be more alarmed than pleased by the events in Belgium.

Obviously, in England communications with the Continent were rapid, frequent and unfettered. Elsewhere this was not always the case. None the less, events in France in particular were still followed very closely. In Italy we can still see hastily written accounts of the events in France which were confiscated by the police from alleged liberals. There is also evidence of the warm welcome the news received in the west, in countries as far apart as Spain and Denmark. In the former a provisional government was optimistically created at Bayonne by exiles, while in the latter not only did Copenhagen give every sign of enthusiasm, but also separatist opinion in Schleswig-Holstein was revitalised. In eastern Europe, apart from Poland, the impact was much less immediate. However, when the news reached opposition circles in Russia, as it did on 18 August, some former Decembrists felt that the popular struggle in Paris offered a new perspective on how things might go in future in Russia. The poet Pushkin, indeed, went so far as to claim that the July Monarchy was the kind of regime which Russia needed. Similarly, intellectuals in other distant regions like Croatia were also moved by the news to launch cultural demands of their own, and supporters of independence and liberalisation in Greece were also, for a while, much encouraged by it all.

At the same time as the July Days and the other troubles were exciting the populace to demonstrate their discontent with their conditions and inspiring the politically aware to seek constitutional changes, rulers and conservative groups were also affected. In some cases the revolutions strengthened the hands of rulers. Most obviously, Don Pedro was moved to accept the inevitability of assisting the liberals in Portugal, and the country moved closer to civil war. The Turks, moreover, felt it wise in the new circumstances not to renege on the undertakings they had reluctantly given to Serbia, and they duly withdrew their garrisons and then agreed to cede further territory to Miloš Obrenović. Other rulers similarly took the July Revolution as a warning and held back from provocative projects of their own, as did Charles John of Sweden, thereby assuring the Norwegians that there would be no further threats to their autonomy and constitutional rights. The new king of the Two Sicilies, Ferdinand II, was moved to offer an amnesty to political offenders on his accession later in the year.

Some rulers, on the other hand, found that the new troubles threatened their positions. Nowhere was this more marked than in the case of Don Miguel in Portugal. But it was also true of Ferdinand VII in Spain; and the July Days may also have made Francis IV of Modena change his mind about pursuing his strange dealings with a coterie of exiles and plotters. In The Hague, Turin and Rome new controls and tighter surveillance were imposed in August in case the troubles should spread. Nicholas I went so far as to try to seal off his empire from all contact with the subversive west. Yet, despite the obvious dangers posed by a new revolution in Paris, the established authorities did not react very positively, which was perhaps the first of their mistakes. The opposition was not so lethargic.

In like manner, although the members of the diplomatic establishment talked a great deal of what should be done, they were not inspired by the news to any drastic measures. Charles X had not been the most popular of rulers, and reactions to his fall were somewhat mixed. Metternich wanted to create a united front of the eastern powers and England so as to confine the French inside their existing boundaries, doubting the ability of Louis-Philippe to stop the forces of revolution in the way his envoys were soon engaged in trying to assure Europe would be the case. Metternich was unable to do this, or to secure new guarantees for the Austrian position in Italy, and had to content himself with warning the French that Austria would fight if France was found to be involved in fomenting revolution elsewhere. Some diplomats believed that this was already happening in Belgium. So, despite the feeling of expectancy in the chanceries of Europe in 1829–30, the powers were taken by surprise by events in Switzerland and France, and took some time to work out their position, thereby enabling the movement to gain strength and spread. The fact that they could not at once stop the new conflagration they so much feared was a further weakness.

Thus, while peasants and artisans acted and reformers enthused, establishments havered. Out of this came the first new challenge to the system. This broke out in Brussels on 25–6 August when the failure of the authorities to deal with riots led to the creation of a local committee of security which was to be the forerunner of a *de facto* native regime, to which much of the country began to look for leadership. That all this happened in Brussels was not the result of French agitators, or even of the lure of money, despite the hot air talked about the annexation of Belgium in Paris. It owed much more to the fact that the July Days had a tremendous impact on an area which had been incorporated in France for twenty years prior to 1814 and in which the long-standing conflict with William I had turned the Belgians into one of the most politically aware and active peoples in Europe. Their feelings had not been assuaged by William's concessions, let alone by the maintenance by the local authorities in the capital of an unpopular tax on milling – abolished elsewhere in the country – in order to pay for fireworks scheduled for the king's birthday. In the prevailing atmosphere of political excitement and economic crisis this also caused immense resentment. The authorities chose to ignore both protests about food-prices and their own fears of excesses to come. Then, when trouble ensued, they panicked.

So they helped to provoke the events of 25 August and then allowed these to liberate a whole series of complaints: about high taxes, factory production and, especially, the unfairness of the factory system. Then, when calls for change were met only in part, and without any evidence of good faith on the king's part, the movement escalated. Political mobilisation was thus encouraged by the way The Hague began to pile sins of commission on top of its earlier errors of omission, so that a real revolutionary movement, similar to that of France in the 1790s, began to emerge. And, once the Dutch, albeit not wholly intentionally, shed Belgian blood in Brussels, the movement became a national one and the Dutch were swept from the southern provinces, creating the question of how a new nation could be integrated into the European political system.

These developments in Belgium obviously reinforced the impact of the events in France on populace and reformers alike, while at the same time considerably complicating the diplomatic dimensions of the crisis. Moreover, before Belgian opposition had shown that it had a life of its own, trouble had broken out elsewhere. In Saxony protests against the inert and pro-Catholic monarchy began on 31 August. They were soon reinforced on the one hand by the corruption of local government and the brutality of the police, and on the other by the high level of taxes and the low level of employment. And, although the tricolour was sometimes flown and a constitution on French lines demanded, local issues were the key ones. They were sufficiently widely understood and expressed to persuade the regime to concede most of the demands.

In Brunswick the highly unpopular Duke had tried to ignore the changing political climate and reacted even more provocatively to requests for constitutional change by trying to use the army. However, he had not counted on civilian disaffection being shared by the military, and when demands for food and a Diet took on a violent form the army refused to support him. As soon as he fled disaffection spread to the peasantry, aggrieved by the burden of internal customs-barriers. Finally, in Electoral Hesse it was the combination of the ruler's besotted behaviour over his mistress, and the fear that he was conspiring with bakers to raise the price of bread, which sparked off successful demands for a parliamentary constitution.

This first wave of revolts, then, owed a great deal both to popular action and to the eccentricities of the rulers involved. What in other circumstances might have been venial mistakes turned out to be mortal blunders in the highly charged atmosphere induced by the revolutions and the mounting economic pressures which the political troubles had often served to aggravate. The triggers were immediate and action spontaneous.

Later challenges were slightly different. In Switzerland there was much popular clamour for change, but to a large extent there were also proper channels for its expression; and, although governments were often slow and hesitant about their responses, they generally gave ground. Social issues were less visible and, whatever the original impulse from Paris, it was the interplay between the cantons which really helped things along. There was thus one model of political change within the Confederation. It begun with petitions, or the circulation of pamphlets calling for change, and went on to meetings of notables who sometimes politely and personally lobbied their rulers and sometimes called mass meetings to do this. The rural districts' demands for fairer and more direct representation in government were crystallised in the process. When governments demurred, or dispatched commissioners to sound out opinion, or tried to undertake reforms themselves, there was often a real, or threatened, march on the capital, after which governments usually gave way and agreed to full, open constitutional revisions, according to the desired forms. In other words, once the trigger had been pulled the whole process proved to be fairly self-contained.

Popular support was much more limited in Poland and, though the dissident military cadets were vastly encouraged when they saw the French consulate flying the tricolour on 6 August, the influence of France was even more indirect and psychological. In any case, the Poles were aware of the diplomatic uncertainties created by the July Days which could all too easily work against them. So, although they decided to continue plotting, they put off immediate action on 12 August in the hope that the situation might improve and more general support be obtained. Neither of these things came to pass, especially as the diplomatic community in general and Russia in particular had begun to take matters in hand, and in the end it was fear, first of having to fight in the west and then of having been discovered, that finally drove the Poles to act in late November. In the event, the cadets' *coup de main* would probably have failed had it not been for the spontaneous intervention by the Warsaw crowd, aggrieved at the way the local authorities had abused their powers and raised the price of vodka. Once the *putsch* succeeded, the revolt began to escalate, somewhat as it had in Belgium.

In Italy the effect of the July Days was more direct. It gave a fillip to the exiles from 1820–1 and, more important, electrified liberals and others in the Romagna and elsewhere. Police reports speak of excited recountings of the Parisian events in the cafés of Bologna, together with fervid readings of the French press and passionate discussions with foreign visitors. The news of the Brussels outburst also caused new demonstrations in Cesena, where the tricolour was flown. All of this caused governments to tighten their police operations and to try to stop possible exile incursions, whether from Switzerland into Lombardy or by landings on the Ligurian coast. In fact, while some Tuscan liberals did plan a kind of *coup* in Florence and the veteran liberal General Pepe wanted to land a force of exiles in Calabria, initially nothing came of either.

The exiles were slow to unite and to act, so that it was only in January 1831 that, having got what they thought were guarantees of support from the French, they arrived at a plan. And, although there was a conspiracy in Modena aiming at making the Duke head of a north Italian state, here, too, it was only in the New Year that any real attempt to create nuclei of support was started, and the attempted rising in Modena was pre-empted by the Duke. So it was actually in Bologna that a real revolution began – a reflection of accumulating social grievances and the weak and inept handling of the crisis by the papal administration. Encouraged to some extent by a forged note, purporting to come from a French envoy, the revolt spread down into the Romagna, as well as back to Modena and Parma.

The lack of success of the Italian conspirators was as great as that of those brave, if misguided, Spaniards who set out to invade the eastern and southern flanks of their country. Deliberate attempts to stimulate revolution had much less success, in other words, than movements emerging because of governmental provocation and popular unease, both of which had been indirectly triggered by the July Days. These did not, however, create the explosive situations themselves. The latter had their own internal dynamics and were not merely domino-like responses to the events in Paris or anywhere else.

The spread of revolution in Europe between the summer of 1830 and the New Year of 1831 can be explained without invoking direct intervention by the French. Indeed, emulation of the events in France was far from slavish. There were conspirators who hoped to stage deliberate revolutionary acts but, as has become clear, they counted for very little. The connection between the July Days and the other outbursts was not organic but symbolic. Metternich was quite right when he said that the July Days were like the breaching of a dike. They blew a hole in the fragile defences of the Restoration system so that all the accumulated frustrations and tensions took the opportunity of forcibly escaping, especially as other rulers had done their best to chip further parts of the dike away.

Politically conscious townspeople and discontented artisans and peasants all took their chance; for, whether or not they understood who Charles X was or what the July Revolution really involved, they all seem to have seen in the July Days a symbol of liberation, sometimes political, sometimes not. The Swiss changes in the early summer of 1830 lacked the emotive appeal of the happenings in Paris, but the other revolutions all played their part in widening the breach in the system. The idea, then, that 1830 was the automatic result of what took place in France that July is quite simply wrong.

The July Days, in other words, were a necessary cause of revolution, not a sufficient one. Such psychological symbols and other governmental and economic triggers would have had little effect had there not been water mounting behind the dam. Local grievances and the ways in which these and the economic depression were handled were essential to the causal process. Without them there would have been no response to the news from Paris or elsewhere. Because of their own problems people were willing, first, to read into the events in Paris whatever suited them and then to exploit local opportunities often created without their real volition. So when the symbolic and psychological triggers of the July Days interacted with existing stresses and strains inside Europe's uneasy social and political life, the whole thing erupted in a series of explosions which were at one and the same time part of a European-wide crisis and responses to quite specific local situations. The year's explosions were the complex product of a prolonged accumulation of fissile material in European society. Paris merely ignited the fuse.

4   A Bird's-Eye View of Revolution

It should already be clear that the complex and multi-layered causes of the revolutions of 1830 allowed the revolutionary process to develop its own dynamic. And consideration of why there were revolts in 1830-1 has inevitably moved the story somewhat beyond the initial outbursts of June, July and August 1830. As the outbreaks became more separated in time and place they became less dependent on the popular agitation and political excitement of these months, and more involved with the general European crisis which was developing. This crisis was increasingly concerned with the diplomatic implications of the outbursts in the west, as the great powers recovered their equilibrium and set about curtailing or absorbing the explosions. So, while the revolts obviously had very marked individual characteristics, they all had a family resemblance and were all affected by the same general European conditions. In other words, the next question we need to ask – what actually happened in the revolutions of 1830? – must first be answered for Europe at large, and an effort made to identify the similarities and interrelationships of the revolutions, particularly at the diplomatic level, leaving their differences to separate examinations later. So an overview of the way matters developed in the fifty months of crisis, in regard both to the revolutionary movements and the general European responses, is a useful prelude to looking at the way events unfolded within the confines of specific regions and countries.

On the European level the crisis was a variable one. It went through at least four phases, and as the character of the revolutions changed, so did the response of the great powers. Initially, as we have seen, the outbreaks were mainly social protests aimed as much against concrete grievances as they were against the French or Dutch monarchies. Because they happened so suddenly and unexpectedly, the great powers, for all their alarm at the possibility of a return to the disastrous days of the 1790s, could do little but acquiesce. However, when events took a new turn and the revolutionary explosions became more frequent, more widespread, more radical and more violent, as they did in the constitutional and patriotic risings of September and October 1830, this tolerance began to fade and some powers, notably Russia, began seriously to consider going to war to halt the further spread of revolution. The continued social disorders added to the general uncertainty of the early autumn.

The outbreak of a third wave of more explicitly nationalist risings in Poland, Italy and – to a much lesser extent – Spain over the winter of

1830-1 changed things. The fact that the first two revolutions were directed against pillars of conservative Europe meant that a general war became much less likely, especially as some of the earlier issues were increasingly dealt with diplomatically. Although there were social elements in the latest revolutions, usually these took on the appearance of a hopeless military confrontation between the forces of change and those of conservatism. By the spring of 1831 the tide began to turn. The early revolts had by then largely made their points, while the later ones increasingly found themselves staring military defeat in the face. And, although this period of aftermath was not free of new troubles, some of which grew out of the revolutions themselves, both the revolutionary movement and the possibility of a general war – which had briefly returned in the spring of 1831 – began to fade. By 1832-3 the crisis was nearing its end.

The crisis had begun in a series of unplanned political outbreaks, directed against abusive governmental initiatives. In Switzerland things initially stayed at this level, but then, thanks to the apocalyptic hopes raised by the July Days, the first phase of the crisis was marked by a major outburst of social protest, such as was the case in the south-east corner of England. But, before that could begin, the phenomenon had made itself felt in Brussels. There on the night of 25–6 August a largely symbolic protest against Dutch rule, orchestrated by middle-class theatregoers, degenerated into a wave of vandalism, directed not just against the establishment, but also against cafés, wine-shops and suburban factories. Because the authorities on the spot failed to stop the disorders, the local notables set up their own administrative and military organisation to safeguard property. They then seized the opportunity to press for the political changes which they wanted, particularly as these might remove one of the ostensible grounds for social disturbances which had meanwhile spread not merely to other Walloon towns like Verviers, but also into Germany, to Eupen, Düsseldorf and Aachen, where many Belgians were employed. The arrival in Brussels of revolutionary volunteers from all over the southern provinces, coupled with William's oscillation between military and reformist responses, meant that the situation became increasingly acute. Administrative separation became the order of the day in Brussels, not just amongst the notables, but also amongst the lower classes who were increasingly hard pressed by the economic dislocation caused by the August disturbances.

This growing radicalism in Belgium was paralleled by the outbreak of trouble in some of the states of north central Germany. Thus in Brunswick political protests began on 31 August. They were soon followed by more violent demonstrations against the brutal police and the catholic sympathisers of the Saxon monarchy. Such protests were soon reinforced by the way the eccentric Duke of Brunswick tried to answer renewed pressure for constitutional reform by military means, only to complete the alienation of the local establishment. Then, on 2 September, social protest began in Saxony. Although it was mastered, this further evidence of regal incomprehension only added to the resistance. The king's advisers decided that he must climb down and concede change. They were confirmed in this view when the violence spread to the state capital. On 6–7 September the middle classes in Kassel had to put down a very violent bread riot against the Electoral adminstration, and within a week the ruler had seen the light, agreeing to reform and to call the Diet. Self-evidently he had learned from the fate of Karl of Brunswick, whose nerve had broken when, on 7–8 September, the army had refused to do his dirty work for him, so forcing him into ignominious flight. The way the Saxons had flown the tricolour, sung the 'Marseillaise', burned police records and seen off *chasseurs* sent to discipline them no doubt also helped wonderfully to concentrate the minds of other of the Elector's princely colleagues.

The manner in which the July Days had not merely led to an outburst of social protest, but also enabled disgruntled subjects in at least four states to extract large constitutional concessions in the face of street violence that could not be mastered, was a matter of very grave concern to European statesmen and rulers, haunted as they were by the traumatic memories of the first French revolution. However, taking action against this very rapid series of revolts was not all that easy. This was not just because of the generally ambiguous attitudes generated by France, but also owed something to problems of communication, especially during a holiday season, and something to the general disharmony amongst the powers consequent on the troubles in south-eastern Europe. Many countries tried to take preventative measures, albeit to little effect. Metternich in particular felt that the July Days threatened his life's work, even if they did justify his warnings about the possibility of revolution, which had been almost derided in the late 1820s. Whatever his feelings about the personalities in France, the overthrow of an established monarchy could not be overlooked, especially when its result was to threaten both Belgium and the left bank of the Rhine just as Polignac had done in 1829.

None the less, he had to tread carefully because of the uncertain and divided state of Europe. Suggestions of a conference were rejected by Wellington as smacking too much of the Holy Alliance, and so Metternich had to be content with agreeing with Nesselrode, the Russian Foreign Minister, on the so-called 'chiffon de Carlsbad' of 6 August. This was a promise to recognise the new French monarchy provided it stayed within its existing frontiers, which, of course, was what Louis-Philippe was soon promising to do. He sent envoys to all the courts of Europe arguing that he had only taken the throne in order to stop anarchy and adventure. Generally he was able to win their tolerance, save in the case of Russia. There the Tsar, on hearing of the news in early August, had attempted to seal his empire from contamination. And, far from confirming his Foreign Minister's initiative, he broke off diplomatic relations with France. Although he was eventually persuaded to relax his stance and approve the 'chiffon', he still insisted that the great powers must stand united against the potential threat and sent out his own envoys to sound out the eastern powers on the possibility of military action.

By then the other powers had acted and recognised Louis-Philippe. Prussia was the first to move, once she had obtained guarantees that the new regime, unlike that of Charles X, had no ambitions in the Rhineland. As a result, Berlin was somewhat embarrassed by the subsequent arrival of a bellicose Russian envoy. The British ambassador in Paris presented his credentials on 31 August and, on 5 September, Francis II of Austria received a French envoy. His recognition, however, was couched in cooler terms, with a heavy emphasis on the need for France to avoid all aggressive action. This trend towards recognition meant that when, on 7 September, the Dutch Foreign Minister invited the powers to consider holding a conference on the Belgian issue there was not much interest. And, by 1 October, Nicholas himself came round to actually recognising Louis-Philippe, albeit in an offhand and slighting manner. Spain followed suit on 13 October, and by the end of the month only Modena still held out. In fact not until early in 1831 did Francesco IV offer to recognise Louis-Philippe, but his tardy overture was to be ignored throughout the life of the July Monarchy.

The first phase of the July crisis had, then, ended in accommodation. Although the powers might huff and puff, the relatively self-contained change of regime in France, even when followed by popular effervescence in Brussels and other cities, was not enough to justify a war, any more than the trouble in southern Switzerland had been. The revolts were too scattered and too limited in nature at that stage to warrant more drastic action. However, almost before the powers had come to this decision, the situation had begun to change rapidly, and for the worse. The dissidence in Belgium took on an increasingly radical tone, and by the end of September had effectively destroyed the Joint Kingdom. Since this had been created in 1815 in order to guarantee the security of the Continent, Belgium became a matter of pressing international concern. The way that trouble continued to flare up in Germany, where it came formally before the Bund in one case, and began to affect Switzerland reinforced such anxiety, especially as new popular disturbances in Paris seemed to call into question Louis-Philippe's claims to have mastered the forces of aggression and disorder. With some rulers feeling it wise to adopt conciliatory measures the crisis spread and deepened. Not merely did the Vienna settlement as a whole seem to be in jeopardy, but also countries not so far affected seem to have felt threatened, as was Austria by the excitement in Italy. Yet, again with the exception of Russia, the powers still considered it was preferable to try to solve the matter diplomatically, in part because many of them were inclined to hold William I more than a little responsible for the major problems they faced in Belgium. And, in the end, the possibility that this second phase of the crisis might issue in war was removed by the outbreak of revolution in Warsaw.

As far as the momentum of revolution was concerned, there is no doubt that this was maintained primarily by Belgium during this phase of affairs. That the situation in Belgium, which had initially seemed to be moving towards relatively pacific administrative separation within the Joint Kingdom, should have escalated in the way it did was due in part to the inherent dynamic of Belgian aspirations and partly to the mistaken tactics of the king. In Brussels there was what amounted to a political vacuum, since many leading figures had gone north to try to negotiate with William during the special session of the States-General. This vacuum coincided with increasing economic dislocation, springing from the general political uncertainty. Thus the administration left in the southern capital found itself besieged by the poor and the unemployed.

The latter proved a fertile source of recruits for the more radical and politically conscious elements who were still pouring into Brussels from Liège and elsewhere. Though they still thought in terms of mere separation, they were willing to extract this by creating a proper army and seizing control of finance and administration from the Dutch, thereby going well beyond the aims of the moderate authorities in Brussels even though they, too, were thinking in an ever more nationalistic manner. The latter were soon overwhelmed by a series of massive demonstrations, attempted sorties against Dutch troops, and clashes with the remnants of the burgher guard in August. Two-thirds of the way through September the town was in a virtual state of anarchy, and the lower classes were being encouraged to build barricades and join free companies as a military confrontation with the Dutch became increasingly likely.

Such a clash was not wholly unwelcome in The Hague. For, although the States-General had by then started to discuss possible constitutional amendments, William had not pursued the task with any great urgency and, at the same time, he had begun to plan military action. He seems to have believed that a military demonstration would dispel resistance in Brussels without undue difficulty. The fact that industrialists and others were increasingly alarmed by the prospect of continuing social unrest and economic dislocation and, in Brussels, apparently made overtures to his younger son encouraged him in this view. Even some of the radical leaders in the south felt that resistance was hopeless and fled when fighting appeared imminent. William also believed that, were the Belgians to attack his forces in the south, this would justify any punitive measures he might wish to take. In all this William seriously underestimated the effects that social distress and patriotic fervour were having on the populace of Brussels, not to mention the impact that his own Machiavellianism would have both there and on the diplomatic community.

So, although Prince Frederick's proclamation on 22 September disbanding the Security Commission and threatening a purge of the militia was meant to cow the *canaille* and encourage the notables to rally to him, it had the opposite effect. Popular resistance was stiffened, and hardly any notables rallied to the Dutch, thereby totally undermining Frederick's strategy. Attacks on the lower town were ignominiously rebuffed by a relative handful of lower-class patriots, while the main pushes in the well-to-do quarters of the upper town were poorly executed, and the bulk of the army found itself dangerously pinned down in the park attached to the royal palace. Further efforts at negotiation failed while the rebellious populace, angered by the fact that they had been assaulted, grew in number and enthusiasm as peasants from the suburban villages and some members of the middle classes joined the volunteers and the large body of workers who were carrying on the resistance. As Dutch attempts to break out from their cramped positions failed, the Belgians were able to establish a provisional government including some of the radical politicians who began to trickle back to Brussels when the news of the unexpected popular success began to circulate throughout Wallonia. Although the Belgians were not themselves strong enough to storm the park, in the end the Dutch commanders decided that it was too dangerous to carry on the fight, since they risked not only even heavier losses but also the possibility of entrapment in the south. Hence they pulled out during the night of 26–7 September.

The Four Days of Brussels represented a crucial defeat for the Dutch. For, not merely had they embarked on a routine punitive exercise and been humiliatingly defeated, thereby losing face amongst the powers, for whom failure was the ultimate offence, but they had also forced the rest of Belgian society to join the struggle. The bloodshed in Brussels produced a wave of nationalist enthusiasm (as the British envoy had warned it would) which mobilised tens of thousands of people from all social groups against a royal army which was exhausted, plagued by bad organisation, and increasingly unable to rely on its Belgian elements. It had, moreover, failed to cope with other challenges in Liège and Louvain during the Four Days, and then proved incapable of utilising its garrisons and fortresses. And so volunteers continued to flock into Brussels to support the provisional government as it set about creating a makeshift national administration for a country which it was able to declare independent on 4 October. By then, not merely had Wallonia freed itself from Dutch control, but even much of Flanders was following suit while bands of volunteers were cheerfully and successfully harassing the Dutch as they withdrew painfully northwards. By late October the whole country outside the citadels in Antwerp and the fortress cities of

Luxembourg and Maastricht was in Belgian hands. William's combination of bluster, weakness and military naïveté thus cost him control of southern provinces which were both much more mature politically and distressed economically than he had realised.

The impact of this second defeat of a royal army within two months obviously made a considerable impression on Europe, especially as it was the result of a movement that was both more sustained and, it seemed, more revolutionary than that of Paris, and entailed a breach in the Vienna settlement. The self-liberation of Belgium gave pace to developments in other parts of Europe. In late September there were further peasant troubles in the Harz Mountains, affecting both Brunswick and Hanover, while in October the Spanish incursions over the Pyrenees got under way. Perhaps even more worrying were the riots of 17–19 October in Paris against the former ministers of Charles X, which seemed to be a sign that the restraint which characterised the first phase of dissent was fading everywhere. Indeed, from 14 September, when the leading citizens of Lenzburg in the Aargau petitioned their Great Council for constitutional reform, the ferment had spread in Switzerland.

By the end of October many more cantons had joined in the movement, backing up initially peaceful petitions by electoral boycotts, as in Aargau and Thurgau, and more rarely by violent means, as happened at Porrentruy in the Bernese Jura. During November mass meetings of several thousand people had become quite common, and many governments came to feel that they had no alternative but to commit themselves to change. By then, too, elections had been held in Belgium for a national congress to consider a draft constitution which created a constitutional monarchy from which, by 24 November, all members of the House of Orange-Nassau had been resoundingly debarred. England also felt the wind of change since the defeat of Wellington over the question of the civil list on 16 November brought in a Whig government, thereby encouraging a renewed outburst of agitation in favour of parlimentary reform. Even Denmark felt the impact of this second wave of revolt, since it moved Uwe-Jens Lornsen to petition the king for autonomy for Schleswig-Holstein.

All of this worried the powers as much as it seems to have encouraged the forces of opposition. For revolts had become more frequent, more interrelated, and more radical, spreading beyond spontaneous anger and social protest towards overtly political demands which threatened to subvert not merely established regimes, but the Restoration diplomatic order as well. It was inevitable that the powers would have had to review their initial, moderate positions. In the event, this was forced on them by a Dutch declaration of 28 September to the effect that they were no longer in a position to undertake the subjugation of their rebellious southern provinces themselves. Then, on 2 October, the Dutch Foreign Minister formally requested military aid to this end from the signatories of the

1815 treaties. Although Field-Marshal Diebitsch offered nearly a quarter of a million Russian troops, the other powers rejected the request. Prussia did so because she would not risk war without a general agreement amongst the powers. There was still little chance that this would be forthcoming. Indeed, Metternich, perhaps surprisingly, was even more trenchant in his refusal. He regarded the Joint Kingdom as a lost cause and sought only to ensure that Belgium would not be reunited with France and, like Wellington (who regarded him as vain and dangerous), had a low opinion of William. On the other hand, he was very concerned about Italy and made it clear on 20 October that, were there to be trouble there, Austria would always intervene if requested and would not respect the proposal of non-intervention which the new French government had derived from Britain. His main aim was to stabilise the July Monarchy and thus to stop it from aiding revolt in Italy. The Austrians therefore recalled the Hungarian Diet that autumn in an effort to gain the men and money needed to do this.

Britain and France, of course were not only totally opposed to any assistance to the Dutch, but were also averse to any kind of military venture. Tallyrand had been sent as French ambassador to London late in September with a brief to steer clear of all threats to the Belgians' crown, lands or stability. Molé, the Foreign Minister, was well aware of inherent British suspicions of French ambitions in the area and sought to do everything to allay them. The French therefore declared themselves ready to accept the decision of a European conference, such as that which had presided over the solution of the Greek war. This was accepted by Wellington and was ultimately embodied in a protocol on 15 October. Two days later the French informed William that there could be no question of military aid – a move anticipated by the Dutch on 15 October when they asked for five-power mediation instead.

William, however, continued to play both ends against the middle, since at the same time he dropped attempts to rally support for his son as ruler of an associated Belgian kingdom and permitted the bombardment of Antwerp on 27 October. To some extent he was encouraged in this course by his impression that Nicholas of Russia had reverted to his original idea of an anti-revolutionary military crusade. The Tsar had indeed been shocked by the loss of Belgium, which threatened the succession of his daughter, the Princess of Orange; and, though his advisers managed to calm him down at first, the receipt of the formal request for aid – and the news of the Belgian declaration of independence – made his attitude harden. The fact that some Russians had been on the barricades in Paris and that echoes of the July Days were now reaching border towns, students and intellectuals in Russia itself no doubt worried him as well.

He was emphatic that the general threat from revolution had to be met, and so on 17 October he mobilised his troops, Poles included, with a view to campaigning in the west not later than 22 December. On 25 October he also indicated his willingness to respond to William's appeal. It may be that he was really engaged in a war of nerves with the French, rather than actually committing himself to the overthrow of the July Monarchy, since he was warned by France on 1 December that any intervention in the west would be regarded as a *causus belli*. None the less, his new line meant that Europe was gripped by a real war-scare, despite the fact that the London Conference had already begun to meet and had, not without difficulty, secured an armistice in the Low Countries by 21 November.

The fear of war was a real one, encouraged by the way some extremists did what they could to bring it on in the hope that it would usher in the general liberation of Europe. But the majority of the great powers remained firmly opposed to resorting to arms; so that it all depended on Russia, and events in Warsaw late in November conspired to make the launching of a general struggle impossible for Nicholas. Although this was not the intention of the cadet conspirators, their *coup* did have the effect of removing the threat hanging over Belgium and other western countries. At the same time, the Warsaw insurrection helped to unleash the third phase of the crisis, which ran from December 1830 until about April 1831. Although the social protest which had been so significant earlier in 1830 remained visible, most notably in Switzerland and Hanover, the revolutions were increasingly a matter of nationalist challenges to the great powers, carried forward mainly by military means. They thus tended to substitute specific challenges for the generalised confrontation feared in the late autumn, though suspicions of France ensured that this demon was only slowly exorcised. There were to be renewed clashes in Iberia, including further armed incursions into Spain; attempted *putsches* in Rome, which were to serve as a prelude to a series of major risings in central Italy and which, before they were put down by the Austrian army, involved a military strike against Rome; while even in Switzerland there was more violence.

The dominant issue, however, was the war between the Poles and Russia which, because it started promisingly for the rebels, gave an enormous boost to exiles and radicals in western Europe. Even some of the western powers were sympathetic, but were powerless to do anything to assist the Poles. The nationalist element present in the Polish struggle for freedom was echoed in the arguments between the Belgian Congress and the powers, who took a much more functional view of Belgian rights than did the self-confident revolutionaries there. Agreement was hard to achieve, and combined with suspicions of French ambitions both in Italy and Belgium to produce continuing tension. Not until the late spring, by which time internal changes had helped the French and Belgians to adjust to the new situation, did the tension ease and the war-scare wane.

The fact that the European crisis evolved in this way, rather than into a general war, was, as we have seen, partly due to the Poles. But the Warsaw *coup* of 29 November did not reflect any particular concern with the diplomatic situation. The July Days had encouraged a long-running conspiracy, yet had not enabled it to acquire much popular support; and in the end the cadets launched their *coup* more because they had to than because they really wanted to do so. It was hurriedly brought forward to avert repression and, not surprisingly, was ill-planned and poorly executed. The attack on the Belvedere Palace was carried out by a bare handful of men and, though the Palace was captured, the conspirators failed to find their main target, Grand Duke Constantine. Equally they failed to carry the fight to the Russian garrison and were unable to create a provisional government. It was only when the artisans of Warsaw, for social and economic reasons of their own, joined the cadets and when Constantine refused to use the forces available to him immediately to snuff out the trouble that the revolution triumphed. And, although a good deal of popular excitement was generated both there and in other centres, it was left to senior generals and moderate politicians to try to run affairs. Many of them, including the leading general, Chłopicki, had no sympathy with the rebellion, and took charge in the hope of negotiating with Nicholas and avoiding a catastrophic breach.

The Tsar, unfortunately, would have none of this. His immediate response on learning of the revolt in early December was to demand the Poles' total surrender. He also increased the readiness of his armies. Thus, when the Polish Parliament met on 17 December to hear the gentry deputies' enthusiastic declaration that the insurrection was a national act which should be extended throughout the lands of the old Commonwealth the breach was consummated. While Chłopicki tried unsuccessfully to lay down his office of temporary 'Dictator' Nicholas ordered loyal troops to concentrate at Płock, thereby making war almost unavoidable. When Chłopicki's attempt to arrest the radical leaders and to halt the increasingly revolutionary enthusiasm of the capital failed, the Sejm cheerfully went on to depose Nicholas on 26 January amidst growing preparations for war. By late January, Russian troops were on the move westwards and war soon became a reality. That it was fought on the Narew rather than on the Nethe was testimony to the gravity with which Nicholas regarded the Polish threat, causing him to concentrate all his energies on dealing with it, and allowing the attempt to reach a diplomatic solution in Belgium to proceed unchecked.

In this manner Belgian independence was preserved and the threats to a growing number of revolutionary movements elsewhere were also lifted. December, in fact, had proved to be a fairly eventful month. In Paris demonstrations against the allegedly mild sentences passed on the ministers of Charles X showed that the radical tide was still running high. A few days previously, on 12 December, there had been an abortive Bonapartist *coup* in Rome, which filled both Louis-Philippe and the

Vatican with alarm. In Switzerland the pressure for reform boiled over into angry gatherings of armed peasants who extorted constitutional reforms in Fribourg, Aargau and the Vaud within a fortnight. In the other cantons the process was a little more peaceful, but still vigorous. The new year brought yet more marches, attempted assassinations and, on 6 January, a bloody clash between the peasants and the urban reformers of Basle, in which the former were worsted. Alarms and excursions continued into February, by which time cantons had agreed to reform and many had started to do so.

Before then the spirit of dissidence had flared up in Hanover, where on 6 January there was a rising in Osterode against William IV's resident minister. Although this was rapidly dealt with by the army, the idea caught on and two days later Göttingen threw out its own unpopular authorities and set up a popular militia. And, although several thousand troops were mobilised to put an end to them, the fact that not merely were the towns seething, but there was unrest in the countryside as well, led the government to look into constitutional concessions. None the less, trouble grumbled on in Electoral Hesse and Saxony, while in late January and early February new attempts were made to invade Andalusia and to overthrow the Miguelist regime in Lisbon. Though resolutely repressed by their respective establishments, they marked an intensification of the crisis.

The authorities in Italy, however, were much less effective, and the real breakthrough came in the central regions, much to the aggravation, not merely of Austria, but also of France. The revolts were the work neither of exiles nor of local conspirators, but the result of a combination of social pressures and political frustrations in Bologna at a time when, because of the papal conclave in Rome, the regional capital was left in the hands of a rash and inadequate acting governor who was outmanoeuvred by local notables into allowing them to set up their own civic authority and militia. This example was copied, not only somewhat tentatively to the north-west in Modena and Parma, but also speedily and enthusiastically to the south-east throughout the Romagna and the northern Marche. There it led to the rapid creation of a regional state. The Austrians, the Papacy and the other local rulers were gravely worried.

The fact that French diplomatic agents in Italy were sympathetic to a movement which, in its new incarnation as the United Provinces, was prepared to allow a force of some three thousand volunteers to try to fight its way from Ancona over the Apennines towards Rome was even more worrying. Oddly enough, the Austrian response was somewhat hesitant, largely because of military insufficiencies, but once its column began to move the rash attacks made on it by the Modenese and Parmesan volunteers soon spelled the end of the western revolts. Although the Bolognesi and their allies were able to check the advance of another Austrian column at Rimini, there was no stomach for a prolonged fight, especially as the advance on Rome had been halted, and by the end of March the rebels had capitulated, allowing the Austrians to re-assert their own influence and to restore the legitimate rulers.

All this was, however, carried out against a background of tense diplomatic exchanges with France. Louis-Philippe himself was very hesitant, but there was a great deal of popular enthusiasm for the Italian cause, just as there was for that of the Poles. Many opposition politicians, not to mention some diplomats, had been deliberately indiscreet in their encouragement of the former. So when Metternich, ignoring Poland as a distraction, set about organising invitations to intervene in Italy and sent Austrian forces marching south in a clear breach of the principle of non-intervention the French were acutely embarrassed. On the one hand, they did not wish to embark on war with Austria but, on the other, they did not wish to lose credibility as defenders of liberal interests and upholders of the idea that the powers should not act against oppressed peoples. Meanwhile the Italians did not get the immediate military riposte they expected.

Metternich refused to give ground and made great play of the fact that Sercognani's force in the Apennines included two young Bonaparte brothers, who were as great a danger to the Orléans family as they were to the Habsburgs. The French hastily redefined non-intervention and agreed to Austrian action in Parma and Modena, and then, less happily, accepted it in the Papal Legations. They harassed the Austrians into a speedy withdrawal and seized the vain hope of a diplomatic conference in Rome which might persuade the Papacy to end the maladministration which had been the root cause of the trouble in the Romagna; but this did little to disguise the fact that France has suffered a humiliating diplomatic rebuff. Only by dismissing the existing cabinet and bringing in Casimir Périer in late February was Louis-Philippe able to survive the crisis.

While this was going on, liberal hopes had been equally raised by events in Poland. However, neither the diplomatic nor the military situation really warranted such optimism. For, if there was some sympathy amongst western statesmen for the Poles, Warsaw was a long way away and acting on that sympathy would inevitably bring a major clash with Russia. In any case, aid to the Poles would constitute precisely the kind of intervention which the French professed to reject in Italy and elsewhere, and might also compromise the attempt to solve the Belgian problem peacefully. So it is not surprising that, as early as 11 December, Louis-Philippe made it plain that he would offer no encouragement to the Poles lest he deprive himself of continuing Russian recognition. Ideas of joint western mediation were also dropped fairly rapidly.

In military terms it seemed in the west that the Poles had great prospects after they halted Diebitsch's advance in battles at Grochow in early February. However, the Polish gains were at best merely pyrrhic. They won a breathing-space in which to consolidate their new government, but hopes of a triumphant march of liberation into western Russia were shattered. This made their unhappy generals even more despondent and inactive, so that they failed to take the offensive when they might have done so. In reality, the prospects for Polish independence were grim, especially since the peasant masses showed little inclination to rally to the mainly noble patriots.

All the same, the fact that tens of thousands of Russian troops were bogged down in Poland did change the diplomatic balance. In particular, it facilitated a negotiated solution of the Belgian revolt. The London Conference had soon got down to work and by 20 December agreed to the creation of a free, and possibly enlarged, Belgian state, albeit one not including the king's private possession of the Grand Duchy of Luxembourg. These decisions were at first resisted by the Dutch, who, like the Russians, still saw no need to go further than autonomy; while the Belgians felt them to be an unacceptably slight return on their military efforts. None the less, they sent delegates to the Conference. By late January the territorial and financial bases for the separation of the Dutch and the Belgians had been agreed. These were accepted on 18 February by the Dutch, who had now implicitly come to terms with their loss of Belgium. The Belgians, on the contrary, felt immensely shabbily treated by the terms and rejected them. Moreover, their Congress turned its back on both the candidature of the Prince of Orange, which was favoured by the English, and the warnings not to offer the throne to France. The Duke of Nemours, one of Louis-Philippe's younger sons, was therefore offered the crown. His father then rejected the offer, despite having apparently solicited it, probably to thwart the rival Bonapartist candidature. The Belgians thus found themselves at odds with a diplomatic community which was also much exercised by its traditional suspicions of French ambitions.

By the late spring of 1831 the diplomatic liquidation of the crisis was still incomplete, although the war-scare was fading after these French humiliations and with the Russians still regrouping in Poland. In Italy, moreover, the cause of revolution had been almost completely checked. There the Conference of Ambassadors began on 14 April and worked to produce a memorandum of guidance for the new Pope on 21 May. Polish revolutionary prospects were declining, while scattered outbursts in the Valais and later in Neuchâtel both failed to shake the establishment. In Britain the launching of the first Reform Bill in March encouraged popular excitement, but the proposals were fought tooth and nail from the outset and made little more progress than did the Pedrista's efforts to eject Don Miguel from mainland Portugal. Similarly, the social protests which had done so much to carry the early outbreaks to success were fading fast. The army had mastered the Swing riots in southern England, and the Orleanist monarchy had managed to cope with the outbursts of anarchy on its side of the Channel.

None the less, the implementation of the important and concrete gains of the early revolutions had not really been held up, let alone reversed. The new constitutional monarchy in France may have had to drop some of its aspirations, but it remained firmly in power. Constitutions had been agreed throughout Switzerland and were moving towards popular ratification, despite the recrudescence of troubles in one or two cantons like Schaffhausen and Schwyz. Reform was also proceeding smoothly enough in all the German states where there had been trouble, including Hanover, and the Bund found it was able to live with the phenomenon, just as the great powers, whatever they felt about the question of kingship in Belgium, found themselves able to accept the constitution agreed by the Congress in February.

In a word, the cause of change and revolution was really marking time by the spring. If there was no immediate threat to what had been achieved, there was even less possibility of the various movements linking up to form the one continent-wide front which had so haunted Metternich. The revolts remained somewhat isolated, and were as much absorbed by the system as they were successful in undermining it. The critical moment had thus passed, and Europe moved into a fourth phase, of consolidation. This aftermath was to last for a couple of years more before complete normality returned; and though the crisis was still to come in places like England, generally the worst was over by the early summer. Conservatism was to become the order of the day, along with renewed co-operation amongst the powers and a revived spirit of counter-revolution. The cramping effect this had on supporters of change often provoked them to new radical outbursts, which generally merely justified further repression, and thereby ensured that the crisis and the excitement came to a dispiriting close for the liberals and the lower classes.

This turning of the tide was first and most dramatically visible in Poland. The patriotic forces there found themselves increasingly isolated, both socially and diplomatically. The peasants, without whom successful resistance was impossible, became hostile, and pressure on the Belgians to accept the terms offered them did not incline the western powers to change their cautious policies as the Polish government had optimistically expected. When its armies did finally push eastwards they were roundly defeated at Ostrołeka in late May, after which there was little chance of stopping the new Russian commander's offensive north of Warsaw in June and July. These failures drove the extremists and populace of Warsaw to a last desperate outburst of violence in mid-August, but this produced neither a new political *élan* nor an escape from the Russian noose then being tightened round the capital. After bloody fighting the city was stormed in early September, and real resistance came to an end, although isolated units and fortresses held out till late October. Well before this happened, however, the Belgians had adapted to the new realities. Following the warning from the powers, a new government had been installed by the acting regent. From April onwards it began to search for a solution to the problem of king-making which might prove acceptable to the country's guarantors. This led the government towards Leopold of Saxe-Coburg, a man who had been offered the Greek throne and who was very well regarded by the British, into whose royal family he had married. The Belgians' co-operative mood helped to persuade the diplomats to offer them the prospect of more generous terms of separation in a new protocol on 21 May. Many Belgians, however, still wanted much grander frontiers, which could only have been extracted from the powers by war, and refused to accept Leopold unless he committed himself to their full claim. Deadlock ensued as he would not accept the throne unless the Belgians agreed to be bound by the offer already on the table.

Not until the end of June was a compromise found. The Congress was persuaded to accept the powers' offer in conjunction with a slightly spurious rider that allowed certain enclaves in the Netherlands to be exchanged for some of the lands the Belgians really wanted. Leopold was then elected. The Belgians' return to the diplomatic fold was confirmed when, in early August, a new and nationalistic Dutch army suddenly fell on the south and brutally exploded the hollowness of the Belgian claims to military prowess. They had to be seen off by a French expeditionary corps, which did little to conserve the diplomats' peace of mind. The French troops were, however, soon withdrawn – although they had later to be called out again to enforce the Dutch evacuation of the citadel of Antwerp. In the wake of their second return home agreement on a more equitable division of territory was negotiated with Leopold, although it was not to be implemented until the end of the decade, William declining to accept the inevitable until 1838.

The powers were much less successful in their dealings with the other remaining centres of disturbance. They had to acquiesce in the re-interment of Poland where, although in theory a modicum of independence was promised by the Organic Statute of 1832, in reality military rule was imposed. In Italy the Vatican refused to be guided by the May memorandum, and the very limited concessions promised served instead only to re-activate liberal energies. The summer and autumn therefore saw an increasingly bitter political confrontation between the liberals of the Romagna and the Vatican. This finally degenerated into a new military clash in January 1832, after which a new papal army disgraced itself by sacking its own cities of Cesena and Forlì. The Austrians were therefore required to send their troops back to protect the local population against the 'Papalini' – a move which caused the French to dispatch a fleet to occupy Ancona by way of protest. This did something to calm the Romagna, but elsewhere again raised fears of French motives and intentions.

Such renewed fears of France played into the hands of Metternich since, when accompanied by a recrudescence of radicalism in south-western Germany, they compelled many German rulers to return to their normal conservatism. Hence in Hesse-Kassel the new Estates were to be suspended late in 1832, while liberal measures and French contacts also came under increasing pressure elsewhere. Revolution now seemed as big a bogey as Metternich had always claimed, and by September 1834 the French were formally warned to keep out of German federal affairs. In fact, it was unlikely that they would have risked meddling since in August 1833 the Convention of Münchengratz had formally renewed the understanding of the three eastern powers about resisting change. Such diplomatic moves, not forgetting the impact of the defeat of the Polish revolution, were part and parcel of a more general reaction. This showed itself quite spontaneously in Switzerland where not merely did the ultra-conservative cantons band together to try to repress by force the attempts of some rural areas to secede in August 1833, but the newly emancipated cantons also refused to back proposals to regenerate the federal constitution as had been considered by the Diet in 1832–3. Similarly, in Belgium the continuing economic difficulties and the failure to achieve extreme nationalist aims led to a revival of Orangism, which even attracted some of the leaders of the initial rebellion. In France and Iberia the movement took on a decidedly counter-revolutionary tone, marked by the Duchess of Berri's abortive attempt to start a new Vendean rising in the spring of 1832 and by continuing public support for Miguelism and Carlism in Portugal and Spain respectively.

Only in Britain did the tide still flow in a more progressive direction, with massive demonstrations in favour of Reform first in the autumn of 1831, and then in May 1832, when the Tories finally decided to accept the inevitable and let the Bill through the Lords. Even so, the narrow limits to the changes meant that many radicals chose to continue their opposition long after the new Parliament had met. Obviously, the English success, even when coupled with the ending of the Tithe War in Ireland a year or so later, was no real compensation to European radicals for the disillusion and defeats they had suffered elsewhere, particularly in Poland. Nor was free but moderate Belgium a sufficient salve to their wounds, any more than was the ultimate defeat of Don Miguel in Portugal by foreign volunteers.

Thus it was to be expected that attempts would be made to renew the struggle. In France and Belgium we can see the formation of new patriotic and radical associations from the summer of 1831, while in the following year the liberal cantons in Switzerland banded together in the *Siebnerconcordat* to guarantee their new constitutions and the liberals of south-west Germany inaugurated a campaign for a freer press which issued in the nationalistic Hambach Festival of 26–7 May 1832. Some of the more extreme leaders, often encouraged by the arrival of bitter and radical Polish exiles, sought to turn the fight into a military one. This explains the attack on the Frankfurt Diet in 1833 and the Mazzinian fiasco in Savoy in 1834. Equally worrying, however, and in the long run more significant, were the revival of secret societies and especially the development of organised social protest, symbolîsed by the troubles in Lyons and Paris in 1834. These were evidence of a growing conviction amongst some radicals that only social solutions would serve their purposes in future.

Such tendencies were extremely counter-productive in the short term. Continuing radical and quasi-socialist discontent meant that the middle classes tended to rally behind their governments and to accept the return of restraints on political life. So by about 1833–4 the impulse of the July Days had rather petered out. None the less, for many months Europe had quavered as spontaneous and largely social protest gave way, first, to radical political movements and then to nationalistic and military confrontations. Yet one co-ordinated onslaught on the Vienna settlement never arose. The crisis had remained a series of isolated movements, albeit all with one inspiration. While this fact seems not to have mattered to Russia, the rest of the great powers were sufficiently consoled by it – despite their continuing uncertainty over the July Monarchy – to refrain from panic and general war. Europe's distemper did not seem to warrant the setting aside of a whole range of other interests which pointed towards peace. And, although Eric Hobsbawm has argued that all these movements were united, including that in Britain, the evidence, particularly in regard to timing, is somewhat against him. The fact that the Reform Bill crisis only gathered pace during the aftermath phase of the Continental troubles is proof that, for all their family resemblances, the events of 1830 were ultimately based on local problems. In other words, to answer the question of what actually happened in these years, we have to turn to individual countries and regions, where evidence of both liberal and social pressures for change had been mounting long before the July Days came along to breach the dam.

5 The Swiss Confederation: The 'Regeneration' of Cantonal Democracy

Well before the July Days there had been clear signs of impending political change inside Switzerland. During the late 1820s the authority of governments began to yield to a growing wave of political pressure. So, while the fall of the Bourbons may have been a sign, it was not really a cause of the events in the cantons. Why this was so needs to be explained in local rather than in general terms. The complexities of cause, process and achievement in 1830 can best be appreciated by looking in detail at the 'Regeneration' as the Swiss call the movement for political reform between 1829 and 1833. And we must remember that the Regeneration was successful at the cantonal level, not at the federal or national level. Indeed, to treat Switzerland as a single and uniform nation is to lose sight of its most fundamental trait.

At first sight congeries of cantons of independent and widely different characteristics is hardly the most likely place to see the birth of a European-wide liberal movement, particularly when we think of the country as traditionally sleepy and insignificant. In fact, Switzerland was neither so peaceful nor so unimportant as we are wont to imagine. Violence was by way of being a custom of the country. It was to play a part in Regeneration as well. Indeed, the latter produced bitter fissures inside Swiss political society, so that it was the prelude to increasing conflict. Again, because Switzerland was a federation of republics, relatively tolerant of religious dissent, possessing a free press and providing a home for political exiles, it had a significance which is often overlooked. William Tell was a symbol of liberty far beyond the frontiers of the Confederation. Geography also made the country a listening-post and source of information at the crossroads of Europe: so what happened there was closely watched by others.

To an extent, however, it may seem odd that there should have been so much protest against a system of government which was infinitely more liberal and democratic than anything else in Europe. The Swiss already had an advanced political system, with a tradition of mass organisation, participation and action, which was far more democratic than that envisaged by any of the opposition movements of the time. Nor was the country tyrannically or badly administered. Dissatisfaction arose more from the origins of the system than from its detail – from what we might call relative deprivation. The Swiss liberals compared themselves with their ideals and their past, not with less fortunate countries. The old Confederation, in which a handful of cities and oligarchies had lorded it over the rest of the country, had been swept away by the French invasion of 1798. Then, after an unsuccessful and anarchic experiment with a unitary structure, Napoleon imposed a system of modified federalism by his 'Mediation'. This worked quite well, but depended on the continuation of the Empire.

When this collapsed things changed. The Allies, despite some doubts as to the wisdom of restoring Swiss independence, were eventually persuaded to accept the federal constitution of 7 August 1815 and the associated cantonal documents. The former set up a system which was as much a treaty of alliance as a federal state. For while all cantons, old and new, were in the Confederation, as Map 2 shows, there was little by the way of a strong and united central power. There was a Diet composed of two jointly mandated representatives from each of the twenty-two cantons (including four half-cantons), which met briefly each year to exercise a very limited number of powers. In between times, there was a federal directory, exercised in turn by the governments of Berne, Lucerne and Zurich. For the rest, the cantons were self-governing and perpetually suspicious of each other and the federal power. The whole system was 'Majestic, solemn and ineffective', and few majority decisions were ever taken. To many liberals this was an enormous insult. They disliked the way that outside interests had denied them national unity and status on the one hand, and had allowed many of the cantons to return to archaic practices and quasi-hereditary patriciates on the other. This was particularly the case with the constitutions of Berne, Fribourg and Lucerne, Nidwald and Solothurn. Elsewhere the élites thrown up by the Revolutionary era managed to ensconce themselves since, as we might expect, the Restoration meant different things in different cantons. However, in almost all there were significant differences in the representation of various areas of the canton, with capital cities usually enjoying the lion's share of seats, thanks to complicated and indirect electoral systems. It was this lack of direct popular sovereignty – which obviously worked to the benefit of conservative and affluent interests – which so offended liberals domestically. No matter how good the administration, their democratic espectations were affronted, just as was their desire for federal independence and self-respect.

The fact that during the first years of the Restoration the country was subjected to continuing censure and pressure from the Holy Alliance merely exacerbated these basic objections to the settlements of 1815. The Diet had, moreover, to make an equivocal adherence to the Alliance in 1817. The fact that the Diet was also unable to stand up to French demands for the expulsion of the regicides from the Vaud and had to endure harassment for its tolerance of refugees from the revolutions of 1820–1 was bitterly resented. Some cantons, however, did go along with

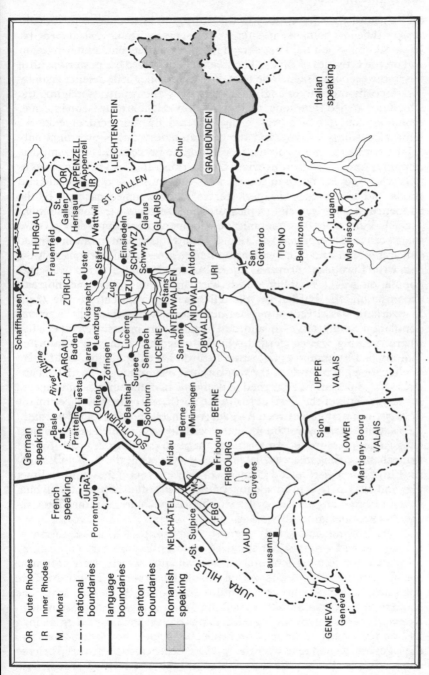

2 *Switzerland*

this because they depended on the supply of mercenaries to foreign armies. The low point of this subservience came with the *conclusum* of 14 July 1823 by which the Diet agreed to impose strict controls on its press and on the activities of exiles. The weakness of the federal power was also felt in the economic field. The Diet was able to offer little defence against the imposition of increasingly high tariffs by the country's neighbours which threatened traditional markets. Nor was it able to insist on internal economic unity, which was badly affected by the recrudescence of internal customs-barriers and the discriminatory tariffs by which one canton tried to penalise another. A canton like Berne could freely impose crippling tariffs on Vaudois wine. Goods thus often had to pay a dozen tolls when moving north to south across the country and, in the Ticino, goods had to be taken off pack-horses to be weighed each time this happened. Similarly, weights, measures and coinage varied considerably.

Such hindrances to economic development were important at this stage because Switzerland was a small country, deficient in raw materials and arable land, and faced with a population growth which, though it was below the European norm, was a great burden. For much of the 1820s the population was 1.97 million and, with little emigration and no real urbanisation, the burden of this fell heavily on agriculture. By then Switzerland was already a peasant democracy with a third of the active population ownings its own land, and farming very intensively, especially where dairying was concerned. On the other hand, most of the main cantons had to import grain, since a third of the population could only survive for eight months of the year on their own produce. To fill the gap many Swiss peasants had turned to domestic manufacturing – of watches in the Jura hills of the west, of silk in the north, and especially of cotton in the east. The triangle between Aargau, Appenzell and Glarus had become the seat of a thriving cotton industry, with looms installed in barns and lofts. The pressure of English competition soon forced the Swiss to mechanise, using freely available water-power, while the tariff policies of the European powers forced them to seek new markets in the Ottoman Empire and elsewhere. This made for some concentration of production, but it would be wrong to think of an industrial revolution, rather than of symbiosis of peasant and worker.

This growing industrial strength was supported by a thriving agriculture and a number of ancillary services. Exports and population pressure brought agricultural improvements which were further encouraged by the profits to be made by exports. This provided manpower and capital for further industrial growth. At the same time the country already had an active banking sector and was, because of the Romantic penchant for 'sitting on an Alp as on a throne', also experiencing its first tourist boom. Better communications, including steam-boats on the lakes and a good road over the St Gotthard, helped also to keep prices down. So the 1820s were a period of growth and relative prosperity.

Exports to France rose from 9.1 million francs to 13.3 million between 1823 and 1828. This had social implications. It encouraged the self-confidence of farmers, peasant workers and professional people, who found the continuing predominance of the old oligarchy somewhat galling, whatever its other virtues. It also concentrated attention on the need for land and for free trade and economic assistance, domestically and internationally.

This restiveness was reinforced by intellectual changes. The first of these was the Protestant revival – an evangelical movement which swept through the country, producing a mystical fervour amongst the eastern peasantry and leading the western middle classes to question the role of the established Calvinist Church. The second was the impact of Romanticism and nationalism, typified by the growth of philhellenism. It produced a new interest in Swiss history and achievements, symbolised by the erection of the famous monument to the dead of the massacre of 10 August 1792 in France, the Lion of Lucerne. All this intellectual ferment was focused by the emergence of a new and active press, the *Neue Zürcher Zeitung* of Zurich in 1821, the *Nouvelliste Vaudois* of Lausanne in 1824, the *Journal de Genève* in 1826 and, especially, the *Appenzeller Zeitung* of 1828. It also showed itself in the development of semi-learned societies, which provided means of political contact and expression. In addition to the old Helvetic Society, which heard discussions of reform involving people who were to be active in the Regeneration, and the Public Utility Society, there was the Zofingen group of 1819, the Union of Sempach of 1821 and the Federal Rifle Club, established three years later. The Zofingen Society was founded by Protestant theological students to celebrate the tercentenary of the death of Zwingli, but developed into a ginger group amongst students in western Switzerland. The Union aimed to further the study of Swiss history, while the Federal Rifle Club, formed to give the militia firing practice, brought together part-time soldiers from all over the country.

This intellectual ferment combined with the impact of economic change and the underlying issue of control of the Swiss destiny, cantonally and federally, to produce a new political climate in the late 1820s. This showed itself first at the cantonal level. In 1826 the government of Schaffhausen felt it wise to put in hand some reforms to enlarge the size and rights of the legislature. Proposals to remedy constitutional defects were also tabled in the Vaud in 1825–6, in Lucerne in 1827, in Geneva and in the Vaud again in 1828, and in the Ticino in 1829. In the Inner Rhoden of Appenzell, where there had been for long bitter factional disputes which broke out into violence in 1827, the Diet was forced to intervene. This helped to produce actual constitutional change in 1829 when the control of the old families over the *landesgemeinde* was loosened. The same year also saw rural unrest in Lucerne which prompted a further constitutional change, constituting the area as a proper canton and republic instead of merely an inequitable extension of the city. In a number of other cantons like Zurich there were moves to free the press and allow proper reporting of legislative debates. There was also evidence of some degree of liberalisation in Basle. Some cantons did swim against the current, as did Fribourg, Schwyz and especially the Valais where the government had taken precautions in 1826 against which the population of the French-speaking Lower Valais protested in vain in 1829.

That year the new mood of liberalisation also showed itself at the federal level in the refusal to co-operate with Austrian interception of post and the revocation of the 1823 *conclusum*. So it is not surprising that in the Vaud the government also felt that pre-emptive measures were necessary. The canton was a prosperous one, largely agricultural but with a flourishing transit trade, although there was something of a depression after 1829. The Vaud had only secured its independence from Berne in 1798 and was still led by people who had helped to create the free canton; they now sought to defend their creation against pro-Bernese aristocrats and liberals, whose disaffection might rock a still uncertain boat. They were able to use the power of patronage to build a 'compact majority' of large-scale landowner supporters in the Grand Council. So when liberals like La Harpe and Clavel tabled reform motions they were heavily defeated. The latter was opposed because, it was claimed, his ideas were not representative. To prove this wrong the liberals organised petitions for reform in the spring of 1829 which attracted over 4,000 signatures. So, although this was again turned down, the government in great secrecy set up a sub-committee to consider whether reforms ought to be undertaken to reassure an aggressive public opinion and an uncertain legislature. They soon concluded that, unless reform was offered, anarchy might result, and they carried the government with them, so that drafting continued throughout the winter.

While pressure for change was developing covertly in the Vaud, it emerged openly in the Ticino. This was a poor mountainous canton, with no manufactures, precious little craftwork and few independent farmers. It regularly exported plasterers and other craftsmen. It had even less tradition of free political life than the Vaud, having been a badly ruled colony of the old Forest cantons, and enjoyed less reform than others under the Mediation. The post-1815 regime, moreover, owed more than most to foreign and federal influence, the latter in a military form. It was particularly uneasy about offending either the Vorot or the nearby Austrians in Milan. Hence, it was run on a tight leash by *landamanns* or two chief executive posts which were usually held by two major figures from the Napoleonic era, G. B. Maggi and the aggressive G. B. Quadri. The latter had a very personal view of what was in the common interest and inherited many of the bad habits of the *landvogts*, the old colonial governors. And, since in such a poor state jobs were very attractive, he was able to build up a tame following of fifty-three in a Grand Council of seventy-six.

Though there was no real liberal movement, people did get restive, particularly when they did not get the jobs they desired. The resentment of some unsuccessful candidates was such as to lead to a series of assassination attempts on Quadri in 1826-7. Since these involved some of Maggi's relatives, Quadri was able to oust him from the government, even though he was not personally involved. There had already been differences between them, and the small canton was not really big enough for two such ambitious personalities. Quadri was also able to rush through curbs on the press, desired by Austria but turned down by the Grand Council earlier in the year, and to conduct a wide-ranging inquiry into the conspiracies. All this greatly strengthened his authority and also forced Maggi to go outside the system in his attempt to regain his position. Hence, in May 1829, no doubt drawing on what had happened elsewhere in the country, he proposed an extension of the size of the Council which would benefit certain hitherto less well-represented areas. Although this was dressed up in constitutionalist terms, it was effectively just a challenge to Quadri's power and, as the Austrians realised, a bid for the succession. The regime rejected the idea out of hand, branding all thought of reform as 'anarchy'. It took the opportunity to muzzle the press further, and also controlled associations and schools.

All this helped to develop opposition to Quadri's regime. Those excluded from power in 1814 – the unfavoured regions and the clergy – were there to be exploited. Since 1827 the capital had been in Lugano, a more cosmopolitan and lively city than Bellinzona with which it shared this status, whose political awareness was stimulated by the newspapers and books published by the Ruggia brothers from 1827. The debate started by Maggi thus fell on fertile ground, as the foundation of a branch of the Society of Public Utility in 1829 shows. By the winter of 1829-30 there was trouble in the bars and theatres of Lugano, notably amongst the young. The rallying-point for this latent opposition was the publication, first, of an anonymous pamphlet, *Della Riforma della Costituzione Ticinese*, and then of a new radical newspaper, the *Osservatore del Ceresio*, both the work of Stefano Franscini, a young teacher from the hills north of Bellinzona.

Attacks on the corruption of government and the unfairness of the representative system had to be met openly. On 24 February, Quadri was forced to call a special meeting of the legislature for early the next month and to declare that only the latter could undertake a revision of the constitution. This might have been enough, but Quadri insisted on going farther, closing the *Osservatore* and prosecuting its editors, despite the demurrals of the rest of the Council of State. The latter began to distance themselves from Quadri, setting the prosecution aside and going on to sponsor reform, aided by the way the new mayor of Lugano was able to win the town as a whole over to the cause. A violent pamphlet war followed in which Quadri was forced to devise his own plan of reform to stay in contention. When he won a small victory in the legislative discussion of change, all the resentment of his domination (and the fears of a *coup* he was rumoured to be staging) came to the fore and he was the object of a threatening demonstration. This was to be the prelude to continuing harassment which all but drove him out of public life. So the government's own reform was agreed by the legislature on 23 June and confirmed in a plebiscite by all circles save Quadri's own on 4 July. Quadri's only means of reply was to seek Austrian intervention. This failed, and his eclipse continued, but the Austrians were aware of the personal elements in the struggle, the times being against such efforts.

Thus, in the Vaud the government, having taken the liberals largely unawares, was able to rush through its projected reform. This merely increased the directly elected part of the Council to a third and removed the worst of the other abuses, yet even these limited changes were staged by a 'transitional' law so that they would not come fully into effect until the 1850s. It is therefore not surprising that it has been said that there was thunder in the air at the Berne shoot in July. This first stage of the Regeneration might have gone further. Clutching at straws, the conservatives were, briefly, much encouraged by the firmness apparently implicit in the issue of the Four Ordinances. The July Days then boosted the hopes of liberals, peasants and others, at the same time blowing away the restraints which had curbed political life since 1814. The fact that the late 1820s saw a sudden spurt in population growth and a deterioration in economic conditions generally also helps to explain why the July Days were taken as a sign that the time was ripe to implement the long-standing programme of extending popular sovereignty and basic rights, still denied to many. The Austrian ambassador told Metternich that the masses were reliable but that, because of their property and other stakes in the community, artisans, shopkeepers and lawyers were not. Spies had therefore to be sent to a country which previously had been considered as safe from upheaval save for foreign intervention.

With so many people behind it, the pressure for reform was not easily to be stopped, whether by police measures or by appeals from the Diet to resist innovation, such as that made on 22 September. So from mid-September the country was gripped by a fever of change which took a very similar form in most cantons. Beginning in Aargau and Thurgau, where the tactic of an electoral strike was used to coerce reluctant executives, the ferment spread to the small towns of the French-speaking Jura, to Basle, Fribourg, Solothurn and Zurich. By mid-October there had been disturbances in Porrentruy in the Jura, planting of liberty-trees in Aargau, and mass meetings in Thurgau to support claims that the country districts should elect two-thirds of any new legislature.

Governments like Berne and Solothurn tried to declare such meetings illegal, but few people bothered about such warnings. Other governments, seeing the way pressure built up in late November and early December, decided to be more accommodating. This was the case in Geneva where reform was again put on the agenda, even though in May the idea had failed to convince the legislators of its merit. Even more significantly, it came to Zurich, a large and more urbanised and manufacturing canton with something of a reputation for liberalism. However, in 1815 its country districts had had to concede economic and financial control to the capital along with a monopoly of ecclesiastical and political affairs. Zurich town had two-thirds of the seats in the legislature, even though its population was only 11,000, compared to 182,000 in the country. Thanks to financial scandals and the influence of German intellectuals, this disparity was challenged in the late 1820s and, not surprisingly, the July Days gave a great boost to the protests. Brochures were published from the traditional rural political centre of Stäfa in October and on the 13th thirty-two Grand Councillors met in Uster and called for a special meeting of the legislature.

This was conceded by the government, which not only summoned the Council for 1 November, but also set up a commission to sound the people out about some possible changes. Since these only envisaged giving the country half the seats, and were urged without enthusiasm, public opinion was aggravated rather than pacified. So while the commission was received with stony silence a German radical was invited to develop demands, in what became known as the Küsnacht Memorandum, and a group of notables meeting in Stäfa on 19 November decided to call a mass meeting in Uster three days later. This attracted an amazing 12,000 people and drew up a petition not merely for political changes, but also for economic ones including the removal of mechanised looms. This was supported by a further meeting of notables. Hence, when the Grand Council finally met on 25 November it immediately agreed to accept the Uster proposals, even though these gave two-thirds of the seats to the countryside. A new Grand Council was then elected on 6 December to do the actual work of revision. Its sub-committee was chaired by Paul Usteri, a man with a distinguished revolutionary past. It sat from mid-January to mid-February, and its proposals were then debated by the Grand Council between 16 February and 10 March. They were approved by 169 votes to four. Although the proposals did not go all the way to meeting the opposition's demands, they were accepted on 30 March by 40, 503 votes to 1,721.

Many other cantons followed suit at this time. Pressures built up in Fribourg, Lucerne and the external districts of Schwyz. In the second a march on the capital to demand revision by a constituent assembly rather than by nominees of the existing bodies set out triumphantly from Sursee on 1 December. The next day, which also saw protests starting in Liestal in Basle and, very significantly, in Nidau in the German-speaking part of

Berne, witnessed a major confrontation in Fribourg. There the peasantry of Morat and Gruyère followed up their petitions for change by gathering in the capital, several hundred strong, and armed with batons. They were faced with cannons and lighted matches, and only an error prevented the order to fire being given. The government was left with no alternative but to agree to abolish all privilege and to call a constituent assembly. Three days later several thousand peasants followed up an earlier decision and marched from Vilmergen on Aarau, supported by some Lucerners. Alarmed government troops fired one volley and then fled in panic and, after a further rally at Lenzburg, the government had to give way. About the same time there was trouble at Frauenfeld in Thurgau and in the Rheinthal in St Gallen. Both governments decided to give way, to some extent but the Bernese authorities would do no more than send out commissioners to take soundings and, at the same time, started to recruit mercenaries, thereby causing major disturbances and calls for separation in the Jura.

Another government which thought it had managed things well, that in the Vaud, also found itself virtually invested on 17–18 December. When a special meeting of the Grand Council was called to draft instructions for delegates to a special meeting of the Federal Diet, liberal forces based on the Casino Club rapidly organised petitions to demand real constitutional changes. Vast crowds flocked in from towns and outlying mountain areas where land holdings were small, insecure and disfranchised, to Lausanne, alarmed by what appeared to be government bad faith. Although they were willing to abjure the transitional law, the Council refused to deliberate under threat and adjourned till the next morning. When it did not reconvene at the time expected the crowd invaded the empty assembly-hall, until persuaded to withdraw so that the Council could in fact agree to call the constituent assembly. This met on 7 February and drafted a constitution which was finally approved on 25 May. Small landowners and those whose resources lay in other forms of property were rewarded by this.

Within a few days of the Lausanne crisis there was trouble in Solothurn and St Gallen with liberty-trees, petitions and meetings in Balsthal, Olten and Wattwil until the governments gave way. Such troubles continued into January. A peasant march on Basle was driven off, with some loss of life, on 6 January, and the 13th saw both an invasion of the Grand Council of St Gallen – which won the countryside a virtual veto – and the defeat of the Bernese government. This had been faced with virtual civil war in the Jura and growing pressure from the German-speaking territories as well, symbolised by a rally in Münsingen on 10 January. By the end of the month the authorities in Schaffhausen had conceded a constituent assembly as well, as had those in Basle.

The New Year was a period of consolidation for the Regeneration in three ways. To begin with, the Federal Diet on 27 December announced its unwillingness to oppose any constitutional changes presented to it, thereby giving reformers further encouragement. Secondly, the process of revision was now largely agreed and in the course of implementation. Thus, elections took place in Fribourg in January so that a constituent assembly could meet, just as happened in Basle, Berne, Zurich and elsewhere. By the late spring most consitutions had been finalised and agreed, by 28,000 to 2,500 in the case of Berne where there were many religious doubts about the new balance of power. Sometimes, as in Thurgau, the process had to be helped by further demonstrations, but generally it went ahead calmly enough, even if it was not always very radical in its outcome. Thus in Fribourg, which was the only one where popular consent was not sought for the changes, elections remained a two-stage affair, with the 80,000 voters selecting 730 'electors' who then voted for the eighty-six deputies. Even in the Vaud liberals never got a monopoly of office after 1830. A third facet of consolidation was that the idea of change spread to other areas. In Glarus there was talk of legal reforms, while the Nidwald experienced some dissent, and Geneva saw the first of a series of amendments to the constitution being pushed through by the chief executive or Syndic, Rigaud. Even in half-Prussian Neuchâtel there were petitions and evidence of a desire for change so that the principle of turning consultative assemblies into elected bodies was conceded.

The aftermath of the Regeneration was not, however, to be as peaceful as this might lead us to expect. The spring of 1831 saw the beginnings of a move by the 'external districts' of Schwyz to sever their links with an oppressive and uncomprehending Old Schwyz. This kind of issue had already led to an armed clash involving the town and country districts of Basle, and the defeat of the latter did little to assuage feelings, even though a constitution was approved. Before things came to a head, however, there was trouble in three other cantons. To begin with, on 23 May the inhabitants of Martigny-Bourg, who, like the rest of the Lower Valais, suffered a severe form of External-Schwyz type of oppression, planted a liberty-tree in protest against the controls placed on free elections. Social and economic stresses, involving food shortages and high taxation, also seem to have played a part in this. When summoned to take it down they refused and were subjected to a large-scale military occupation which left the Federal Diet somewhat uneasy, and did nothing to appease the agitation. Then in Schaffhausen the rural populace rejected the proposals which emanated from the Constituent Assembly in May, both in a plebiscite and in an armed march on the capital. It was not until the autumn that a second version was submitted and approved. Thirdly, the unrest in Neuchâtel helped to persuade the Prussians to change the Audiences-General into a more parliamentary body, the Corps Législatif, for which the initial elections were held in late June. For republicans, however, this was far from enough, as it left unresolved the question of the territory's dual status. So, while in August the forces of Basle town made an unsuccessful sortie against their rural opponents, on 12 September in Neuchâtel a group of some 450 republicans seized the château and held it until it became obvious that, whereas they had little popular support, the royalists had a good deal. A withdrawal was negotiated by federal emissaries. As in Basle and Schwyz, however, this was no more than a truce – and, indeed, a further rising was even more emphatically dealt with in December 1831.

This evidence of renewed conservative strength, combined with the relative lack of enthusiasm in the Diet when it came to giving the federal guarantee to the new constitutions, worried some of the Regenerated cantons. Seven of them – Aargau, Berne, Lucerne, Solothurn, St Gallen, Thurgau and Zurich – therefore signed a pact on 17 March 1832 to preserve their gains. This helped to introduce a new and very dangerous division within the body politic, at a time when new issues were being posed. On 22 February 1832 the town of Basle withdrew its administration from forty-six rebel communes, in the hope that the resultant anarchy would lead them to see the error of their ways. In the event, it merely encouraged the rural population to create their own half-canton on 17 March – a move which was copied by the external districts of Schwyz in Einsiedeln a month later. The Diet had little option but to accept the two new half-cantons. This was held to be unconstitutional by many of the conservative cantons, who were equally alarmed at the success of the proposals, first aired in 1831, to set up a commission to draft a new federal constitution which would complement the revised cantonal documents. This led between June and November of 1832 to the emergence of the Saarnenbund of Basle town, Neuchâtel, Schwyz, Unterwalden, Uri and the Valais. And when the Diet proceeded to allow the rebel half-cantons to participate in its debate they withdrew from it in March 1833 and set up a rival body in Schwyz. This proved to be the prelude to a two-pronged attack on Outer Schwyz and Rural Basle in July and August 1833. Federal troops intervened to stop the former, but the latter were humiliatingly defeated at Pratteln where sixty-three of their men were killed. This bloodshed prevented any hope of reconciliation there, although the Diet was able to encourage Old Schwyz to make concessions which succeeded in uniting the two halves around a revised constitution in the autumn. Although the Diet was able to dissolve the Saarnenbund but not to carry through the constitutional revision since the cantons chose to reject the suggestions, as even Regenerated ones like Aargau, Lucerne – the capital designate – Ticino and the Vaud felt that revision was either unacceptable unless agreed unanimously, or presented too much of a threat to their new independence. The Regeneration neither united the country nor made itself felt at a federal level. So stormy times continued, especially with a period of what Hughes has called 'a democratic conservative reaction' over the next few years.

Yet it had led directly to constitutional revisions in twelve cantons, which between them counted for two-thirds of the total population, and indirectly to rather more limited changes in Geneva, Neuchâtel and, in 1836, Glarus. As a result, cantonal democracy could claim a better balance between town and country, more direct elections, a wider franchise, a clearer separation of powers and stricter limits on office-holding, and an extension of political rights such as that of petition. If some of the old restraints on popular sovereignty remained and the changes in personnel were neither so extensive nor so dramatic as might have been expected, partly because of the conservatism of the peasantry, it was none the less a significant reordering of the political system. The term 'regeneration' therefore seems a very apposite description of the process - a process much more legalistic and procedural than that in many other areas at the time. In a way, it was more the reversal of 1815 than anything else, and it does not seem right to call it the Swiss 1848. The divisions which were eventually to produce the Sonderbund were the development of the situation created by the Regeneration, and were not implicit in it.

The men of 1830 in Switzerland turned out to be agreed only on the need to overturn the Restoration. The next few years thus saw a polarisation of politics at the expense of the liberal front of 1830, with the emergence of a new radicalism which renewed foreign concerns about Switzerland. Although the Regeneration was basically a localised and rather introverted set of political movements, it did also have a social side. The front of 1830 involved peasant farmers and workers, who made up the rank and file, the traditional craftsmen - such as those who burned Kunz's cotton factory in Uster in 1832 - the ordinary middle class of the small country towns, and the emerging intellectuals. It was an inherently unstable alliance generated by the mistakes of the old patricians and the conflicts of the Revolutionary era and liable to division on issues of economic and religious freedom. It was aimed as much at excluding the major capitalist interests from monopolising power as it was at developing the interests of a capitalist bourgeoisie of an industrial kind. It drew on social issues, like the impact of falling population and textile depression on the Neuchâtelois republicans, but essentially liberalism was a political movement owing much to the factions of 1798–1803. And the Regeneration thus had its ultimate roots and character in the political system which, even in the restrictive years of the Restoration, so many foreigners had envied.

6   France: Political Calculation and Social Protest

To some extent, the events of July and August 1830 in France owe their position in the historiography of the subject more to the role of the country in which they took place than to their nature. As Riballier has observed, 'The revolution of 1830, in contra-distinction to that of 1848, was not a European or general movement. It was a local French affair, best studied in a French context.' That context had two particularly striking features. The first was the emergence of a dynamic political opposition well before the actual crisis, while the second was the considerable depth of social awareness and protest. As a result, miscalculations leading to the surprising military humiliation of Charles X's government in Paris led to immediate political experiment and to an explosion of social dissent. The two were much more closely connected than in many other countries at the time.

The emergence of a liberal opposition in France was not inevitable. It owed much to the way in which the right used its domination of political life in the 1820s. After the dissidence in the army and elsewhere, symbolised by the assassination of the Duke of Berri in 1820 and the conspiracy of the Four Sergeants of La Rochelle, the forces of accommodation had been checked. Under the government of Villèle a series of measures was passed which many moderates chose to see as presaging a full-blooded return to the *ancien régime*. The law on sacrilege, the curbs on the press, the compensation paid to former owners of church lands, and the toleration of religious orders all worried the markedly anti-clerical middle-class liberals. And, in Paris at least, their views were shared by the lower classes, whose radicalism was renewed by a deliberate campaign of education and propaganda, as well as by the passage of time. The late 1820s saw a number of quite serious clashes between the opposition and the government. When new elections were held in 1827, the revival of the opposition and the internecine divisions in the government camp cost Villèle first his majority and then his premiership. This crushing reverse, which further divided the royalist camp, was celebrated by popular demonstrations in the capital which the government was hard put to master. It took its revenge by disbanding the National Guard, which had made its oppositionist sentiments plain. Such growing confrontation led one politician to call for the Duke of Orléans to assume power, although he was speedily repudiated by the Duke himself.

The king felt it necessary to return to a relatively moderate cabinet headed by Martignac. Unfortunately, he never really trusted what was really a somewhat motley collection of centre-right politicians, even though the change did much for his popularity. So when liberal press criticism became even more aggressive he withdrew his support from the government and allowed it to be overwhelmed by a coalition of ultra-royalists and extreme liberals on the question of local government reform. As soon as he was able, Charles ditched Martignac and, on 8 August 1829, replaced his cabinet with a new one which included two pillars of the counter-revolution, La Bourdonnaye and the Prince of Polignac, the son of Marie Antoinette's favourite and nephew of Charles's last mistress. The liberals greeted this as a sign that the long-dreaded return to the *ancien régime* was finally upon them, and much of public opinion seems to have shared their view. In fact, the cabinet was both mixed and divided and one which, even after Polignac was designated as Premier, seems to have had no clear and calculated aims. So, over the winter of 1829–30, nothing decisive happened, save that political polemics grew ever fiercer, with both ultras and liberals talking of a royal *coup* to come.

This political tension was experienced by a country which was rapidly running into social and economic difficulties. After the general postwar slump, the French economy had enjoyed a period of relative prosperity in the 1820s. Large-scale capitalist agriculture began to make itself felt, and trade began to recover its pre-Revolutionary levels. And, if there was no real industrialisation, manufactures did grow considerably in both size and scale of organisation. The Lyons silk industry, for instance, doubled in size. These structural changes, however, often had a deleterious effect, particularly on the lower classes, when the economic climate began to change in the second half of the decade. As a result, political opposition began to be underwritten by social dissent. The downturn in the economy was in part a product of the way the English bank crash of 1825 caused French interest rates to rise, thereby causing investments, share values and prices to fall. Some industries which had expanded rather too fast in the good years, like the Haut Marnais iron foundries and Alsatian cotton manufacturing, could not endure the new conditions and went to the wall. All this had marked social effects. The level of petty crime in Paris rose sharply in response to increased competition, falling wages and unemployment, while working-class organisation and activity became much more militant.

The manufacturing crisis coincided with an agrarian depression. From 1826 there was a string of bad harvests, and the winters of 1828–9 and 1829–30 were glacial. Food-prices, as a result, rose by something like 75 per cent in the late 1820s. Rural workers were often as badly hit by this as their urban counterparts, particularly so since because of the manu-facturing slump they could not fall back on their traditional refuge of domestic textile-working, since this, too, had already been gnawed away. Even though the harvest of 1829 was a little better than its predecessors, things were still tense early in 1830, with grain riots in the Loire valley, forest disturbances in the Ariège (which is down in the Pyrenees as Map 3 shows) – in response to the way large-scale entrepreneurs were monopolising woodlands to provide fuel for charcoal furnaces – and, above all, the wave of arson in the Norman countryside. Significantly, this last was often blamed on the government. So, with bands of unemployed workers wandering the countryside and some 40 per cent of the Paris population reported as indigent, it is not surprising that a version of a traditional satire on the Lord's Prayer circulated in some areas: 'Our father, who art in the Tuileries, eliminated be thy name; thy kingdom cease, thy will be disregarded, on earth as it is in heaven; leave us this day our daily bread and forgive us our victories, as we forgive those who have failed us; lead us not under the weight of your domination, but deliver us from your presence.'

3 *France*

Given this mood, it is understandable that the government was distrusted in Parliament as well as in the countryside. But neither Charles nor Polignac would give way to a liberal cabinet. As the latter said after his fall, those who urged this made the mistake of having 'seen in 1830 a question of tactics rather than one of fundamental principle'. Rather than accept the realities of parliamentary government, the cabinet, in early March, issued a calculated warning to the liberals in the speech from the throne. The opposition majority then drew down the gauntlet, in an address carried by 221 to 181 on 16 March, which, in effect, called on Charles to replace Polignac by ministers who enjoyed the confidence of the Chamber. Charles, as might have been expected, refused. He had, after all, once said that he would rather be a woodcutter than king on such English terms. Yet the cabinet merely prorogued Parliament and only lethargically agreed to dissolve the Chamber on 16 May. New ministers were brought in to organise the elections called for 23 June and 3 July. Their efforts were not very successful, and Charles felt it necessary on 13 June to issue an inflammatory appeal to the electorate, thereby committing his own fate to that of the government. But neither this appeal nor the successful capture of Algiers outweighed superior liberal organisation.

The elections were then postponed and, when this failed to reverse the tide and the liberals went on to triumph by 270 seats to 145, thought began to be given to the idea of using the powers allegedly given to the king by article XIV of the Charter to make special 'regulations and ordinances for the execution of the laws and the safety of the state'. Though the decision to use this was taken on 6 July, there were many hesitations and reservations before four new ordinances were finally agreed on 26 July. These dissolved the recently elected Chamber and called for new elections to be held in September under a much reduced franchise (which might have cut the electorate from some 90,000 to about 25,000), since the press had rendered the summer's elections invalid. The press was itself punished by being subject to pre-publication censorship by the authorities.

Chantelauze, the minister who suggested this strategy, had coupled it with making large-scale military preparations, but this was not done. The Prefect of Police guaranteed 'on his head' that Paris would remain calm, and Polignac talked cheerfully of having over 40,000 men available. In fact there were no more than 15,000 in the vicinity of Paris and only 7,000 –8,000 of those were available immediately. So it is hardly surprising that when the Ordinances produced outraged resistance the authorities could not contain it. Their basic and fatal calculation was that the opposition had no substance and would be cowed by a show of force. They were wrong in this belief. They also ignored social dissent. The result of their fallible calculation was disaster.

Admittedly things started quietly on the Monday morning when the

Ordinances first became known in Paris. Businessmen meeting for elections to the Commercial Court decided to close their shops and manufactories, partly as a sign of dissent, partly out of fear and partly, perhaps, to encourage their workers to resistance. The few deputies who were in the capital met to discuss the Ordinances but merely agreed to meet again. The only real action came from printers and journalists, who were the most directly and immediately affected by the changes. A group of the latter published a proclamation claiming that the Ordinances ended the king's right to expect obedience from his subjects, but even they stopped short of actually calling for insurrection. It was police attempts to close newspapers which led to the first disturbances in the evening, when there were scuffles with demonstrators who stoned ministers and flew the tricolour flag for the first time in years. However, the security forces were able to master this, and by midnight all was quiet.

Things deteriorated rapidly on Tuesday, 27 July, which was to be the first of the *Trois Glorieuses*. By the afternoon, when the police began to act on warrants for the closure of those newspapers which had defied the Ordinances and published, and tried to break up their presses, they met a variety of legal and violent resistance. Groups of students, printers and others tore down royal insignia, flew the tricolour from Notre-Dame and began to erect barricades. The first deaths occurred in the late afternoon as the gendarmes sought to dismantle the barricades, but this merely fuelled the fire. By 5 p.m. a virtual state of siege had to be declared by Marshal Marmont, who had been pitchforked into command of the security forces without much warning. Since he was widely held to have betrayed Napoleon in 1814, the demonstrators felt even more aggrieved. Hence, though the troops sent to occupy strongpoints were able also to clear a few barricades, their situation was very uneasy, since the disturbances had cut them off from their food, forage and ammunition supplies in Paris. The telegraphs were also being cut, and the building-sites abandoned in the slump provided the crowds with useful ammunition. The troops fired back, so the crowds went further, tearing down street-lights and breaking into shops, particularly armourers'. Although the crowds were eventually dispersed by about 11 p.m., the police were exhausted and some elements of the army were unhappy about the role they were being asked to play. Charles, however, refused to call up adequate reinforcements.

Came the dawn and barricades were to be found throughout popular districts of the city and firing was to be heard everywhere by mid-morning. Marmont reluctantly declared martial law, only to find he could not get the official notification printed. Although it was baking hot, his troops had no bread and little to drink. They were then asked to assault the centre of the city to try to break up both barricades and resistance. One column was sent around the northern boulevards to the Place de la Bastille, but once there it found it could not penetrate into the Faubourg

St-Antoine and had to retreat westwards along the left bank. The central detachment soon got bogged down in the web of narrow streets and separated in the course of attempts to fight its way out. The third push along the riverside Quais reached the Place de Grève, but proved unable to retake the Hôtel de Ville and took three hours to get back to the Champs Elysées. By 1 a.m., when the firing died down, the royal forces had lost some 2,500 men, not to mention command of the city centre, thereby posing the question of who was really in control.

While the fighting was going on, the deputies met twice, agreeing finally to issue a general protest on the Thursday. But they also sought to negotiate with Marmont, whose known preference was for a political solution. Polignac, however, would not even talk to them. Indeed, he still expected Marmont to launch a new offensive. The latter, however, with his men forced on the defensive by the sniper fire directed against his makeshift redoubt in the Louvre – Tuileries complex, which resumed at 5 a.m. on the 29th, still hankered after negotiations. He therefore sought to arrange a ceasefire with the mayors of the metropolitan boroughs but, as before, he could not get the agreement printed or publicised. On the other hand, Marmont would not agree to depose Polignac on his own authority as he was urged, and the Prince was able to retire to join the king at his suburban palace of St Cloud. Although the court was aware that things were going wrong, Polignac was able to persuade them that the willingness of the mayors to deal with Marmont pointed to the weakness of the rebels, so that the struggle should be continued.

In fact quite the reverse was true of the military situation. On what was to prove to be the last of the *Trois Glorieuses*, pockets of royal resistance were viciously mopped up in the capital and even the new defence-line wavered. Two regiments, in fact, went over to the rebels and, by retiring to their barracks, left other unreliable units exposed. In an attempt to take these out of the firing-line a crucial mistake was made which left part of the Louvre undefended. Before reserves could be brought up the crowds broke into the Louvre and the whole garrison, believing that they had been overrun, panicked. By the time Marmont could regroup them they had reached the Etoile, and it was obvious that no further resistance in the city was possible. The army may have lost only something like 150–400 dead, compared to at least 500–800 civilians, together with at least 600 out of anything up to several thousand wounded, but large numbers had also melted away, and there was no doubt that the army was demoralised and defeated. So the army fell back on St Cloud, leaving the capital in the nominal control of self-appointed leaders, including a makeshift Municipal Commission elected by the deputies.

In face of this, Charles finally agreed to replace Polignac by a moderate diplomat, the Duke of Mortemart, but negotiations with the Municipal Commission on the acceptance of a new ministry and policy proved difficult to conduct because of the conditions. And, in any case, the king showed no urgency to act. It was not until 7 a.m. on Friday, 30 August, that the Duke was able to set off for Paris. Not only did he find it difficult to get there, but also neither the Commission nor even the representatives of the peers ultimately proved keen on dealing with him, so the initiative collapsed. Into the vacuum came the idea of bringing in the relatively liberal Duke of Orléans as a new king. Some of his supporters issued thousands of bills to this effect at 8 a.m. on 30 August and, after some debate, the deputies agreed to invite him to serve as lieutenant-general of the kingdom, or temporary head of state. Louis-Philippe himself arrived in Paris late that night, a rather hesitant claimant because he was aware of the hostility of many of the crowd to any notion of royalty. Meanwhile a Bonapartist challenge was quickly squashed and the left-wing republicans of the Café Lointier thwarted, partly because they looked to Lafayette for a republican lead – and he was too ineffective and too afraid of a new Jacobin anarchy – and partly because their own ideology of doing nothing until the people had been consulted played in some measure straight into the hands of the moderates and Orleanists. So, early on the morning of Saturday, 31 July, Louis-Philippe accepted the invitation to act as lieutenant-general. By going alone to the Hôtel de Ville about noon and appearing on the balcony with Lafayette and the tricolour, he also won at least the tolerance of a hostile left-wing crowd for the ratification of his new role the following day.

That same day, Sunday, 1 August, Mortemart finally and formally gave up his attempt to form a new government for Charles. The latter, again deciding not to act on Marmont's advice that he should fall back on the Loire valley and try to carry on armed resistance from there, had moved the court, first to Versailles on 31 July, then, when his rearguard defected, to Rambouillet on Sunday. There on Monday he finally decided to abdicate and invited Louis-Philippe to act as regent for his ten-year-old grandson, the Duke of Bordeaux. However, Charles refused to send the boy to Paris, so that Orléans was able to ignore the invitation when, on 3 August, he announced Charles's abdication and formally took up the reins of power. The Chamber then invited him to fill the royal vacancy. The Charter was rapidly revised in a not terribly liberal way on 6–7 August and, on 9 August, Louis-Philippe took an oath to the new Charter as King of the French. Well before then he had established provisional government and begun both to purge the administration and to secure his authority throughout the country. In attempting the latter he was at least spared the problem of royalist – or Carlist – resistance outside one or two isolated places like Nîmes and Parthenay in September. Charles, meantime, had retired slowly to the Cherbourg peninsula between 4 and 16 August, once his base at Rambouillet had been threatened by a popular march from Paris, but contrary to his hopes there had been no movement of support and he had to sail for England and exile.

The apocalyptic explosion of rural and popular violence presented the new regime with more than enough other problems in its efforts to restore order throughout the country. Because basically similar conditions applied as in Paris, neither troops nor officials showed a great desire to resist change, even when it was urged, as it was in Chaumont, by demonstrators who could be bought off by a few francs for a drink. But change meant both a political interregnum and even greater economic dislocation and uncertainty. This moved the poor and underfed rural population to strike a blow, not so much against Charles X as against all the forces which exploited them, whether grain merchants or the state itself. The fall of the Bourbons was equated with the coming of freedom: from dues, taxes, tolls and police records, not to mention from hunger and high prices. In the north-western half of the country grain merchants were the main targets; in the wine-growing south government officials and tax collectors suffered; while in the east and the Pyrenees trouble flared up in forests. Housewives, innkeepers and peasants were often joined by workers seeking better conditions. Hence there are stories of machine-breaking and, in Roubaix, of an orgy of window-smashing in order to secure higher wages. The reviving National Guard was unable – and perhaps unwilling – to deal with this, while the government's attempts to remould the administration meant that it, too, could not be relied on. In the end the new regime had to give way and lower taxes on inns and cafés, reform indirect taxation generally and either import or subsidise grain. These measures and the passing of time gradually restored some kind of normality, but new threats like the war-scare and cholera outbreak of 1832 caused a new *grand peur*, showing how uneasy the country remained.

This rural anarchy was not linked to any precise ideology and therefore did not prevent the consolidation of the Orleanist regime. However, the July Days had provoked more overtly political aspirations, and these did threaten the process of consolidation. In the first instance, the question of what penalties should be visited upon the leaders of the old regime became the key issue for assessing whether or not the new order was living up to expectations. It helped to break up the first ministry in October, but the new government under Laffitte (though regarded as being more adventurous) still found itself under increasing pressure from discontented popular elements and radicals, leading to street demonstrations in the capital against the mild sentences passed on the ministers of Charles X on 21 December and anti-clerical violence in many towns in February 1831. That spring saw also the emergence of a more radical and nationalist pressure-group, the Association Nationales, groupings of officials and others desirous of taking the revolution further and, especially in the east of the country, worried by the possibility of invasion.

The fear that the government, influenced by the 'Parti du Mouvement', as such people were known, might lead France into a war that could not possibly be won, reinforced by Laffitte's handling of the Italian imbroglio, finally moved Louis-Philippe to dismiss his premier. He was replaced by the much more conservative Casimir Périer in March. The revelation that the Parti de Résistance, where members believed that no more change was needed, was in power forced active opposition to take to the streets. In the autumn of 1831 there were troubles in Grenoble, Rouen and especially Lyons, where the economic problems of the *canuts*, or silk weavers, played a particular role. Then in 1832 Paris was the scene both of an abortive attempt to fire the North Tower of Notre-Dame in January and of a brief republican seizure of power in the Cloître St-Merri and other districts in June. All this was a great deal more threatening to the new regime than the sad wanderings of the Duchess of Berri between April and December 1832 as she tried to start a new Vendean war, and explains the savagery of the repression.

Political activists, feeling increasingly betrayed, were driven underground into secret societies like that of the Droits de l'Homme, only to find that the government was determined to break them by legal means or, as when Paris rose in sympathy with the Lyons *canuts* in April 1834, by even more brutal force. Workers in Lyons and other major towns began thereafter to turn away not merely from the regime, but also from political activity, since petty bourgeois republicans and others did not really share their desire for public intervention to improve conditions, enforce agreements negotiated with employers and restrict foreign competition – as had been very clearly visible from early in the regime's existence. While the republicans could only resort to isolated attempts at assassination, like that of Fieschi, the workers moved towards self-help, co-operation and socialism.

Thus, as Sewell remarks, 'class consciousness first emerged during the agitation which followed the revolution of 1830'. The political crisis resulting from Charles's refusal to accept the realities of parliamentary government led to a political change which, as has been said, made 1789 legitimate. It also switched power, not to the capitalist bourgeoisie but to a new political class deriving from the Empire and the Restoration opposition: a new class of notables, libertarian and nationalistic in politics but socially conservative. They thus reacted very strongly to the way that social grievances and political hopes mobilised so many people in 1830. And, like Charles X, they calculated that they could disregard the social protest which played so large a part in the events of 1830. For a while they succeeded, but the July Days opened another phase in social history, and the divisions of 1830 were to reappear in 1848. The role of social protest and the advantage of having an official opposition ready to exploit a totally misconceived political calculation was, however, unappreciated outside France.

7 Belgium: The Revolutionary Creation of a Nation

The generally mistaken impressions of what happened in France were bound to have an impact on adjoining countries. This was particularly true of the strategically senstive Joint Kingdom of the Netherlands, which had been deliberately created by Britain and the other great powers to keep the peace and balance of Europe. In fact some contemporaries blamed the troubles there on French agitators, while there has been a school of thought which sees the events of 1830 as creating a new state which only benefited French-speakers. Any discussion of 1830 in Belgium thus treads on ground which remains politically very sensitive. Yet it has to be said that, just as the July Days can only be understood in local terms, so there were spontaneous local forces behind the troubles in Belgium in 1830. Those forces again included marked social pressures, although questions of religion, language and constitutional rights were even more significant. When conflict over these things exploded in 1830 it produced, first, a revolutionary movement akin to that of 1789 in France and then a new nation. The Belgian experience, therefore, falls halfway between the internal restructuring found in France and the more formal, albeit still limited, war of liberation fought by the Poles.

The roots of Belgian nationality have been much debated, but there was certainly no Belgian state before 1830. For centuries the area had been a mosaic of quasi-separate provinces ruled in part by the Prince Bishop of Liège and in part by more foreign rulers like the kings of Spain and, after 1714, by the emperors of Austria. As a result of the Revolutionary wars the whole area was annexed to France. Initially there was a good deal of resistance to this and, although things improved somewhat under Napoleon, with the return of prosperity and with the development of gallicisation, many Belgians still welcomed the Allies as liberators in 1814. And, while the Dutch rose spontaneously in support of the return of the House of Orange, the Belgians showed no desire for autonomy. Indeed, they sent delegates to Francis II to seek the restoration of Austrian rule. When he refused they had to accept the idea of participation in a joint state with the Dutch. On 21 June 1814 the Allies laid down eight principles which should guide the creation of what they clearly envisaged as a unitary state. Its actual creation owed much to William I of the Netherlands, who declared himself king on 16 March 1815 in response to the news of Napoleon's return from Elba. As a result, Belgian troops fought against the latter and Belgian notables played some

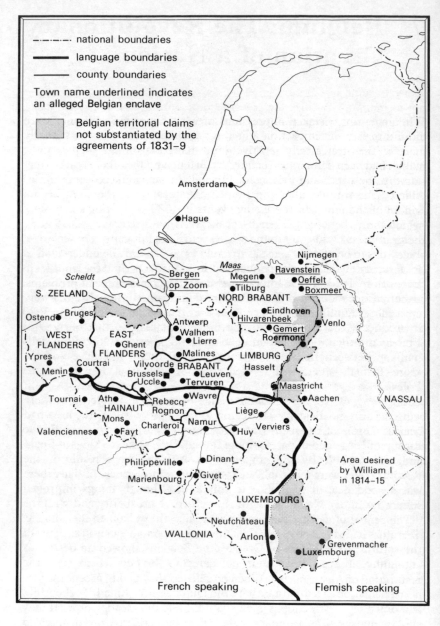

- national boundaries
- language boundaries
- county boundaries

Town name underlined indicates
an alleged Belgian enclave

Belgian territorial claims
not substantiated by the
agreements of 1831-9

Amsterdam

Hague

Nijmegen

Maas

Scheldt

Bergen op Zoom

Megen
Ravenstein
Oeffelt
Tilburg
Boxmeer

NORD BRABANT

Eindhoven
Hilvarenbeek
Venlo
Gemert
Roermond

S. ZEELAND

Ostend
Bruges
Antwerp
Walhem
Lierre

WEST FLANDERS
EAST FLANDERS
Ghent
Malines

LIMBURG

Ypres
Courtrai
Vilvoorde
BRABANT
Hasselt

Menin
Brussels
Leuven
Uccle
Tervuren

Maastricht
Aachen

NASSAU

Tournai
Ath
Wavre
HAINAUT
Rebecq-
Rognon

Mons
Liège

Charleroi
Namur
Verviers

Valenciennes
Fayt
Huy

Philippeville
Dinant

Area desired
by William I
in 1814-15

Marienbourg
Givet

LUXEMBOURG

Neufchâteau

WALLONIA
Arlon
Grevenmacher
Luxembourg

French speaking
Flemish speaking

4   *Belgium, the Netherlands and Luxembourg*

part in redrafting the *Grondwet*, or fundamental law, establishing the structures of the new kingdom.

So the amalgam, as the Joint Kingdom was known in Belgium, does not seem to have been doomed from the outset. Indeed, it had certain things in its favour. The Belgians never turned it down in principle. They did also gain some representation in the formal bodies of the new kingdom, not to mention considerable educational and economic assistance from William I – a man not inaptly termed 'a king for the new century' by one of his supporters; for, although he was authoritarian at heart, he showed more willingness to tolerate a relatively free parliament and press than many rulers of the time. So, although the kingdom got off to a very bad start because of Belgian Catholic resistance to a constitution which – at Allied behest – enshrined relogous freedom, things settled down in the mid 1820s.

However, there was a number of issues which did cause general and continuing conflict between the two halves of the kingdom. The Belgians objected to the high indirect taxes and low tariffs which weighed heavily on agriculture and industry. They also felt that they bore an unfair proportion of the old Dutch national debt. A second range of problems concerned education and language. The expansion of state education had to be paid for by Catholic communes whose children preferred to attend church schools, so that Dutch school policy was regarded as a costly way of trying to proselytise for Protestantism. This impression was reinforced by the gradual extension of the use of the Dutch language in all official business – a move which also threatened the prospects of young professional men from Wallonia and even from Flanders, where French occupation had led the middle classes to use French much more, despite being, as the map shows, somewhat removed from direct contact with France. During the Restoration, of course, French lost some of its association with free thinking because of the Catholicism of the Bourbon monarchy. With the Dutch setting up an association to promote the use of Dutch at the expense of both French and Flemish, language was always a delicate issue, even though the policy was not fully or rigorously enforced.

The religious fears it aroused were reinforced by decisions made in 1825 that all intending priests should attend a state-run Philosophical College and that all unapproved secondary schools – that is, Catholic ones – should be closed. Since the king was also flirting with the idea of establishing a separate Dutch Catholic Church and failing to implement the Concordat agreed with the Pope on 18 June 1827, many Catholics believed they were facing a dual challenge of Protestantism and secularism from The Hague. At the same time, other elements in Belgian society were alarmed by matters like the prosecution of outspoken journalists and pamphleteers, changes in the penal code and alterations in the organisation of the Burgher Guard – things which in 1826 caused violent opposition in the streets of Brussels. All were seen as part of what was known as 'Dutch arithmetic', that is, the way in which Belgium, despite having well over 3 million people compared to the 2 million in the Netherlands, was granted only half of the seats in the States-General and only a tithe of posts in army and administration.

Yet, if these grievances were very real, they involved matters of policy rather than the principle of the kingdom's existence. There were also channels available for their resolution. They were also experienced against a relatively favourable economic background. After the general postwar economic and subsistence crisis the patchy growth already visible in eighteenth-century Belgium seems to have resumed. Mechanisation began to appear; steam-power in Liège, for example, rose from 4 horsepower in 1803 to 1400 horsepower in 1830, and there was a general shift from Flanders and cottage-based production to Wallonia and factory production, making the latter area as important in continental terms as an industrial centre as was Alsace. Because of the strength of rural industries, the educated work-force and the relatively low wage-levels, there was a marked growth in businesses like the metallurgical industries of Charleroi and Liège, the cotton industry in Ghent, the woollen industry in Liège and especially coalmining in the Borinage around Mons and Charleroi. However, the Flemish linen industry was badly affected by increasing French tariffs, and nail production also encountered difficulties.

The situation on the land was much less satisfactory. Agricultural prices fell until 1824, while the population rose by some 20 per cent during the Dutch period, from 3.38 million to about 4 million. Since there was little urbanisation the result was growing pressure on land, employment and profit. By the late 1820s prices had begun to rise, with the result that indigency became common in the southern countryside, whereas in the Dutch half of the kingdom the towns suffered more. The government did little to aid agriculture – a fact which was resented not merely by farmers and rural workers, but also by the large-scale noble landowners, who were fairly common in the south. And, although William did much to aid industry through grants, loans and general encouragement, the fact that he went outside Parliament to do so was a cause for concern. In any case, Dutch industrial policy seems to have assisted entrepreneurs rather than workers, probably because the rising population kept wages down at a time of high food-prices. In the industrial centre of Huy the cost of food rose threefold between 1824 and 1830, by when 1,900 of the 4,900 work-force were dependent on public poor relief.

These weaknesses in the political economy ensured that people did not overlook political problems, especially when these affected the professional middle classes and the Catholic peasantry of Flanders, neither of whom benefited much from industrial progress. By 1829–30, when industrial growth began to slacken and food-prices soared, political problems may well have seemed harder to bear. Yet it was a change in the organisation and attitudes of the opposition which really made the late 1820s a time of a new and dangerous confrontation. By then the Catholic population had become seriously alarmed about its position and prospects in the Joint Kingdom, deprived of a Concordat, while being exposed to threats to its educational provision and priesthood by a regime which, to some extent, still enjoyed the support of the Vatican merely because it was an established monarchy. Their only hope seemed to be to change the political system so that public opinion might have a greater effect on policy; in other words, to create responsible government.

This tactic, which may have owed something to the inspiration of the Catholic Association in Ireland, would have much more chance of success if the Catholics had the support of other forces in Belgium. Consequently, some Catholic leaders began to put out feelers to the liberals and, after some hesitation, a new generation of liberals, associated with the Liège newspaper the *Mathieu Laensbergh*, responded favourably in March 1827. They agreed that the rather different freedoms they sought also required ministerial responsibility if they were to be achieved, and that co-operation towards these ends was worthwhile. So, although for a time some more anti-clerical liberals continued to play William's game and snipe at the church, others came round, perhaps because they became aware of how important religious motivation was in the Greek War of Independence. By November 1828 the Union, as it was called, was consecrated when Louis de Potter, the leading Flemish anti-clerical, declared himself in print in favour of attacking the supporters of government rather than the Jesuits.

De Potter was immediately prosecuted for this article, which simply threw into relief the alleged unfairness of government. And, when a liberal motion in the States-General calling for more freedom for the press was rejected, and those involved were disciplined, the struggle was taken outside Parliament. The Union replied with a wave of petitions calling for freedom for education and the press, together with a lowering of taxes. Between January and March 1829 some 70,000 people signed these petitions and, very significantly, 45,000 of them came from Catholic Flanders. The Union also drew intellectual strength from the views of the radical Catholic Felicité de Lammenais, whose *Progrès de la Révolution* of 1829 – in part inspired by events in Belgium – argued that Catholicism would always triumph in a free polity. The tactic thus became a principle.

William himself was made particularly aware of the strength of the Union when he visited Belgium in May 1829. He was sufficiently impressed to promise to abolish some of the most hated indirect taxes and to relax the controls on the press. He also began to implement the Concordat. These concessions simply emboldened the Union. It began to take on an organisational form and, even though many people felt it had already achieved its main aims, was able between December 1829 and

February 1830 to persuade a further 360, 000 people to sign a new series of petitions calling for minsterial responsibility and other civil liberties. The king, however, rejected such drastic demands out of hand on 11 December and took the battle to the opposition by prosecuting those who supported dissident opposition deputies and creating a tame newspaper, *Le National*, to urge his case in the south. This caused more trouble, particularly in the universities, and one anonymous pamphleteer called for the throne of a separate Belgium to be offered to the very popular heir, William, Prince of Orange. As a result, in May 1830 the king made further concessions on language and education, effectively setting aside the Collège Philosophique.

Some observers, like the papal nuncio, felt that further trouble was bound to come, and the police that spring were worried both about public reaction and about stories of mysterious couriers from France. Things were made worse by the deteriorating economic conditions which prompted an increase in the crime rate in Brussels and food riots in the Namurois as over-production in industry led to wage-cuts, redundancies and bankruptcies. Against this background it is not surprising that the July Days caused great excitement. At once the government placed the barrier forts on alert and ordered extra surveillance, but the flaunting of the tricolour and local flags and badges became common in early August. The papers were totally given over to the news from Paris, and its significance was much debated. There was a dull resentment that Belgium had still not really achieved the liberties reconquered in Paris.

Yet, although exiles and radicals in the Café Belge in the Galerie Vero Dodat in the French capital talked cheerfully of aiding the Belgians and issued fly-sheets in Brussels on 10–11 August saying, 'Frenchmen, one step and Belgium is yours!,' such efforts seem to have had little effect. William was quite well received when he visited the industrial exhibition in Brussels between 12 and 16 August and appears to have returned to The Hague unworried about the state of feeling in Belgium. He was both right and wrong in this, since political grievances seemed to have been less significant than economic ones. Knyff, the Chief of Police, repeatedly drew attention to the dangers posed by the lowering of wages amongst spinners, the laying off of hatters, and the way the July Days halted building operations, not to mention the slowness of the municipality in providing public works to relieve the crisis. With the municipality amidst rising food-prices also maintaining a tax on the milling of flour – everywhere else abolished – in order to pay for the royal birthday fireworks display, there was more than enough evidence for Knyff to prophesy trouble.

When a poster appeared on 22 August threatening that the fireworks, if they took place, would surely be followed by revolution, the municipality decided to call off the display. Trouble still followed on 25 August. Towards the end of a performance of an opera called *The Deaf Girl of*

Portici, which dealt with the Neapolitan rising against Spain in 1648, an aria praising the 'sacred love of the fatherland' was used as the occasion for a demonstration by members of the middle-class opposition. They streamed out of the Mint Theatre, to be joined by others outside, including some printing workers organised by someone with connections in Paris (although police records make it clear that there were fewer French visitors in the capital than was usual at that time of year and the demonstration was essentially Belgian). They demonstrated and stoned the offices of the *National* and the houses of its editor and other government supporters. With both local authorities and the forces of order failing, or refusing to intervene, things got out of hand. As the night wore on, the middle-class elements began to vanish from the streets, and more workers and hooligans were seen. Thus basically symbolic demonstrations against the regime gave way to looting, indiscriminate attacks on local government intallations and, once trouble spread to the suburbs, to the sacking of country houses and factories, some of which used new machinery. By the morning of the 26th tens of thousands of people were on the streets, expressing social and economic grievances more than political ones, although by 27 August royal insignia were indeed being torn down.

Knyff's repeated efforts to get the security forces to deal with this incipient anarchy having failed, middle-class notables began to take the law into their own hands. After a meeting on 26 August they called on all good citizens to illuminate their own houses, to make up for the now destroyed street-lights. Then vigilantes began to appear and, by 27 August, at least a thousand of them were operating in a makeshift Burgher Guard. Though they sympathised with the political aims of the Mint demonstration – and much use was made of the ancestor of the modern Belgian flag from the beginning – they dealt ruthlessly with looters and others. Since the leadership of the Guard was the only real political authority in the city, it fell to it to send delegates to The Hague in an attempt to improve the shining hour and get the king to accept reforms and the administrative separation of the two parts of the kingdom. Although William did agree to call the States-General for 13 Steptember, he would not give any more ground and, in fact, sent his sons south with enough troops to restore order and to supplant the Burgher Guard.

By the time the angry and disillusioned delegates returned home, Brussels had fallen prey to turmoil once again. The arrival of 6,000 royal troops at Vilvorde on the outskirts of the capital on 30 August caused a wave of panic. Barricades went up in the popular quarters, and the Prince of Orange was refused entry with his troops. When he and a small escort did enter on 1 September he was greeted with great hostility by thousands of armed citizens. Their attitude first scared him into fleeing to the safety of his palace, and then into agreeing to plead the cause of separation with his father. As he did so, the violent euphoria was increased by the arrival of volunteers from the rest of the south. The first group from Wavre arrived on 1 September and was followed by larger detachments from Liège on 7 September. Towns like Liège and Huy, in fact, had gone much the same way as Brussels, and the middle classes had taken over control from the establishment. The royal army had also been forced to abandon Louvain rather ignominiously on 2 September. Succeeding days were to see attacks on royal authority in Grevenmacher, in Luxembourg and in many other places, notably, but not entirely, in Wallonia, and rather on the lines of the rural troubles in France. Even some French volunteers came to join them. In the capital and elsewhere there were abortive plans for attacks on the Dutch, and tension and radicalism grew as the uncertainty caused increasing economic difficulties with the withdrawal of tourists and nobles. Banks stopped making payments, and there were more lay-offs. From 9 September there were demonstrations demanding food and work, and these were echoed in places like Bruges and Charleroi. Authority in Brussels had to be transferred to a more acceptable Security Commission on 11 September, but this, too, found it difficult to maintain order as it became clear that the political situation was deteriorating. Little seemed to come from the meeting of the States-General, and pressure on William to resolve the crisis by military means was growing. This often came from worried industrialists and notables.

The growing number of volunteers founded a political club, the Réunion Centrale, which urged the increasingly uneasy authorities to arm the peasants, subvert the Dutch army and create a unified revolutionary government which would take over state funds and seek to create a separate government, by force if need be. Such ideas appealed to the underfed and unemployed artisans of the capital, who staged massive demonstrations on 17-18 September and, when the authorities disowned a sortie to Tervuren on 19th, they occupied the town hall for a while. Finally, on 20 September, they disarmed the Burgher Guard. Skirmishes with the Dutch resumed while the middle classes, and even more radical leaders, withdrew in dismay at the sight of this threatening militancy.

News of these latest upheavals merely confirmed the king in his decision to resort to military action and to disregard the States-General's growing suport for an administrative separation. On the afternoon of 22 September a workman repairing the cathedral tower in Brussels saw the Dutch begin their advance and rang the alarm-bell. Yet, despite the immense lower-class enthusiasm for the fight which ensued, the initial exchanges went against the patriots, and many of their leaders fled to the safety of France to avoid what promised to be a complete rout. So a planned provisional government never emerged, and only some 350 people seem to have been left guarding the capital against some 14,300 royal troops. The remaining leaders sought desperately but unsuccessfully to negotiate with Prince Frederick to avert a massacre.

They were saved, however, by the activities of a number of nobles and others, including a certain Colonel Delescaille, who went out frequently to the Dutch cantonments and assured the Prince of the support of hundreds of armed burghers if he would at once advance and restore order. Whether this was a deliberate trap or a flight of fancy, it seems to have been what Frederick wished to hear. As foreign envoys reported, he feared the losses and opprobrium that an assault would bring and warmed to the idea of restoring order in collaboration with responsible elements of society in such a way that the extremists would be ridiculed rather than martyred. In order to minimise bloodshed, Frederick organised his assault in a way which one Swiss observer described as an unpardonable imprudence after the July Days. The Prince was so misled as to misconceive his whole strategy. And, since it had to be executed by a staff who were opposed to street fighting and by troops who were young, inexperienced and uneasy about fighting their fellow-countrymen, it is not surprising that it resulted in total disaster.

The advance, which began at 6 a.m. on Thursday, 23 September, was designed to make minor demonstrations in the lower town, the popular quarters, while the major pushes were made in the upper town where the well-to-do tended to live. All of these moves were concentrated on the north in the hope that those radicals who had not been disarmed by the middle classes and local authorities – as the Prince had urged in a proclamation on 22 September – would be able to leave easily enough, thereby limiting the need for proscription. So in the north-western corner of the lower town some 800 men attacked the Flanders Gate and a further 900 that of Laeken. The larger units consisted of 2,500 men at the Louvain Gate and finally 4,500 at that of Schaerbeck, both in the north-east of the upper town. However, instead of finding active support from local authorities and men of good will, the Prince found only Delescaille and one or two others to encourage them at the Louvain Gate, plus a few more in the lower town. Moreover, the main detachments at once met fierce resistance, even though there may only have been about 500 rebels then manning the barricades. Hence, the Louvain Gate force remained pinned down on the outer boulevards, while the main strike-force, after a successful charge into the town, failed to carry the crucial Place Royale, which would have enabled it to deploy into the lower town. The tired and inexperienced young recruits hesitated fatally and finally took refuge in the royal park where they were subject to constant sniping from the tall terrace houses facing the park on its western side.

In the lower town the royal army suffered even more heavily. At the Flanders Gate, where there was some evidence of support, they were able to penetrate a distance into the town, but at the Marché des Porcs they were held up by barricades. Since this was only a diversionary attack the commander decided to withdraw, but as he did so his troops were defenceless against attack from all sides, and even from above, with furniture as well as bullets coming from high tenement blocks. The soldiery panicked and did not stop running till they reached Asse, several kilometres distant. The last detachment was not able to make any real inroads because of barricades in the narrow streets and, though it was pulled back more successfully, it still remained very exposed. By 5.30 or 6 o'clock, when the firing seems to have died down, the Dutch plan was a total and humiliating failure. Nobody had rallied to them, they had only an insecure foothold in the town, and all hope of administering a short, sharp shock to the rebels had gone.

The only courses left to Prince Frederick were to bombard the town with his heavy artillery or to take it house by house. He baulked at the former and, given the exhaustion and heavy losses already suffered by his men, he would not, or could not, contemplate the latter. Instead he tried again to negotiate, as the middle classes still seemed to want him to do. This got nowhere, but none the less he issued a new proclamation calling for middle-class support and offering an amnesty. When a local *curé* toured the town with this on the morning of the 24th it elicited no response, and the combats recommenced. Refreshed by a night in the taverns, the insurgents were fresh and were able to mount more barricades, attract more support, and use their few cannon inside the town while some volunteers from outside began to threaten the Dutch rear. Firing continued all day round the park and the Place Royale and, while some notables were moved by it to discuss a ceasefire with the Prince, some of the radicals, notably Charles Rogier, the leader of the Liègois volunteers, returned and offered command of the rebels to a Belgo-Spanish exile, Juan van Halen. On the morning of 25 September the rebels came forward in ever-increasing numbers and, despite some difficulties, tried to take the offensive. But, while they were able to carry more houses round the park and even make raids into it to plant flags, they were not strong enough to carry things farther. The Dutch meanwhile were able to strengthen their position on the boulevards, although Frederick still tried to negotiate, this time with the makeshift administration which was emerging in the Hôtel de Ville. But, as the latter pointed out, too much blood had by then flowed for anything other than a withdrawal to be acceptable.

Frederick was thus compelled to mount his offensive at the worst possible moment, when his tired and dispirited men had to face several thousand enthusiastic and increasingly well-organised rebels, led by a provisional government. When the élite Dutch grenadiers assaulted the Place Royale at about 10 a.m. on the 26th they were driven back by Belgian artillery. The Dutch initially resolved to stand firm until relieved by the remaining 5,000 men of the Prince's command, but afterwards, in the absence of the main proponent of resistance on the Prince's staff, it was decided to withdraw to avoid being cut off altogether by a more general rising – a wise decision given that it turned out that the relief force had been held up and whittled away by desertion and obstruction. So, when van Halen finally mounted his major assault on the park on the Monday morning, he found that the Dutch had silently slipped away while his men had been again in the cafés and inns of the lower town. Poor morale, a lack of stomach for the fight amongst both officers and men, and a series of tactical errors had led to the Dutch suffering a signal defeat. Out of nearly 9,000 men involved they had lost at least 2,000, including 400–600 dead, 800–1,200 wounded and between 100 and 450 prisoners. Against this the Belgians, whose numbers, after the initial exchanges, had fluctuated between 3,000 and 8,000 all told (although only about 1,200 were engaged at any one time), lost 450 dead, 1,200 wounded and 100 prisoners. Most of the casualties were skilled artisans, peasants from surrounding villages like Uccle, volunteers from Liège and elsewhere, and, eventually, a few members of the middle class. Economic motives seem thus to have become fused with political ones.

The effects of these 'Four Days' of combat inside Belgium were dramatic. Although the States-General voted on 29 September to accept the idea of administrative separation, this was now too little and too late. A movement for total freedom and independence spontaneously swept the country, Flanders included, although there was some resistance to the tide there. October in Belgium saw a genuine national uprising – somewhat similar to the way the Regeneration was to sweep through Switzerland in December 1830 – and Belgium moved from revolution to a war of liberation. However, the Provisional Government did make use of temporary institutions rather like those of 1792–4 in France, and social pressures continued because of the way the troubles intensified economic uncertainty and food shortages. So, while one or two places had effectively thrown off Dutch suzerainty before late September, it was really the Four Days which changed things.

As soon as the fighting started, volunteers began to flock in from Wallonia and beyond, many of them wearing the blue blouse of the Belgian artisan. Thus the line of Wellington forts was soon in rebel hands. If Flanders was slower to move, this was due in large part to the presence of larger numbers of royal troops there and more active government handling of the crisis. None the less, the Provisional Government soon had a growing body of supremely confident men available to it, facing a Dutch army which was rapidly losing heart. Resistance therefore crumbled from within rather than succumbing to outside pressure. However, two bodies of rapidly organised free corps struck north in pursuit of Frederick's demoralised armies. The left-hand column went via Malines and on 23 October captured the crucial Pont de Walhem, which – as Map 4 indicates – controlled the approach to Antwerp. The next day it linked up with the right-hand column which had stormed Lierre on 16 October *en route* to Antwerp. After two days of fighting the united columns were able to force their way in, aided by a popular rising inside the town. All but the citadel fell into Belgian hands. Although a ceasefire was agreed, friction between the townspeople and the garrison led the latter to bombard the town, inflicting heavy casualties and damage until Charles Rogier arrived to negotiate a more lasting armistice on 5 November. By then only Venlo, Maastricht and Luxembourg were left in Dutch hands.

The bombardment of Antwerp killed any remaining chance of separation being acceptable to the Belgians. The Provisional Government, indeed, had declared Belgium independent on 4 October, and less than a week later elections were called for a National Congress to draft a constitution for the new nation. Although this immediate appeal to the people was the kind of thing for which the radicals in Paris had yearned in vain, the elections turned out to be unkind to the left in Belgium. Their one representative in goverment, de Potter, resigned soon after, and the Réunion Centrale club folded up late in November. The elections also dashed the hopes of those who believed that there could be a member of the House of Orange on the throne of the new nation. On 10–11 October, William had agreed to revise the *Grondwet* so as to allow for separation, and he also sent the Prince of Orange to Antwerp to try to rally support. But, with the Prince proving too ready to make concessions, his powers were soon revoked, and the bombardment was a further blow to Orangist hopes.

The fact that the revolution was consolidated on a basis of national independence made Belgium an international problem, thereby circumscribing the freedom of action of its new leaders even more than did their difficulties in reforming their army and attaining fiscal stability. The Belgians were only partly aware of their uncertain diplomatic status, and in the euphoria of their revolutionary and military triumphs resented these curbs. Their relations with the great powers thus became extremely bad, even though their very efforts to deal with the powers annoyed many extremists and helped to distance the new order from the people who had actually made the initial breakthrough to freedom in late September. Significantly, when the elections to the Congress took place on 3 November, only 45,000 people were entitled to vote, and about 30,000 of these turned up to do so, with the small towns of Flanders being especially well represented.

Not surprisingly, this small electorate opted for men of substance rather than for the men of the hour. They produced a relatively young and inexperienced body of landowners, clerics, lawyers, tradesmen and intellectuals, nearly two-fifths of whom were nobles. Many were practising Catholics and, although there were no formal parties, it seems that the largest number were supporters of the Union. The composition of the Congress is important since it was effectively to run the country over the next few months, somewhat downgrading the government, as well as considering the draft constitution placed before it by the Provisional Government on 27 October.

Their most pressing problems were, however, on the diplomatic front, where the powers had called a conference of ambassadors in London on 4 November to preserve peace and the balance of power against threats from possible Russian military assistance to William or from a Franco-Belgian *Anschluss*. The Belgians got off to a bad start in their dealings with the Conference by their territorial claims of 18 November and by their formal rejection of the House of Orange a week later. The latter clashed particularly with the ideas of Britain, which aimed to install the Prince of Orange on the throne. Lord Ponsonby, the Conference representative in Belgium, worked hard for this end, and the Prince himself was to issue a more encouraging proclamation in January. However, in November, with the Dutch attempting to break the siege of Maastricht, there was little chance of this and the Conference's first task was to achieve a ceasefire, which was accomplished on 24 November. By 20 December the powers had also agreed on the shape and status of an independent Belgium; and, though the Belgians themselves contested the terms, they were largely confirmed on 20 January as the Bases of Separation. This granted a neutral Belgium only those territories not part of the old United Provinces in 1790, thereby denying the Belgians southern Zeeland, North Brabant, much of Limburg and the Grand Duchy of Luxembourg. The powers compounded the difficulty by going on to rule that the Belgians would have to accept both responsibility for $^{16}/_{31}$ of the national debt of the Joint Kingdom and the exclusion of all members of the ruling houses of the major states from the new throne.

At this there was an immense protest from radical nationalists who were able to persuade the Congress to reject the Bases and then, in early February, to vote to offer the throne to the Duke of Nemours, a younger son of Louis-Philippe. As tension with the Dutch was also rising after the explosion of a Dutch sloop in the Scheldt, the Belgians had thus isolated themselves from the rest of Europe. Their position was worsened when, on 24 February, Louis-Philippe declined their offer, which his agents had probably encouraged so as to block the rival, Bonapartist, candidature of the Duke of Leuchtenberg. With the Conference having already ordered the Belgians to lift the blockade of Maastricht and to accept the Bases of Separation, the revolution reached its lowest ebb. Even some revolutionaries turned to the reviving cause of Orangism, and there were attempted *putsches* in Ghent and elsewhere in early February. These were immediately answered – first by counter-demonstrations in Ypres, Antwerp and the south, and then by the formation of Associations Patriotiques or Associations Belges, which sought to emanicpate both country and lower classes from a treacherous establishment under the slogan 'The blouse not the epaulette. On the frontier, not in the Swiss Café.' The powers were antagonised further.

The constitution was approved on 7 February and implemented later that month, with Baron Surlet de Chokier, a lawyer of somewhat limited capacity, acting temporarily as regent, but the crisis persisted. However, the new constitution, derived in the main from the *Grondwet* and the French Charter, established a genuinely limited monarchy, with two powerful chambers and a cabinet responsible to the chambers, in which, although the new nation was constructed on a unitary basis, large powers were given to local government and a wide range of civil liberties was guaranteed. This was to prove popular, successful and influential well beyond Belgium. Perhaps significantly, it was when the Young Turks who had actually drafted the constitution – Liègois intellectuals like Lebeau, Devaux and Nothomb – entered a new government in April that the *impasse* began to be broken.

The new ministry supported the idea of Belgian independence rather than liaison with France, but it was also aware of the English interest in the fate of Belgium. They therefore looked for a candidate for the throne acceptable to England. They found one in Leopold of Saxe-Coburg, a German prince and a widower who had married into the English royal house, and who had previously been canvassed as King of the Hellenes. But, while Leopold was willing to accept the role the constitution marked out for the King of the Belgians, he could not accept the Belgian territorial claims because these threatened war with the Allies. For, on 10 May, the Conference had issued Belgium an ultimatum: either the Bases were accepted or the Grand Duchy of Luxembourg would be transferred to the German Confederation and the Allies would rule in favour of the Dutch on other disputed issues. Ponsonby persuaded the Conference that to act on this would simply provoke the Belgians to a more radical outburst. Hence, on 21 May, a new protocol held out the hope of compensation for the Belgians and, by somewhat exceeding his authority and negotiating around this, Ponsonby led the Belgians to elect Leopold without his having agreed to their territorial claims.

However, the concessions eventually offered by the Allies in the so-called XVIII Articles Treaty of 26 June did not go very far, and another crisis arose. It was solved by Nothomb, who pointed out that, in strict legality, the old United Provinces had not actually enjoyed sovereignty over a number of places north of the Moerdyk frontier, like Tilburg, Eindhoven, Bergen-op-Zoom, part of Maastricht and a string of estates round Nijmegen as depicted in Map 4. The Belgians somewhat spuriously offered to surrender these in return for part of Luxembourg and, although the claim was ridiculous in itself, the Conference was glad enough to accept it in order to get off the hook. And, on the understanding that this would be so, the Belgians accepted the Treaty on 9 July and Leopold made ready to ascend his new throne.

All this infuriated not just William, as we might suppose, but a majority of Dutchmen as well. Hence a wave of patriotic fervour led to a new army of 39,000 men marching on Belgium on 4 August. The Belgian army failed to live up to either its reputation or its rhetoric and fell apart.

Leopold was only just able to hold on until a French relief force arrived. Faced with this unexpectedly rapid and diplomatically accepted action William had to accept a ceasefire. So, although the Ten Days War cost the Dutch only 661 men as against 925 Belgian losses, the Belgians actually gained by it. The military collapse was a tremendous psychological blow to Belgian radicals, who were tamed by it, while, at the same time, the attack itself greatly displeased the powers. The latter, on 14 October, therefore offered the Belgians 60 per cent of the Grand Duchy in return for their rights in Limburg and elsewhere. When all the Allies were persuaded to underwrite this new treaty, of XXIV articles, the Belgians accepted the offer. However, it needed, first, a new Anglo-French expedition in the autumn of 1832 to free Antwerp and then the passage of time to force William to accept the settlement.

The consolidation of the new monarchy in the 1830s thus took place within an enlarged Belgium, for William could not take possession of Limburg and the rump of the Grand Duchy until he accepted the Treaty. But consolidation there was, presided over by Leopold and his new French wife, and a series of Union cabinets, and aided by the economic revival which began about 1833 and owed much to government investment in railways. When it became clear that the new kingdom was working and that the powers would not change their minds, William eventually, in 1838, accepted the Treaty. As a consequence the Belgians had to agree to hand back Limburg and that part of Luxembourg which had been theirs for nearly a decade. Despite the appeals from the radical nationalist left for a new holy war, they did so, though it was a traumatic experience for them.

Such national questions remained the dominant issues in Belgian political life for some time after 1830. This does not mean, of course, that 1830 was the product of a fully formed Belgian nationality and consciousness as has been argued. On the other hand, the claim made by some extremists that the creation of an independent state was the work of French aspirations or of English malevolence does not fit the facts, either. There is no truth in the stories of French agitators causing the revolt. This was due to concrete grievances. There is also plenty of evidence to suggest that Flemings took part in the revolutionary moment. Most of the Brussels artisans would have been Flemish-speakers. Significantly, Flemish nationalists like Henrik Conscience fought against the Dutch in 1830, and it was really industrialisation which began to divide the two communities.

The movement of 1830 was thus a spontaneous and local one, owing a great deal to social and economic causes. Yet, at the same time, it could not have been possible without some pre-existing concept of 'Belgian-ness', even though this had never taken political form before and owed a great deal to the events of the 1820s and, especially, to the traumas and euphoria of August, September and October 1830. So, while the lower classes carried the revolution to fruition for their own reasons, they seem to have done so as part of a much broader national movement. And it was political questions rather than social ones which really divided people then. Thus, 1830 was neither a beginning for Belgian nationality nor its end-product. It was both. The whole thing was a product of circumstance. It was the revolutionary situation itself which generated a patriotism which had only been latent beforehand and which might not have been created a few years later. William I was thus responsible both for the creation and for the problems of the new nation.

8 Northern Europe: Adaptation inside Constitutional Monarchies

To brigade together Britain, the Scandinavian kingdoms and some of the German states is unusual, but they did have common features. They all had relatively advanced political systems in which constitutions often figured, and their governments proved more adaptable than many. Even the much maligned German princes were willing, albeit under duress, to embark on political changes. Furthermore, their social patterns, involving sometimes large numbers of independent peasant farmers, active artisans and middle-class liberals, and even flexible upper classes, made them structurally, if not geographically, part of the heartland. Social dynamics played a significant role, even if the timing of political change could differ from that in countries to the south and west.

Obviously Britain had the longest and richest tradition of political activity, but that in Sweden went back a century and more. Throughout Scandinavia this was widely built on in the latter stages of the Empire. Thus Bernadotte had to accept the revised Swedish constitution of 1809 and the even more liberal Eidsvoll draft of 1814 in Norway, which gave the Storting large powers. Alexander I himself had to issue an Act of Assurance to the Finnish Diet at Porvoo Borga in 1809 guaranteeing the Grand Duchy the rights it had enjoyed under Swedish rule. Only in Denmark did absolutism remain more or less entrenched, although a royal commission did apparently consider granting a constitution to Schleswig-Holstein. In Germany article XIII of the Founding Act of the Germanic Confederation provided that 'in all confederate states there will be a constitution providing for representation by estates'. Some attempt was made to implement this rather ambiguous statement in Nassau in 1814, Saxe-Weimar in 1816, Bavaria and Baden in 1818, and in Würtemberg and Hesse-Darmstadt in 1819. Saxony, Mecklenburg and Hanover, moreover, preserved Estates of some kind from the past, although only in the south-western states can we talk of any kind of real parliamentary life.

These constitutions reflected a general mood of postwar reform which embraced mass agitation in Britain - with a quasi-insurrection in Scotland - student unrest and political murders in Germany, and cultural and regional restiveness in parts of Scandinavia. However, the excesses of this phase and the general revulsion against the revolutions of 1820 provoked an equally general reaction, symbolised by Austria's imposition of the Carlsbad Decrees against universities and the press in Germany. The early and mid 1820s were a period of political calm. Reform debate died away in Britain; the Finns were happy with new career opportunities and did not query the 'frozen constitutionalism'; and, as for Germany, one writer remarked sadly that one could hear the country snore when coming northwards across the Alps. To some extent this calm correlates well with the gradual return of prosperity after the severe crises of the immediate postwar years. Thus mechanisation developed apace in Britain, while the Scandinavian countries were able to revive their old timber, corn and pig-iron trades.

Both prosperity and political calm seem to have come to an end in the later 1820s. Thus in Britain growth seems to have slackened after 1826, causing unemployment, wage-cuts and ever more ruthless competition, particularly in London. Distress was intensified by high food-prices, especially after the bad winter of 1829 which hit not merely the towns, as the revival of trade unions shows, but also the countryside. The latter was already suffering from the spread of large-scale farming using Irish labour and machines. In Norway and Sweden population pressure also conspired to increase the proportion of land in large estates, at the expense of smallholders. In Germany, where the population of the Confederation rose from 24.8 million in 1816 to 29.6 million in 1830, productivity still rose thanks to emigration, whether to towns or overseas, and to an increase in large-scale operations, whether on the land or in traditional crafts like tailoring.

Given this intensification of social and economic pressures, it is perhaps not surprising that the political climate began to alter in the last year of the decade. Even in states like Brunswick and Saxony liberalism revived, amongst students and officials, just as it did, more notably, in parts of Scandinavia. In Norway, 17 May 1829 saw the so-called 'Battle of the Market-Place' in Oslo in which nationally and constitutionally minded students clashed with the forces of order. On an infinitely larger scale was the Catholic Association in Ireland, where the collection of the Catholic Rent and the election meetings forced the Union government to concede Catholic Emancipation in 1829 after O'Connell had won the County Clare by-election. And in mainland Britain the Reform movement began to revive in a more organised way through the political unions, including the Manchester Reform Association of 1827 and the Birmingham Political Union, founded in December 1829. So, on the eve of 1830, there was a good deal of political activity as well as the flammable social conditions typified by the Scotch Cattle movement in south Wales. The former was just as important in determining the reaction to the news from Paris and Brussels as was the latter.

Everywhere the July Days influenced established opposition politics. Thus in Britain, if the news did not influence the elections of 1830 it had an effect on the way Members behaved once Parliament met. In Norway

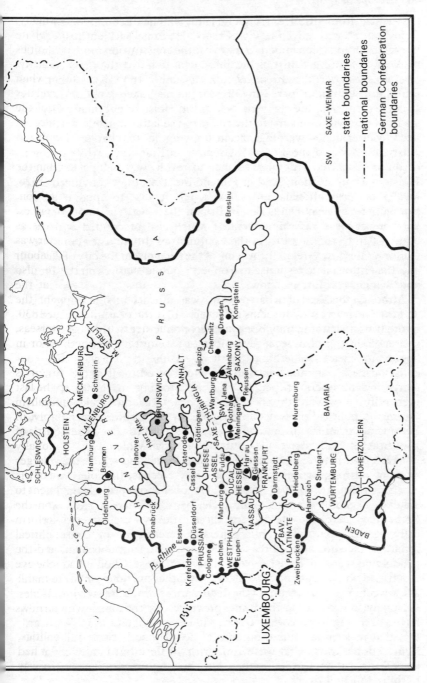

5　The German Confederation

the critical Romantic Henrik Wergeland, who had been involved in the Oslo 'Battle', was moved to visit France. He came back enthusiastic for liberal ideas and determined to try to use the constitution more positively in Norway's interest, just as did those who founded the great Swedish liberal newspaper, the *Aftonbladet*, in December 1830. Karl-Johan thus found himself under increasing pressure in his linked kingdoms: and in Denmark political life revived, as it did in Holstein and many German states. The revolutions made the rulers of the latter much less willing to heed Metternich's warnings against giving in to change. Even the Austrian envoy to the Federal Assembly in Frankfurt, while trying to organise concerted federal resistance to revolt, was willing to concede Holstein a constitution. And in Finland the Tsar, once convinced of the loyalty of local officials and soldiers, felt it wise to appoint a more sympathetic governor-general. In Britain there was an almost unparalleled lower-class radical movement which also responded with great enthusiasm to the news from the Continent as the monster demonstrations on Glasgow Green, the waving of the tricolour in the city of Armagh and the enthusiastic response to Cobbett's public lectures on the French and Belgian revolutions show.

Although this kind of urban response was unusual outside Copenhagen and the German cities, it seems that everywhere the peasantry responded to the stimulus, not merely because of economic stress, although this was real enough, but also because the idea of revolution and liberation had begun to mean something to them. Thus in Norway this new consciousness was much encouraged and showed itself in the return of increasing numbers of peasants to the Storting in the early 1830s. Generally, however, the peasant response was more elemental. In Germany, political protest was associated with machine-breaking, anti-Semitism, troubles over conscription in places like Bremen and Zweibrucken and, above all, a surge of agrarian violence.

Much of this took place in the Prussian Rhineland where there was a wave of burning of rent, tax and military records, but there was also trouble in Brunswick, Württemberg, Hanover and especially the Hessian states – a goodly part of central Germany as appears from Map 5. Sometimes, as round Heidelberg, these protests were directed specifically against the towns, but generally resentment of conscription, inflation, the shortage of bread, and competition from mechanised craft production seems to have been the motor of protest. Chopin had to write to a friend on 22 September 1830 that 'my father did not wish me to travel a few weeks ago, on account of the disturbances which are starting all over Germany; not counting the Rhine provinces, the Saxons – who already have a new king – Brunswick, Kassel and Darmstadt and so on. We heard, too, that in Vienna some thousands of people had become sulky about flour. I don't know what was wrong with the flour but I know there was something. In the Tyrol, also there have been arguments. The Italians do nothing but boil over.'

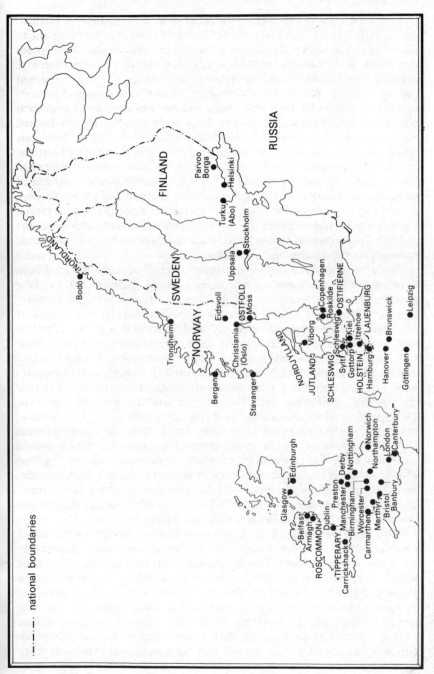

6 *Scandinavia and the British Isles*

national boundaries

In reality, none of the social disturbances was on the scale of those in the British Isles. Not merely were there food riots in isolated areas like Cornwall, Limerick, Roscommon and the Highlands, but, more significantly, in eastern Ireland attempts to enforce the payment of overdue tithes to the Church of Ireland began three years of extreme and bloody violence. At the outset, however, the epicentre proved to be in south-east England. There agriculture had been long involved in a brutal transition from peasant farming to large-scale commercial production relying on wage labourers. This had over-expanded during the war years when food was at a premium. Thereafter prices began to fall and farmers sought to cut wages and bring in threshing machines which meant even less work during the winter months for the already abused and distressed workers. And, with the combination of poor harvests and parishes trying to cut down on the relief they paid under the Speenhamland system, trouble was bound to come. It was sparked off by incidents like the hiring of Irish workers round Canterbury, and from there a wave of arson spread throughout the county and into Surrey.

By the middle of November virtually the whole of the south-west from Worcestershire to Somerset had been affected. Stories that all these assaults, burnings, marches, meetings and menaces were deliberately instigated by the French were malicious fabrications. However, feelings of expectancy amongst urban radicals and the farm labourers themselves may well have made it seem that at last something might be done about the appalling conditions which English agricultural workers had to endure. Eventually troops were called out; but, though 2,000 labourers were arrested and many were ultimately transported, this failed to stop the troubles spreading into East Anglia and the East Midlands by December, prior to petering out generally the next month. This revolt of the fields, in the end, failed to do more than hold up the introduction of threshing machines, but it momentarily frightened the establishment even if it was eclipsed by urban pressure for parliamentary reform. This also built up in the autumn, as riots in Banbury, Bristol, Northampton and Preston – where cholera and food shortages played a part – show. Both movements convinced the Whigs there was enough support for them to start drafting a Reform Bill that winter.

While they were doing this, things moved on politically in a number of German states, so that there, too, the rural and social unrest was somewhat overshadowed. The first to move was the Duchy of Brunswick which, as can be seen on Map 5, was a set of enclaves inside Hanover and Prussia, where the regency for the young Duke Karl had been exercised by Count Munster, George IV's resident in Hanover. When Karl came of age he immediately revoked the constitution Munster had granted four years earlier since he believed that a ruler had no obligations to his subjects and resented what he felt had been an undue extension of his minority. The next three years saw the Duke assault his subjects by removing social curbs on the nobility, denying the army full pay, purging the government and civil service, interfering with the judicial system and selling off his estates to the detriment of both nobles and peasants. By May 1829 the local Diet, or Landestande, was so alarmed that it met without his permission in order to petition the Confederation against him, while leading officials refused to take an oath of loyalty unless the constitution was restored.

Hanoverian annoyance at all this forced the reluctant Bund to rule against the Duke; but, rather than yield, Karl took himself off to Paris, from where he continued to snipe at the establishment, disbanding the fiscal administration and reorganising the judiciary. In May 1830 the Landestande formally protested against his maladministration and absence, but in the end it was the July Days which drove him back. Since he brought an offensive new favourite with him his return merely fuelled the fire, and on 31 August he was again petitioned for the restoration of the constitution. His response was to station cannon and extra troops in front of the Residenzschloss. This was too much for the local élite, who began to think of replacing him with his brother. To win the peasantry to the idea they spread the rumour that Karl was guilty of not merely perversion, treason and pro-Catholicism, but even of causing the hailstorm which had recently savaged their crops. Not surprisingly tension mounted, and on 6 September the Duke and his mistress were stoned on leaving the theatre. Crowds gathered the next day, demanding a Diet, lower taxes, bread and work. Since the army proved sympathetic to the demonstrators the Duke agreed to provide public works and relief, even to withdraw the cannon. This did not suffice. Calls for his removal were heard, and the army commander refused to obey the order to fire unless it was given by the Duke in person at his side. Rather than do this Karl fled. The army then stood by and let the crowd sack the palace that evening.

The local élites at once set up a civic militia and summoned the Landestande so as to ensure law and order. They also sent envoys to the Duke's brother, William of Brunswick-Oels, who was then serving in the Prussian army, asking him to replace Karl. He arrived on 10 September and was appointed Governor-General. A policy of limited reform was begun. The Bund somewhat reluctantly acquiesced in all this and then, when Karl tried one final throw in November, unsuccessfully invading the Duchy offering universal suffrage and other concessions, it agreed to ratify William's accession to the Dukedom ahead of Karl's son. All this was ultimately ratified by a new constitution in July 1832.

Events in Saxony were much more the product of social and structural problems than of mere personalities. As a result, conflict there was the more bitter and long-drawn-out. The government of King Anton had been unable to develop a rational and acceptable system for ruling a country which had been greatly reduced in size in 1815. Local autonomies and privileges remained; the Landestande, while dominated by the nobility, was denied real influence; and nothing was done to protect once flourishing industries against British competition. Moreover, because of its earlier Polish connections, the royal family was Catholic not Lutheran, and the king's patronage of the Jesuits on the one hand and the banning of celebrations of the Confession of Augsburg on the other were much resented by the population at large, particularly when their protests in both Leipzig and Dresden were very roughly handled by the police. Similarly, the way demands from younger nobles in the Diet to be allowed to see the budget for 1830 were rejected increased resentment and popularised the idea of parliamentary government.

Trouble actually developed partly because of news from Paris and Brussels, and partly because of the underlying social crisis. On 2 September there were clashes in Leipzig between apprentice ironsmiths and the police when the former waved the tricolour and cheered the French as part of a protest against the corruption and inefficiency of the local authorities. The municipality had allowed the import of foreign iron bedsteads and mechanised printing presses, not to mention imposing high taxes and favouring royal coach services – all of which meant unemployment. Although the police mastered the demonstrations, the authorities thought it wise to sound out the middle classes, but this did little to quiet things. So, when on 5 September there were new attacks on the police headquarters and the homes of unpopular councillors, the authorities had to withdraw the police in favour of a middle-class guard. They also lowered taxes, freed arrested rioters and sent the popular Prince Frederick Augustus to the town to consider further changes.

Before any of this could really take effect, however, disorder spread to Dresden, the capital. On 9 September crowds of weavers and peasants, again flying the tricolour, broke into the town hall and burned police and other records. The army was unable to repress this, and the king felt it wisest to retire to his fortress of Königstein, leaving the Prince, as co-regent, and some of the more sympathetic members of the old administration to look into all grievances. The new regime committed itself to excluding the Jesuits, entering the regional customs union, lifting some of the feudal burdens on the peasantry, and drafting a new constitution. This did not, however, prevent further troubles amongst artisans, farmers and even some elements of the middle classes to whom political radicalism began to appeal. Other elements of the bourgeoisie, however, were alarmed by this and rallied to the new regent and the army when a further assault was mounted on the town hall in April 1831. None the less, a slightly more liberal constitution was to be agreed on 4 September 1831.

In Hesse-Kassel the difficulties were due to a combination of structural problems and personal eccentricity. William II, who in 1821 had become Elector of a state which had also suffered in the wars, ruled in a somewhat authoritarian way and, more significantly, flaunted his mistress, Emilia Ortlopp, the daughter of a Berlin goldsmith, whom he raised to be the Countess Reichenbach. This was ill received by Prussia, since the Elector was married to a Hohenzollern princess. The Countess also became a scapegoat for all the regime's failings, notably its tendency to spy on its own subjects and the high and arbitrary taxes levied on a rural population already in straitened circumstances to pay for a large court and army.

Thus, although the winter of 1829–30 was a particularly hard one, the government insisted on raising cereal taxes and, when news came of the Paris events, on sending the Countess's brother to Kassel to remove the family and their possessions from the firing-line. On 6–7 September the artisans of the town rioted in the belief that the Elector was conspiring with local bakers to push up bread-prices even more. A fearful bourgeoisie put the riots down, but the state had to open its grain magazines and respond to the crowd's desire for political change. Receipt of a petition about popular misery on 15 September gave the returning Elector the chance to give in gracefully and avoid the fate of Karl of Brunswick. He agreed to call the Landestande, establish a civic guard, abolish the tolls in the enclaves of Hanau and Fulda and, above all, to dismiss his mistress and her family.

These concessions were not enough to stop the peasantry from turning on noble manorial rights and the hated excise-posts. A veritable *jacquerie* broke out in Hanau in Upper Hesse involving attacks on local nobles, the expulsion of Electoral officials and forays into neighbouring Ducal Hesse. After achieving some success against the nobles the movement degenerated into mere looting. As a result, while the Crown Prince was sent to suspend the excise duties the Bund mobilised troops and sent them into Upper Hesse in Early October to complete the dispersal of the rioters. This was also done because the troubles in the Electorate had stimulated some 6,000 peasants in the Grand Duchy to march on Darmstadt late in September. Workers and artisans in many of the smaller towns were also restive, although the middle classes rallied to the government. Some two hundred demonstrators were arrested and nearly eighty were sentenced to terms of imprisonment of up to fifteen years. While this repression quietened the Duchy, Hesse-Kassel remained uneasy.

The Landestande, supplemented by new rural delegates, met on 16 October and set about drafting a new constitution which clearly divided the ruler's revenues from those of the state, gave the Landestande the right of initiative and even freed the remaining serfs. Such liberal provisions, the work of Sylvester Jourdan, a professor from Marburg, worried the Bund and the Elector's family when they were inaugurated on 5 January 1831. Since this almost coincided with demonstrations against the return of the Countess Reichenbach, the Elector in April retreated to Hanau and set up a counter-government. Because he refused to maintain his separation from his mistress, arrangements had to be made to make his son co-regent. And as he was very firmly opposed to constitutionalism he used his powers to curtail its working. By early in 1832 it had largely been set aside.

Elsewhere rulers proved more amenable. The Duke of Altenburg on 14 September conceded tax changes, curbs on officials and greater representation to middle-class petitioners. Similar changes were made in Saxe-Meiningen, Gotha and Reuss, although petitioners in Oldenburg later in the month were less successful. Even in Prussian Westphalia concessions on municipal government were made, although a United Diet was refused. Many smaller states, of course, managed to ride out the storm, notably in Nassau where the Duke signally defeated the Diet's demands for control of his estates in 1831–2.

The last major example of restiveness came in Hanover, whose southern domains overlapped the epicentre of disturbance as Map 5 shows. There the peasantry began to petition for relief and the citizens of Osnabrück to withhold taxes – protests against the way the regime refused both to grant a constitution and to restrain noble exploitation of the rural population. In January trouble spread to Osterode and Göttingen, where students and burghers took over the town and barricaded themselves in on the 8th. Although this was soon dealt with by the army, the government felt it had to dismiss the resident minister, Count Munster, and sent the Duke of Cambridge to look into grievances. In the end this was to issue in a constitution of sorts, although by the time it was agreed the tide was beginning to run against such liberalism in Germany.

Before this happened there had been similar constitutional gains in Scandinavia and, more strikingly, in Britain. In Norway the liberals were much encouraged by the way the July Days made Karl-Johan more amenable on symbolic issues, while also preventing the eastern powers from sniping at the Eidsvoll constitution. The very lack of constraint seems to have made the royalist-inclined peasantry lose interest in politics, so that no real liberal party emerged. In Sweden, however, the liberals were able to politicise the peasantry who, by 1834, went over to the opposition, thereby subjecting the king to increasing harassment as the decade ended.

The most notable change came in Denmark where, in October 1830, a young Frisian administrator called Uwe-Jens Lornsen persuaded a number of German intellectuals in Kiel to join him in petitioning for Norwegian-style autonomy in the increasingly Germanised duchies of Schleswig and Holstein. When Lornsen refused to be ordered back to his post in Sylt and thus silenced he was dismissed and then imprisoned in 1832. This made him a martyr to Danish overlordship, a fact which was to have tragic implications. In the first instance, however, his protests helped to persuade the Crown to make the first changes in absolutism so as to prevent any post-July troubles in Denmark. On 28 May 1831 it was decided to establish four consultative regional assemblies on the Prussian model, elected on a narrow franchise. They were to be in Viborg (for Nørrejylland), in Roskilde (for Ostiftierne or the islands), in Schleswig town (for Schleswig) and, finally, in Itzehoe (for Holstein and Lauenberg). Although the ducal assemblies had more rights than the other two, the fact that there was no united Diet for Schleswig-Holstein as a whole rankled with many Germans, especially when the pan-Scandinavian political and cultural revival began to make itself felt in Denmark.

Long before this the Whig government in Britain had come forward with quite radical proposals to abolish many small and rotten boroughs on 1 March 1831. Their seats were to be bestowed on counties and hitherto unfranchised towns with a basic qualification of £10 for householders applying throughout. This went much too far for the Tories, even those who took umbrage at the pocket-borough system. Hence the bill was rejected by the Lords in the spring. New elections were held amid considerable disturbances, like those in Carmarthen where troops were called in after pitched battles caused by the victory of an anti-Reform candidate. Scotland saw more monster meetings as did the south-east of England. With the election going in favour of the Reformers a second bill was brought in amidst immense political excitement.

When the Lords again rejected Reform on 8 October 1831 there was a massive explosion of anger and frustration. New political unions were created, several hundreds of thousands of people attended meetings in Birmingham and London, and some peers were attacked. In places like Derby, on 8 October, and especially Bristol, between 23 and 31 October, protests took on a violent turn with twelve people being killed and hundreds of thousands of pounds' worth of damage being done. All this encouraged some radical leaders to try to persuade government that revolution would be a real possibility unless Reform went ahead. There was even talk of setting up a Continental-style national guard and of calling a Constituent Assembly.

The Whigs dealt very firmly with such un-English proposals, which were in any case more rhetorical flourishes than real threats. They did, however, persevere with a bill, albeit in a watered-down form. This cost them the support of the lower-class radicals. Yet, even so, although the bill got safely through the Commons between 12 December 1831 and March 1832, it again faced defeat in the Lords. The Whigs resigned when William IV refused to promise to create enough new peers to ensure the passage of the bill. But since the Duke of Wellington then found himself faced with widespread civil disobedience, symbolised by the cry 'To beat the Duke go for gold', there was little chance of his forming a successful government. In the event, he and other Tories decided to abstain rather than risk either the creation of new peers or yet more disturbances, and a bill suppressing the worst of the pocket boroughs and increasing the electorate by some 80 per cent – making it about 366,000 – finally went through in early June 1832.

Considering that the parliamentary tradition was so well established in Britain, it is not surprising that the passage of the Bill has been hailed as the supreme example of political adaptation, particularly when there was so much regret that change had not gone farther. In a way, the concessions by Frederick VII of Denmark were just as remarkable and significant. However, it is true that in Britain and Scandinavia there was to be no going back on the liberalisation achieved in the early 1830s. This was not so in Germany. To some extent, the reversal of opinion was due to the way in which the events of 1830 had not merely produced the changes in the centre and north of the country which we have already noted, but had also stimulated students and liberals in the more advanced states of south-western Germany to press for yet further changes. There were particularly tense struggles for political rights in Bavaria. This worried rulers everywhere. Even in Württemberg, where the king was very sympathetic to the idea of a league of constitutional states which might balance France and the eastern powers, demands for further liberalisation were resisted. Such pressures also led to the creation of a powerful Association for Press Freedom which was responsible for the calling of a mass meeting in Hambach in the Bavarian Palatinate in late May 1832 when 20,000–30,000 people gathered to hear talk of further constitutional changes and even of the need for a federal unification of Germany. Notwithstanding this most rulers followed the Crown Prince of Hesse and set their faces against change.

Since the possibility of war was still exercising them, and Metternich was emphasising the suicidal nature of constitutional concessions, their envoys met frequently at federal level to lay down new controls on political expression during the winter of 1831–2. After Hambach these were reinforced by the Ten Acts of 5 July 1832. This was to be the prelude to mounting repression, especially after the abortive attempt of German and Polish radicals to overthrow the Frankfurt Assembly in April 1833. Yet, although constitutional gains were rescinded, the educational and psychological effects of 1830 in Germany remained significant. In Scandinavia and particularly in Britain, where lower-class dissatisfaction began to show itself with increasing force, the impact was even greater. The lesson seems to be that, without a fully developed political system, concessions by rulers could not be relied upon to produce the desired effect. None the less, 1830 began a long process of adaptation in Germany and Scandinavia, just as it did in Britain.

9 Poland: A Limited War of Liberation

Many Poles might have felt that their problem was that, although they had not merely a constitution but also a quite well-developed political system, they did not have a ruler who was willing to implement the former, let alone to allow adaptations in the latter. Their clash with Tsarist Russia was often explained as a reaction to the way their grievances were ignored and they were denied the constitutional privileges which were rightfully theirs. In fact it seems that they rather misinterpreted the nature and purpose of the constitutional Charter enunciated by Alexander I in 1815. The reason that they did so lay in their deep-rooted and fiercely held patriotism, which made them insistent on what they believed to be their rights. If maladministration had been the cause of revolt in the far east of Europe, it should surely have led to one in Russia which, at the time, was much less generously treated than Poland.

So, although the sense of grievance was sincerely felt by the Poles, there can be little doubt but that the events of 1830–1 really represented an assertion of national pride. The Polish revolution was a classic war of liberation, albeit a limited one. It was limited in that the whole of Polish society was not involved in the struggle, so that the latter was dogged by internal friction and uncertainty. And, at the same time, it was limited by the way the Poles had to contend with an equally assertive nation with a claim to some of the lands involved in the uprising. These limitations on the Polish effort at liberation need to be remembered, even though the military conflicts were on a far larger scale than anything else in 1830.

The creation of a quasi-separate Kingdom of Poland in 1815 had been largely forced on Russia and the Allies by Napoleon's handling of the Polish question. For, although his Grand Duchy of Warsaw had not always been wholly accepted by the Poles, the fact that for the first time since the Third Partition in 1795 had extinguished the Old Polish Commonwealth there was at least a focus for nationhood had encouraged patriotic hopes of re-creating the old national boundaries which, as can be seen from Map 7, were vast. This threatened the partitioning powers and, in the expectation of avoiding further upheavals by a discontented population, they grudgingly acquiesced in the creation of a kind of halfway house between an independent Poland and one wholly incorporated in Russia. Enough territories were released to create a small kingdom, with the Tsar as its hereditary ruler, whose linguistic and religious rights were recognised. There was also talk of free trade between it and the other parts of the Commonwealth which remained in

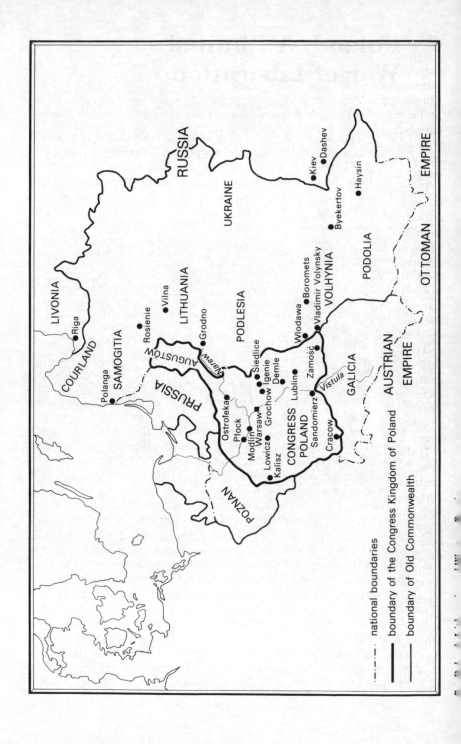

national boundaries

boundary of the Congress Kingdom of Poland

boundary of Old Commonwealth

RUSSIA

UKRAINE

LIVONIA

COURLAND

Riga

SAMOGITIA

Polanga

Rosienie

Vilna

LITHUANIA

Grodno

Narew

AUGUSTOW

PRUSSIA

POZNAN

Ostroteka

Plock

Modlin

Warsaw

Lowicz

Grochow

Kalisz

Demle

Igenie

Siedlice

PODLESIA

CONGRESS
POLAND

Lublin

Sandomierz

Cracow

Zamość

Vistula

GALICIA

AUSTRIAN

EMPIRE

Wlodawa

Boromets

Vladimir Volynsky

VOLHYNIA

PODOLIA

Byekertov

Haysin

Kiev

Dashev

OTTOMAN

EMPIRE

foreign hands. Similarly there was a simulacrum of representative government with a bi-cameral parliament, or Sejm, composed solely of nobles. The realities of power lay with the Viceroy, the Tsar's commissioner, the army commander – who was the Grand Duke Constantine, Alexander's younger brother – and the Polish Secretariat in St Petersburg. The Charter was thus largely symbolic, but the Poles naïvely saw it as the harbinger of further concessions such as reunification with Lithuania and the acceptance of free speech. Whatever the rights and wrongs of the situation it is clear that the existence of a separate state encouraged Polish pride and hopes.

Relations between the Poles and the Tsar were smooth at the outset, but rapidly deteriorated when in 1820 voices were raised in the Sejm in criticism of Alexander's ministers. The Tsar regarded this as no different from an attack on himself, and promptly suspended the Sejm for five years, even though the Charter required more regular meetings. This, the non-replacement of the first viceroy, and new pressures on education and the Catholic Church, not to mention the consideration of using Polish troops in a projected Army of Surveillance to operate in western Europe, alarmed some Poles. Since it all seemed like a change of heart on Alexander's part they began to join the secret societies which had sprung up in student and army circles, even though these were often penetrated and prosecuted by the Russians. This dissidence also had economic roots since in the early 1820s the western grain-market on which the 300,000 gentry, or *szlachta*, depended to pay off the huge debts and mortgages incurred during the war years dried up. At the same time, Russia and Prussia imposed new tariffs on Polish exports. All of this made the situation of the gentry, who made up the political nation, very hard to bear.

It also reduced government income, and the Tsar therefore appointed a new Finance Minister, Prince Lubecki, to restore the position of the gentry and at the same time to increase economic resources generally. Although this was to mean both that the few advantages gained by the serfs during the Napoleonic period were cancelled, to the benefit of the gentry, and that the country was endowed with a modest manufacturing base and an improved infrastructure, discontent amongst the gentry and the intelligentsia was not assuaged. Some Poles therefore made contact with the Decembrist movement, talks taking place in Kiev in 1823–5. Although none was involved in the actual risings in St Petersburg and Byekertov in December and January 1825–6, one Pole who had taken part in the talks was arrested by the authorities. However, the Poles would neither try him for treason, as the new Tsar Nicholas wanted, nor inflict a heavy sentence. The Tsar bitterly remarked that 'they have saved the criminals but lost the country'.

Many Poles were also reinforced in their patriotic feelings by the upsurge of literary and historical Romanticism, symbolised by the poet

Mickiewicz, the historian Lelewel and, of course, Chopin, and even some conservatives were convinced by this that accommodation with Russia was no longer possible. The Grand Duke Constantine, now the effective governor of the country, often complained of the envenomed criticism directed against him and the regime. None the less, Nicholas did come to Warsaw to be crowned in 1829 and then, in 1830, allowed the Sejm to voice new protests. So, while he was coolly received on both occasions, there does not seem to have been any real support for schemes for a *coup d'état* which evolved from December 1828 onwards amongst military cadets in the capital. Coming from active *szlachta* families, they found the inactivity, austerity and lack of promotion imposed on them by Constantine's handling of the army a very galling contrast with their Romantic ideals. They considered trying to assassinate Nicholas in 1829 but were dissuaded, and there was even less backing for the idea the following year.

However, the cadets, as Zajewski says, were transfigured by the stimulus from Paris, which was received in Warsaw on 6 August when the French Consulate there flew the tricolour. At once there were exuberant demonstrations in the streets, but the cadets decided against precipitate action. News was hard to come by as none of them read French and the Russians had closed the border and banned discussion of the events at first. When it proved impossible to suppress the news the latter put out a doctored version which implied that Charles X had voluntarily relinquished his throne, although this did not stop Russian liberals from enthusing over the new possibilities of a popular revolution which were revealed. In Warsaw the cadets felt they could not count on a war breaking out, and felt it wiser to wait, in the hope that they could attract a 'name' to their cause who might help them to overcome the loyalty of the army and those with vested interests in the often profitable link with Russia. Deteriorating economic conditions in the capital itself might even encourage the populace to support them, too.

Nicholas, on the other hand, came round to thinking about military action of his own, and in mid-August ordered Constantine and Lubecki to look into mobilising the Polish army. When they demurred, largely on financial grounds, he had to go back to playing a waiting game throughout September and early October. But then the news from Brussels, Germany and Paris seemed to suggest that the contagion was spreading eastwards and would have to be resisted. So on 17 October he decided that mobilisation would have to take place no later than 22 December. When this became known in Warsaw about 20 November, the cadets felt they had to act, even though the diplomatic situation offered no more assurance than in August, and their own preparations were not much further advanced. Their numbers had crept up only to 200 by October, and the only 'name' in their discussions was Lelewel, who was both reluctant and profoundly unmilitary. The police meanwhile had already arrested some of their number, late in September. None the less, on 26 November they hesitantly fixed their *coup* for 10 December. Constantine had been made aware by the police that something was afoot, but he preferred to regard it as youthful foolishness best dealt with by the Poles themselves. When pressure to have the cadets court-martialled grew to the point that the Vice-President of the Military Region made an appointment to see the Grand Duke in order to present him with evidence on the extent of the conspiracy, the cadets were forced into pre-emptive action. Fear and police action thus played more part in starting the rising than any disinclination to fight in the west, let alone a desire to save Belgium.

Indeed, their plans remained ingenuously vague, not going much beyond the fond hope that the assassination of Constantine and the seizure of army supply-dumps would rouse the people to act. Their view of revolution was closer to a Decembrist-type *putsch* than to the more widespread revolts of the western heartland. Their efforts were very badly executed in any case. Hardly anyone turned up at the rallying-points at the new time set for the revolt, 5 p.m. on Monday, 29 November. An attempt to set a brewery alight as a signal also failed, and a mere eighteen people assaulted Constantine's residence in the Belvedere Palace at 7 p.m. Even though it was unguarded, they failed to catch the Grand Duke, who escaped by hiding in the attic. Not surprisingly after this demonstration of ineptitude, local notables locked their doors and the army refused to budge, even though some loyalist generals were murdered in the streets. The rebels could not disarm Russian troops, nor yet establish a provisional government, and by 10 p.m. they were in desperate straits.

It was the sad sight of the rebels falling back from an unsuccessful attack on the Lazienki barracks which saved them. The lower classes of the capital took pity on them and, with 30,000 rifles made available by the seizure of the arsenal, took the chance to express their own grievances while the authorities stood by. The artisans thus took delight not merely in baiting the Russian bear but also in getting their own back on a corrupt and unpopular municipality which had tried to provoke them to violence and then, despite the fact that things were tight because of the bad rye-harvest, had raised the price of vodka and beer that very day, which was always an unofficial holiday. Soldiers, who had also found food-prices outstripping the ration allowance paid to their colonels – thereby also denying the latter their profits – joined them. Overnight the city passed into their hands, with food- and wine-shops being sacked and Jews attacked.

The muncipality, chastened, left it to Constantine to restore order, but instead he withdrew his troops from the city centre. Even though Russian artillery and other units joined him, giving him the advantage of numbers, he refused to accede to the demand of his Russian advisers to crush the disturbances. This was because there was a long-standing agreement with Prussia that Russian troops should not be used in Polish affairs, and Constantine professed to regard the affair as a mere riot against the municipality. Rather than make war on subjects of whom he was genuinely fond, since his morganatic marriage to a Polish countess, and, in so doing, damage the army of which he was so proud, he left the task to the Poles. As a result, no one did anything, and riot escalated into revolution.

Constantine's advisory Administrative Council was left holding the baby. It decided to make a gesture and, as well as appealing for calm, invited a number of popular figures including Josef Chłopicki, the most respected general, to assist in its deliberations. This failed to halt the looting, and the slide into anarchy continued, with worried young radicals joining the middle classes in setting up vigilante forces to try to restore order, and with provincial troops called up by Constantine to establish a *cordon sanitaire* round the city themselves joining the revolt. The Administrative Council persevered in its attempt to stabilise matters, transforming itself into an Executive Commission – since legally only the Tsar could nominate members to the previous body – and inviting Lelewel and other radicals to join. Then, despite a previous failure, the Commission set about persuading Constantine to agree both not to increase or move his forces without notice and to intercede for them with his brother. This was far too cautious a policy for some radicals who, on 1 December, formed a Patriotic Society which began to campaign for war with Russia, marching on the Commission offices to press home their point. The latter went as far as to turn itself into a virtual provisional government and to make itself responsible to Chłopicki, who was appointed Dictator on 5 December in a final effort to restore order and hold back the rising tide of radicalism from finally compromising them with the Tsar. Unfortunately, when news of the events reached Nicholas on 7 December he could not appreciate their restraint. For him it was a simple case of revolt, and Field-Marshal Diebitsch was ordered to move his western forces directly into Poland. And, with the provinces rallying to the support of the capital, his view seemed more realistic than Chłopicki's protestations that he and his colleagues were seeking to lead the revolt simply in order to control it. War began to appear a real danger.

The Dictatorship struggled on for six weeks, caught between the two stools of Nicholas's growing disapproval and rising Polish nationalism. Nicholas, in response to Chłopicki's protestations, would go no further than to promise an amnesty, and on 17 December ordered all loyal troops to concentrate at Płock. In Warsaw the more radical elements rejected Chłopicki's attempt to resign and his effort to control the government and thus continued to threaten his conciliatory policy. Even the Sejm, which was soon in permanent session and took effective charge of government, could not be persuaded that the very idea of resistance to

Russia was impossible. Despite the growing factional disputes in its midst and outside – which had seen the student guard close down the Patriotic Society at one stage – it issued a pugnacious statement of the nation's grievances on 3 January. It also refused to heed Chłopicki's demands for action against the radicals, and when on 11 January he arrested Lelewel and others on his own authority it refused to support him. Six days later Chłopicki laid down his powers.

The final barrier to conflict with Russia was swept away when the Patriotic Society began to campaign for the deposition of Nicholas. On 25 January demonstrators, carrying a coffin as a symbol of the martyred Decembrists, went to the Sejm. Cheered on by excited crowds in the gallery the excited *szlachta* delegates decided to copy the Belgians and depose the ruling house. This act, performed in a state of high emotional excitement, proved to be a diplomatic error as it threatened the Vienna settlement and made it impossible for sympathetic countries like Britain and France to take the Poles' side. Unfortunately, too, the deposition did not lead to really decisive action in support of the national cause. A proper National Government was set up on 30 January under Prince Adam George Czartorywski, a moderate constitutionalist with a European-wide reputation. But the government was internally divided and distrusted both by the army, whose leaders still felt that armed resistance was a delusion, and by the Sejm. The latter was keen on civil rights and therefore suspicious of any executive authority. As a result, the government was never given a free hand and, while the deputies talked enthusiastically of guerilla warfare, little was actually done to organise real defence.

Another trouble was that, if the Poles were to have had any chance of victory, they would have had to call on the total resources of the country. But this meant mobilising the peasantry – something which was against the interests of both *szlachta* and intellectuals, many of whom were of gentry origin. They rejected the idea of making concessions to the peasantry in order to assuage the already visible hostility of the countryside. In any case, the Sejm felt that the urgent need of supplies of food and men on the one hand, and of political support from the provincial nobility on the other, demanded the maintenance, even the increase, of levies and controls on the peasantry. So it is hardly surprising that mild proposals to curtail labour dues and endow the peasantry with a modicum of land were regarded as excessive and, ultimately, were not even considered when they were due to come before the Sejm on 18 April. There was, as a result, no response from the peasantry to the call for a *levée en masse* in early July.

The agrarian situation was also one of the reasons why the Austrian and Prussian zones of the Old Commonwealth played so little part in the revolt. The Polish élite in the free city of Cracow were sympathetic but cut off by diplomatic hostility and peasant opposition. A rising in

Vladimir-Volynsky and Haysin in the Ukraine was quickly extinguished, so that only around Riga in Lithuania was there a real movement of support, beginning in late March. And even this was too weak to capture Vilna on 17 April. Polish support was too much of an afterthought to save the area from a Russian advance which probably in any case pre-empted peasant violence against Polish landlords.

The mobilisation demanded by radicals and crowds in the capital was thus not a practical proposition. The war had to be fought by the professional army created by Constantine, together with a few volunteers. The army's strength, which had been some 54,000 at the outset, eventually rose to 85,000, of which some 65,000 were in the main field-forces. This was a somewhat limited basis for a successful war of liberation, especially as the commanders had little desire to tangle with the Russians on behalf of extremist civilians. So when Diebitsch crossed the frontier, 110,000 strong, on 6 February no concerted resistance was attempted. Augustów in the north was overrun, and Chłopicki, who was still in command of the army then, was caught unawares and had to stand and fight at Grochow to save the capital on 3–6 February. Although the Poles lost fewer men than the Russians, this proved to be a pyrrhic victory since the Russians remained in possession of a large amount of territory. Only in the south was their advance checked, thanks to a victory at Stoczek in mid-February; but despite later gains at Iganie and Dembe late in March the Poles were unable or unwilling to exploit their advantages, and finished up by losing control there, so that no help could be given to the Ukrainian revolt. Operations in the north were equally lethargic for a while, but when the Poles did finally launch an offensive Diebitsch was jolted into an emphatic riposte. His army caught the Poles at Ostrotela and divided them by capturing the crucial bridge over the Narew. As a result, the Poles lost 20,000 men – whether dead, forced to go into internment, or lost in the unsuccessful foray into Lithuania which followed – and any chance of victory, a point duly noted by foreign powers.

However, a pause followed in the high summer, due in part to the cholera epidemic which carried off both Constantine and the discredited Diebitsch, and caused army mutinies in St Petersburg and some of the military colonies. However, even Russian liberals had little sympathy for the Poles – whom they felt had always been too generously treated – and remained loyal to the Tsar, who, of course, never wavered in his determination to crush the rising. His new commander, Paskievitch, reorganised his forces and set out on a long sweep round the north-west to take Warsaw in the rear. By 8 July he had reached Płock, the Vistula was crossed on 21 July, and by 1 August he was encamped at Lowicz. Yet neither of the Polish commanders, chosen by the increasingly dissatisfied radicals, was willing to risk an engagement. Instead they withdrew most of their forces into the capital, allowing the Russians to reach its outskirts largely unopposed at the end of the month.

This brought to a head the conflict between the generals and the increasingly undisciplined *szlachta* and their popular allies in Warsaw. Their alarm over the generals' inaction was reinforced by the lack of diplomatic response to their cause and the way the government's imposition of conscription, requisition of supplies and additional taxation had provoked peasant unrest in Kalisz and Sandomierz. Dembinski's attempt to arrest the leaders of the Patriotic Society was the last straw, and on 14 August calls for a purge of all conservatives were heard. The next day several thousand gentry and others marched on the government buildings in support of a call for a new government which would be in resolute resistance. Negotiations failed to satisfy the crowds, who first sacked the government offices and then massacred many of the political prisoners in the town until the army stepped in and restored order on 16 August.

The radicals thus destroyed the government – Czartorywski fleeing to the safety of the Army – and themselves. For Krukowiecki, the left-wing general who emerged as provisional President, refused to heed them and, when two sorties in search of food had failed, began to negotiate with the Russians. The Sejm joined in the talks, deliberately dragging them out, until the Russian advance resumed and the city had to be evacuated on 8 September in face of a savage artillery bombardment. The remnants of government and army retired to Płock where the former found that neither officers nor men were willing to continue the struggle. The government went bitterly into exile later in the month, while the army either surrendered or crossed the frontiers to be interned in early October. The last fortresses in Polish hands, Modlin and Zamosc, capitulated on 8 and 21 October respectively. Three days previously Nicholas had officially pronounced the war over.

The fall of Warsaw and the subsequent repression by Paskievitch, the new Governor-General, caused immense despair. Chopin was allegedly moved to write a soulful piano study to echo his lament that 'the suburbs are destroyed, burned ... how many corpses is this minute making in the world?' The country lost its separate status by the Organic Statute of 15 March 1832, not to mention its Charter, parliament, army and tariff-walls. Education and culture were to be russified, although there were few executions and attempts at land confiscation proved ineffective. In fact many peasants, and even some landlords, came to terms with the new order.

Europe was made very aware of the new Polish travail because of the number of exiles who fled westwards. Not merely were they gallant symbols of a martyred nation, but they also developed close links with radical and socialist movements in the west – participating in new movements in Frankfurt and Savoy, for instance. This was not to the taste of all the exiles, particularly of the 'whites' who gathered round Czartorywski and the government-in-exile. The emigration in fact mirrored the social and political divisions of the rising itself, as well as its preoccupation with unenforceable principles and gallant gestures, which were particularly prominent amongst the 'reds' of the Polish Democratic Society, some of whom veered towards a kind of communistic populism. The basis for a war of liberation thus remained very limited. None the less, the Polish effort in 1830–1 became a model for foreigners and a source of almost mystical inspiration to many Poles. This reinforces the impression that the November revolution was revolutionary in role rather than in content. It was concerned only with national liberation, being too socially and politically divided to agree on much else. Yet it was revolutionary in the way in which, despite these limitations, it posed a symbolic and dangerous challenge to the conservative east – a challenge which cost the Russians 180,000 men to overcome.

10 The Southern and Eastern Peripheries: The Limits to Pressure from Without

Unlike some other regions the countries of southern and eastern Europe did not have real grass-roots movements for change in 1830. Prior to the July Days there was no effective opposition inside the Turkish and Habsburg domains, nor yet in the Two Sicilies. In Portugal the majority of the population would happily have allowed the continuance of fierce reaction, while in Spain the development of a large-scale liberal movement came later in the decade. As a result, the impact of the revolutions of 1830 was largely a matter of external and diplomatic pressures. As the abortive invasions of Spain show, the relatively weak regimes of the peripheries were able to cope with such pressures without undue difficulty. In the absence of supporting internal forces, such pressures produced very little change. Even in Portugal, where the July Days brought a sudden accretion of support and sympathy for the liberal cause, a long and painful process was required before Don Miguel could be ousted. The experience of the southern and eastern countries of Europe therefore throws into relief the special conditions of the heartland which enabled change to go so much farther.

To some extent, the absence of change can be explained by mere distance, since the impact of something like the July Days was very much muted by the time it reached Bucharest or Braganza. Much more important, however, was the way social structures and social control conspired not merely to limit, but often to render impossible rapid or radical change. In peripheral areas which were often arid and mountainous, social structures were polarised and retarded. Almost without exception the southern countries were dominated by large-scale noble landholdings, whether those of Romanian boyars or the *latifundisti* of Iberia and the Mezzogiorno. In some cases, as with the Magyars, the nobility numbered hundreds of thousands so they enjoyed a triple domination of land, political life and peasantry. Indeed, the peasantry could often be a class of virtual pariahs, subject to corporal punishment, labour services and a range of feudal restraints which had largely vanished in the north. Even where peasants were sharecroppers or wage earners their revenues were minuscule, and it is not surprising that there was often considerable rural dissent, typified by Tudor Vladimirescu's rising in Wallachia in 1821.

In the Ottoman Empire – which, as Map 8 shows, was still extensive – social enmity often took on an ethnic and religious colouring since landlords were frequently Turkish and the peasants Christian. Moreover,

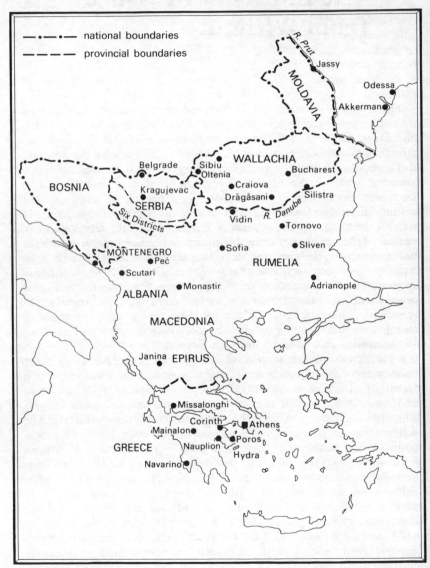

8   *The Balkans*

the old *sipahi* system in which a cavalryman was entitled to enjoy a tithe and labour dues from the free peasants of his jurisdiction, or *timar*, had given way, because of the weakness of the Porte and the attractions of the western grain-market, to a system of hereditary ownerships, or *çifliks*. A new Muslim élite, the *ayans*, were able to use their retainers both to force an increasingly tied peasantry to work on capitalistic farms and to resist central authority. This could mean a virtual second serfdom, and one which changes in the ethnic composition of the landowning élite did little to ameliorate. Thus even the merchants and military leaders of Serbia sought simply if unsuccessfully to claim for themselves the landed status of the departing Turks, while the Organic Regulations in the Danubian principalities merely strengthened the position of the noble boyars.

This polarised social system was, not surprisingly, hard pressed to cope with the burden of rising numbers. In the Habsburg Empire the population rose by a quarter between 1819 and 1843; and in Spain, where growth was low in European terms, it rose by 4.8 per cent a year in much the same period. Tension was greatly increased but, at the same time, misery and social control made political protest even more unlikely – at least, without external intervention. Moreover, such simple social systems did not leave much room for trade, towns, manufactures or even reliable central authorities. In regions like Bulgaria there could be virtually nothing but the moneylender or village notable, or *chorbadzii*, as intermediary between peasant and élite. Trade was often carried on by outsiders, whether Germans, Jews or especially the Greeks, whose ships and interests dominated the eastern Mediterranean in general and the grain trade with the west in particular. However, such Greeks rarely participated in political affairs, and it was left to clerks, pedlars and petty merchants to support the secret societies.

Towns were often small, and industry virtually unknown. Even in 1850 the Hungarian population of 12 million included fewer than 60,000 miners and factory workers. Outside Bohemia and Catalonia manufacturing was a matter of localised crafts, still organised on the guild system and hard pressed to compete with British imports or Turkish artisans. The upheavals of the revolutionary and imperial period had also dealt a series of catastrophic blows to the peripheral economies. In the Habsburg domains, the wars cut the Hungarians off from traditional textile and mineral outlets, as well as driving the state into bankruptcy and unpopular experiments with unsecured paper money. In Portugal war ended a notable economic spurt which had been gathering pace up till the 1790s. It meant physical disruption and enforced concessions on imports and colonies so as to buy British military aid. Textiles and other crafts were soon undermined, so that Portuguese exports were halved while imports from Britain doubled. Wages, employment prospects and the exchange rate all collapsed along with prices. In Spain colonial policies added to the disruption since the mother country had become dependent on the rebellious Latin American colonies for both imports and exports. Without the support of the colonies import penetration could not be resisted and prices fell there, too, reaching their nadir in 1828–30. Both countries also suffered from a backward and refeudalised agriculture, so that Portugal for the first time became a net importer of grain and the Spaniards found it hard to feed their growing population. Recovery did not really begin until the later 1830s.

The sheer pressures of social life inhibited both the growth of active intermediary groups and much concern for politics. The strength of local and noble interests was also difficult for weak states to deal with, hence the frequency of banditry in Spain and amongst the *klefts* and *armatoli* of Greece. Governments, even that of Vienna, showed little understanding of economic problems and even less desire to take remedial action. If the Habsburg government was typical in this, it was less so in the way it found itself on the defensive in the 1820s. For, though there were no overt challenges, the regime was much less impressively based than appears simply from looking at a map. It could only afford to maintain 105,000 men in Italy and 70,000 in Germany, compared to the 250,000 available to Prussia. Nor could the Empire afford a Landwehr of its own to support the regulars. So when the Magyar gentry became restive about the way Vienna levied men and monies without formal consultation the regime had to allow the Diet to meet and express its grievances, especially over the lack of status then accorded the Magyar language.

Elsewhere governments sought to be more active, although often restricted by traditionalist churches and armies. In the chaotic conditions of Greece no initiatives could secure general acceptance, and independence led to gathering anarchy. Miloš Obrenović in Serbia was able to quell opposition to his growing authority by conceding a Senate which the Russians hoped would restrain him. In the Ottoman Empire it was the bloated Janissary corps which was the main obstacle to initiatives to strengthen the central power, and they had to be bloodily suppressed by the Sultan in June 1826, after which they were replaced by the more professional *mansure* force. This proved to be the prelude to a larger programme of reform, which caused a hostile reaction not merely amongst foreign powers, but also in traditionalist regions like Bosnia. Similarly, the Second Restoration of Ferdinand VII in Spain failed to satisfy right-wing extremists, who made their feelings known through a series of associations and *pronunciamentos*.

Social polarisation thus often stopped both reform from above and protest from below. It also invited foreign powers to intervene. Thus the growing alarm amongst the powers about the Greek revolt, which had been reinforced by the creation of the *mansure* corps and the non-implementation of the Convention of Akkerman, ultimately led to Navarino and the Russo-Turkish War. The new army did well enough in parts of Bulgaria, despite the way the Russians were able to attract local

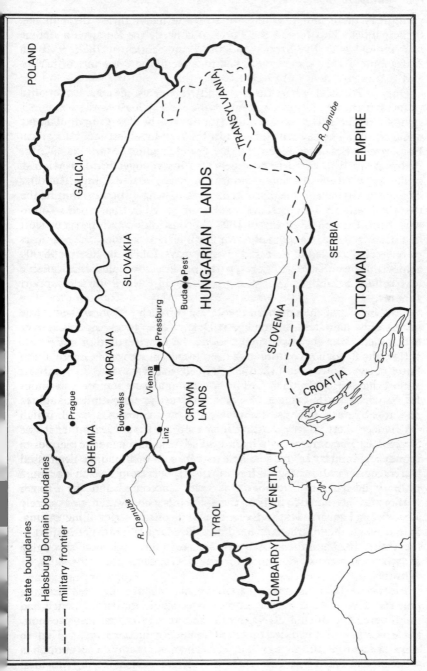

9 *The Habsburg Empire*

volunteers there, but it could not stop the major thrust through the Principalities. This forced the Porte to concede the Russians a virtual protectorate over the Straits and the Principalities by the Treaty of Adrianople. At the same time it had to agree to the autonomy of Serbia and the independence of Greece.

Only in Portugal, where the monarchy retained some constitutionalist traits after the revolutionary events of the early 1820s, was there any real sign of liberal restiveness. Even then it proved to be highly unpopular and unsuccessful. The death of John VI in 1826 left his eldest son, Pedro, the Emperor of Brazil, as regent for his granddaughter, Maria da Gloria. Pedro decided to entrust the regency to his younger brother Miguel, under a revised constitution, pending a marriage between him and Maria. This gave Miguel and the discontented right-wing *apostolicos* the chance that their military activities, even when supported by Spain, had failed to win them. By the late spring of 1828 the constitution and the succession had been set aside in a reign of terror in which tens of thousands of people were arrested, exiled or harassed in other ways. Liberal opposition to this achieved little outside the Azores, partly because Portuguese rural society was solidly behind Miguel and partly because there was no foreign support.

The impact of the northern revolutions on such peripheral states was necessarily slow and unsure. As Dakin says, 'whereas the delays occasioned by Leopold's resignation, by the July Revolution in France, and by the Belgian revolution had been to the advantage of Greece, these latter delays allowed the situation in Greece to develop into civil war and almost indescribable chaos'. The most immediate response came in Iberia where Pedro came under great pressure to aid both his daughter and the Spanish liberals. However, this was countered by Brazilian resistance to any suggestion that their emperor should leave them. The Spanish exiles got more help from Louis-Philippe, who made passports, money and military advice available to them so as to pressurise Ferdinand into recogising him and withdrawing his support from French legitimist military designs. By October this tactic succeeded and the French authorities then acted to restrain the Spaniards who, by then, had created a provisional government in Bayonne and planned a series of incursions. In the event, the marriage of Ferdinand to Maria Christina of Naples in December 1829 and the subsequent change in the succession laws on 27 March 1830 were to do more for the liberal cause than any military ventures.

Elsewhere 1830 did not threaten any such changes in the balance of political force. As a result, some government initiatives continued unhindered. Ferdinand of Naples offered an anmesty on his accession, the Russians continued drafting the Organic Regulations, and the Turks went ahead with the recognition of Serbian autonomy. The Ottomans were not dissuaded by the news from the west from massacring Albanian chieftains at Monastir on 26 August, nor from launching punitive actions there and against Montenegro in October. The Habsburgs appear not to have worried about their hereditary provinces, despite troubles in the capital over taxation and police action during the spring and summer. So, although there were reports of dissent in Milan, Pavia, Pest, Prague and other towns in Bohemia, the Empire did no more than strengthen the German military units in Vienna and urge policemen and tax collectors to combine stricter surveillance with great humanity on 9 September. The way the Hungarians forgot their dissidence and voted the men and money required by Vienna for use in Italy when the Diet met in October suggests that the government's diagnosis was correct, even if the Magyars did ask for language concessions in return for agreeing to crown Francis's son during the former's lifetime. On the other hand though there was sympathy for the Poles in Catholic and Magyar circles, this did not stop Vienna maintaining its envoy in Warsaw as a protest against Russian interference in Italy and elsewhere in earlier years. The threat of internal dissent was so slight that such risks could apparently be taken.

Vienna may also have been consoled by the way the impact of revolution began to work against the forces of change as the year drew on. This was visible in the Magyar change of heart and the effects of the Ottoman onslaught in Bosnia. As this resulted in the flight of the leading rebel, the so-called Dragon of Bosnia, Husein Aga Gradaščević, and the installation of a strong garrison in Scutari, Miloš Obrenović seems to have drawn the lesson that it was worth staying on the Turkish side. So he aided them in Bosnia and ensured that the withdrawal of the *sipahis* and the garrisons went ahead and that disputed territories on his western border were added to Serbia. In Greece the news from the west similarly encouraged opposition to Capodistrias' regime and, whereas tax revolts early in 1830 in Mainalon were put down without difficulty, renewed violence at Hydra and Poros culminating in the revolt of Tsasmis Karatassos on 1 May 1831 posed an almost insurmountable threat to the new state. When Capodistrias appealed to Russia for aid he was assassinated, while the unpaid soldiery dissolved the Assembly and the peasants preferred to desert their fields, finding even Turkish rule preferable to the prevailing anarchy. The enthusiasm generated by the renewed sight of the tricolour in the Morea thus proved counter-productive, and ultimately led the great powers to impose a much more conservative monarchy and much less generous borders than might have been the case.

The fate of the Spanish liberals proved to be equally tragic. Despite the efforts of the French authorities, six to eight groups of exiles, numbering perhaps 2,000 men, crossed the frontier or staged *pronunciamentos* inside Spain. All failed, often horribly. In Navarre, Chapalangarra was shot by royal troops he hoped would join him. Then, in mid-October, Valdes' more radical band crossed the Bidassoa, only to be surrounded by royal forces at Vera. Mina advanced to relieve him but, though he took Irun, he was soon driven back with heavy losses, leaving Valdes to take to his heels. South of the Pyrenees the French seized weapons intended for an invasion, while the units who set out in late October and November under Vigo, San Miguel, Plasensia and Guerra were easily frightened off, and took refuge in the mountains. Milan's invasion of Catalonia was equally unsuccessful, while nobody responded to Rodriguez' *pronunciamento* in Orense in Galicia. Despite all these checks Mina and others continued to plan for new incursions, possibly involving the Portuguese as well. Early in the New Year, therefore, Torrijos sailed from Gibraltar with 200 men, only to be forced straight back by the superior forces he encountered at Algeciras. In late February and early March 1831 there were attempted *coups* in Ronda and at the military base in Cadiz. When the port stayed loyal those involved tried to link up with Manzanares in Ronda, only to be caught *en route*. Thereafter there was a lull in liberal pressure.

Such failures were typical of the fate of unsupported liberal efforts. Where there was some success it was often due to foreign intervention. Thus it was with the implementation of the Organic Regulations in Wallachia and Moldavia in July 1831 and January 1832 respectively. However, their success was very limited since the new structures were highly conservative and thrust the peasantry ever more firmly under the political and economic control of the boyars. Hopeful of a peasant revolt, Czartoryski canvassed the Romanians as allies in 1833, and a year later a Polish–Romanian society was established in Sibiu. Russian influence also counted for something in the final accession of autonomy in Serbia, although Miloš's ruse of provoking a revolt and then stepping in to subdue it was responsible for the transfer of the remaining four of the six southern districts lost in 1813. Where Russia chose not to act, as was the case in Bulgaria, thousands of people were forced to emigrate to avoid Turkish reprisals. And Russia was one of the powers involved in selecting Otto of Bavaria as King of Greece in May 1832 – a decision ratified on payment of an indemnity two months later and implemented from January 1833.

Similarly, although Austrian students in Germany, like their fellows in Hungary, sympathised with the Poles as the Budapest riots of 7 July 1831 showed, without real public support or outside sympathy they could do little of any practical importance. Yet things like the way Polish exiles were hidden on noble estates in Hungary did stimulate both reformers like Szechenyi and supporters of Croatian autonomy like Ljudevit Gaj, whose national song 'Nó Croatia' was derived from the songs of the Poles. But the creation of a new linguistic consciousness here and in other parts of the Habsburg domains merely began with 1830. Had such people tried their luck in 1830 it is likely that they would have been as unfortunate as Torrijos and his fifty comrades who were lured to their deaths in a hopeless last landing near Malaga early in December 1831.

Even in Portugal, where there was outside support, liberalism had immense problems. By early 1831 the pressure on Don Pedro had become such that he had to abdicate and come to Europe. But a liberal rising in Lisbon shortly before this failed and, though he was able to attract volunteers from Britain, Belgium, Poland and Italy, diplomatic and commercial interests were cool, even in Britain, despite the differences with Miguel, which led to the forcing of the Tagus by Anglo-French fleets in the spring of 1831. Then, although Pedro's men were able to seize Oporto from an unprepared and unpaid garrison in June 1832, they found the populace hostile and were soon beleaguered by Miguelists and cholera. Despite the way in which the succession crisis of La Granja on 17-18 September deprived the Miguelists of Spanish support, the liberals were soon on the verge of defeat. Only the incompetence of the Miguelist generals and their own control of the sea-lanes saved them. In January 1833 they rashly broke out of Oporto, and landed a force in the Algarve – which, as a glance at Map 10 shows, is at the other end of the

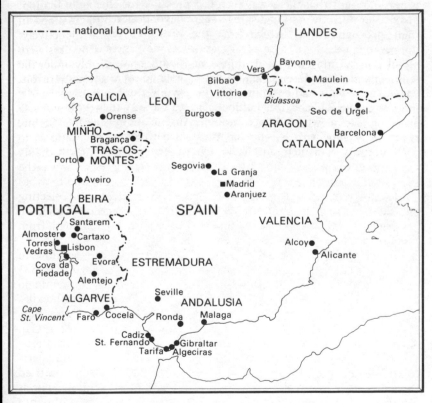

10 *Iberia*

country – where a provisional government was established despite local hostility. With the steam-ships of the British admiral Napier defeating the Miguelist fleet off Cape St Vincent the liberals were able to assault the capital, which fell after a crushing night victory at Cova da Piedade on 23 July. Assistance from both the populace and French and Spanish Carlists notwithstanding, the Miguelists failed to retake the capital, and were gradually forced back into the barren inland areas, finally surrendering at Evora on 24 May 1834.

Liberalism was thus very lucky in Portugal. It was self-evidently not part of the body politic and it was more or less a matter of chance that foreign aid overcame this. For in Iberia social polarisation meant that the peasantry was not simply uneducated or uninterested in politics as elsewhere on the peripheries, but resolutely hostile to change. In Spain it took an even bloodier civil war between July 1834 and June 1840 to overcome such forces of conservatism. Further east there may not have been the same populist resistance, but the lack of social and educational progress meant that there was even less pressure for change in the first place. Not until the nationalist revival got beyond mere intellectuals and their propaganda, by which time the pressures on the land were unbearable, was there to be a real grass-roots movement. And even then social polarisation continued to present it with grave problems. Much still depended on foreign aid, which remained as contradictory and conservative as it had been in 1830. For, while the French took a new interest in the Balkans, this hardly balanced the way the revolutions, by arousing fears as well as hopes, brought Austria out of isolation and into renewed *entente* with Russia and the German states. Pressures from without thus remained unreliable, even when pressures from within began to develop.

11 Central Italy: Responses to Maladministration

The events of 1831 in Italy involved a set of separate movements rather than the single nationalistic uprising denounced by traditionalist historians of left and right. The image they have established is of a pathetic affair, stimulated by secret societies, and led by effete old gentlemen who preferred particularism to patriotism and, therefore, betrayed the Risorgimento. In fact, as the emphasis on their regional nature shows, the movements of 1831 were not truly national at all. Nor were they really due to clandestine conspiracy. Basically, they were more or less open attempts to profit from circumstances to replace regimes which were more incompetent than oppressive by something closer to the semi-participatory political systems of the French era. The response to the maladministration of the 1820s was to seek to return to idealised, and scaled-down, versions of the Napoleonic Kingdom of Italy. Had real oppression been the target, then it is likely that revolutions would have broken out elsewhere than in the small states of what is now Emilia-Romagna, most of which had been under French control in one form or another for longer than other parts of Italy. And, although traditional historiography accords pride of place to Modena in the events of 1831, the reality is that Bologna and the Papal Legations – so called because they were ruled by cardinal-legates rather than by lesser ecclesiastical luminaries – were the real epicentres of opposition. General maladministration was aggravated in the latter areas by the fact that virtually all administration was in the hands of the clergy.

The existence and character of the Legations and the Duchies of Modena and Parma were part and parcel of the way the Vienna settlement had affected Italy. Whereas by 1810 all of Italy excluding Sicily and Sardinia was in the French orbit, whether annexed to France in the case of Parma and the north-west, subject to the Kingdom of Italy in that of Modena, the Legations and the north-east, or ruled by Napoleon's brother-in-law Murat in the south, the Restoration returned the peninsula and islands to no fewer than ten separate states, and to a world of political disaffection and economic stress. Thus, the failure of the restored regimes to live up to their promises promoted violence in many places in the early years of the Restoration, such as the abortive upheaval in Macerata in 1817 and, more important, the revolutions of 1820–1 in the Two Sicilies and Piedmont. These last were the work of small élites with specific grievances, notably the military, and for this, amongst other reasons, they failed.

Yet, even though they were localised socially and geographically, everywhere and everybody seems to have suffered in the subsequent repression. There were show-trials in Lombardy and Modena, for example, and under the Papacy of Leo XII, during which the Vatican swung sharply to the right, there were the Rivarola and Invernizzi commissions of inquiry in the Romagna between 1824 and 1828. The first of these condemned over 500 people for political crimes, half of them artisans, a third landowners, and a sixth lawyers or employees, together with some soldiers, nobles and clerics. Although most of the sentences were commuted, they left a bitter taste, reinforcing resentment at the general inefficiency of the Papal States. They also show how deeply reformist feeling had penetrated in urban society and the lay establishment. Such repression made any kind of political activity very dangerous, and, in the case of Lombardy and Piedmont, seems to have stopped it altogether. Elsewhere it was driven underground, thereby creating the impression that it was the work of subversive secret societies. None the less, the basic rejection of misgovernment often came to the surface, notably at Cilento in Naples in 1828.

Political malaise was paralleled and encouraged by economic problems. These were, in themselves, a glaring example of political and administrative mishandling of affairs. The Restoration logically entailed a return to a plethora of internal customs-barriers, weights and measures, inefficient protectionisms and continuing high taxation, often required to support extravagant courts, even in Rome. It is reckoned that the tax burden doubled between 1815 and 1845, and that the majority of this was passed directly on to the peasantry. This and the way that high tariffs did more to assist smuggling and corruption than they did to encourage what few industries there were, or even to build up government revenues, produced apathy and economic stagnation. Attempts to stimulate industries like shipbuilding and silk, not to mention agriculture, rarely paid off in the Papal States, for instance.

Government shortcomings came on top of both long-continuing secular decline and new structural problems. The peninsula economies had long suffered from marked backwardness: medieval crafts had decayed, and the whole of the country had become dependent on an old-fashioned and inefficient agricultural system. Communications and infrastructure were very poor, capital and investment were lacking, and the work-force, particularly on the land, was largely illiterate. Then, although the French occupation had brought some gains in terms of new industrial crops and quickened business activity, these were often cancelled out by the way blockade and French policy cut Italy off from the wider world economy and turned her into a French agricultural colony. The decline continued under the Restoration both because of the barriers it re-established and the way it allowed international competition, whether from British manufactures or Russian corn, to make itself felt despite the protectionism we have already noted.

All this meant that there was little if any growth and no change in the economy, and all this at a time when the population rose rapidly: from 18 million to 21 million between 1815 and 1830. On the land, where increases in productivity were only half those of the population, the result was pressure on smallholdings and rising food-prices. In the towns, it meant a further decline in manufacturing – the number of people employed in the woollen industry in the Papal States fell from 12,000 to 3,700 between 1823 and 1827, for example – falling wages, unemployment and cut-throat competition amongst artisans. After 1823 the once great fair of Senigallia collapsed, and by 1831 some 44 per cent of Bologna's population of 66,000 were recorded as paupers.

Most classes must have been affected by the continuing stagnation and were no doubt made all the more responsive to news from Lugano, Paris and Brussels in the early autumn of 1830 – a time marked by outbreaks of brigandage and the failure of the crucial hemp-harvest round Bologna. Both members of secret societies like the Carbonari and the general public were electrified by the news. Three youths were arrested in Reggio on 7 September for waving the French flag and singing the 'Ça ira', while the Italian 'tricolore' was seen in Forlì and elsewhere, and the cafés of Bologna and Ferrara were reported by the police to be full of people excitedly discussing the latest events. There was much talk of secret meetings and mysterious visitors, as well as shouts of 'Long live the Cisalpine Republic' and 'Death to the Germans' – as the Austrians were called. The response was best summed up by Terence Mamiani, who was to be a minister in 1831, when he wrote, 'I have read in the Lausanne press about the insensate decrees of Charles X. The moment has come. Before long the drama will be acted out and we shall know if the nineteenth century will be slave or free.'

All the pent-up frustrations of the previous years were thus encouraged to take a political form by events in other countries. In Tuscany there was thought of a *coup* to extract a constitution from the Grand Duke; the ruler of Lucca considered granting one until the Austrians warned him off; and in Genoa the Carbonari revived. Outside Italy exiles began to reorganise and, while hopes of a landing in the south did not materialise, arms were stored and propaganda intensified. By the end of the year the very divided exiles were able to form a Central Committee in Paris to co-ordinate their efforts. Yet the exiles were not able to exercise any control over events in Italy. In part this was because of the extra-watchfulness of regimes like those in Turin and Rome, behind which stood the Austrians, whose readiness to act against any revolutionary outbreaks was made quite clear. In part it was because the real causes of disaffection ran deep and were related more to local conditions than to outside ones. So, while the July Days increased general ferment and dissatisfaction, they were not enough to produce an immediate upheaval.

Indeed, the news may actually have held back what many people have seen as the real cause of revolution, the so-called Modenese conspiracy. This was organised by a young lawyer, Enrico Misley, who seems to have gained the approval of the Duke, Francesco IV of Este, to explore the feasibility of getting liberal support for the creation, by insurrection, of a new central Italian monarchy. At first sight Francesco was the least likely candidate for such a role. He was known as a 'hammer of revolution', and many people have doubted his motives in authorising these conversations. However, it is also possible that he felt piqued by Austria over various of his personal and dynastic ambitions and was genuinely interested in the possibility. There may also have been a Russian hand in the affair since, at that time, it would have suited Russia's interests to have Austria embroiled in Italy. In any event, he allowed Misley to travel widely beyond the frontiers of the Duchy, and in late 1828 and early 1829 he seems to have persuaded the exiles in Paris and London at least to consider the idea. However, at this point the diplomatic situation changed; the Russians lost interest and so did the Duke. Misley went on to Paris with the idea of getting the Duke of Orléans to sponsor the plot, but it seems that, despite all the ink devoted to it, the conspiracy existed only in the most notional sense, and amidst great insecurity and insincerity on all sides.

The July Days, not surprisingly, made the Duke even less keen on the idea. But Misley's local agent, a minor manufacturer from Carpi called Ciro Menotti, was encouraged by the news and kept in touch with the Duke in the early autumn of 1830, allegedly to keep him inert while Menotti began to journey through the region seeking support. He was apparently able to set up groups of sympathisers in many towns from Venetia through Emilia to Tuscany, but he was also attacked as a spy in Bologna, like Misley before him, which rather casts doubt on the story. In any case, it is unlikely that he could have laid down much of an organisation in December and January alone, although he did have a quite radical Jacobinical view of the future of Italy which was common in parts of the Duchy. And, while he was planning his operations, the Duke was strengthening his security forces and moving openly to a reactionary posture.

By the New Year it was clear that the Duke was aware of what was afoot and that he was determined to crush it. As a result, Menotti brought forward the date of his *putsch* in Modena city, only for the Duke to launch a pre-emptive strike of his own. Menotti's forty supporters (youths, artisans and peasants from the heavily taxed lower Modenese) were soon cannonaded into surrender late on the night of Thursday, 3 February 1831. Menotti himself was caught when he tried to get to the gates to let in his main body of rural supporters, who had seized Carpi and marched on the capital. Although he had obviously nipped the local plot in the bud – and none of the other towns mentioned stirred at this time – the Duke was still uneasy and requested Austrian aid. However, the local commander was not ready to act, especially without authorisation from Vienna and, without the certainty of such reinforcements the Duke panicked in face of a rumoured march of several thousand Bolognese on the 4th. He fled to the safety of the nearest Austrian garrison, leaving a provisional regency to cope with the vacuum in his capital. It was to be several days before a revolutionary regime emerged there.

When it did, it was really in response to events in Bologna, which suggests there was very little support for Menotti in Modena and, by extension, virtually none elsewhere in the area. The situation in Bologna, however, was much more explosive. Economic problems were more acute, with fractionalisation on the land and crisis amongst the hemp artisans and the traditionally violent *birrichini*, or porters. Such lower-class discontent was at the disposal of the urban élite, who bitterly resented the way the restored Papacy had deprived them of their autonomy, privileges and Senate. The authorities were aware of this widespread disaffection, which was no doubt heightened by reports of abortive Bonapartist plots in Rome itself on 12 December and again in early February, but the legate was immured in the Vatican for the Conclave, and his young pro-legate, Nicola Paracciani-Clarelli, seems to have courted disaster by being too clever by half. For, having on 4 February confirmed the previously agreed military plans to deal with trouble, which had been brewing for months if not years, and had now reached fever pitch, he changed his mind. By the evening news had reached Bologna from Modena, the sound of cannon having been heard at Castelfranco, the Bolognese frontier-town some fifteen miles from the Ducal capital. The pro-legate called a number of local notables together, believing that they were more scared of social disorder than anything else, and hoping that, by appealing to them to take responsibility for government and order, the latter through a new Civic Guard, he would be able to maintain control more easily and successfully than by using the weak and unpopular security forces.

But by the time he issued a 'Notification' to this effect late on the 4th the crowds had got out of hand, the troops had either joined the demonstrations or were disarmed, and the Italian tricolour and cockade were being worn everywhere. Paracciani-Clarelli refused to associate himself with these developments and demanded a safe-conduct out of the province from the new commission of notables, who happily agreed. Then, after some consideration of re-establishing the old Senatorial city state, the notables turned themselves into a Provisional Government on Saturday, 5 February. They also proceeded to institute a Civic Guard, to lower the price of salt, and to replace papal sovereignty with new symbols of authority. The pro-legate had thus been completely outmanoeuvred as a result of his change of mind, and he was to be bitterly blamed for it by his military advisers and by leading cardinals in Rome. He had indeed provided the opposition with the supreme opportunity for achieving its long-cherished dreams of change. This opportunity was rapidly exploited down the Romagnuol coast in almost every town marked on Map 11 from Ferrara to Senigallia. A million people threw off their allegiance in town after town as papal authority either crumbled or was simply thrust aside as the news of Paracciani-Clarelli's humiliation percolated through. Only in Forlì and Ancona did this involve violence.

Significantly, none of these newly freed towns looked to Modena. In any case, there was no lead available there. The Bolognese authorities kept the frontiers shut, and it was two days before they learned of the Duke's flight. They also refused to listen to the entreaties of their agent in Castelfranco, who was allegedly one of Menotti's contacts in Bologna, when he talked of Italian independence sweeping the north-west, Modena included. In fact there was hardly more movement against the Ducal regime than for it in Modena. Not until Sunday morning were demands heard there that the gates should be opened, prisoners freed and a Civic Guard set up. This was not really acceptable to the regency and the military, and not until after the arrival of some thirty youngsters from Bologna and volunteers from Spilamberto was it decided to create a Provisional Government. Even so, this was composed of nobles with no connection with Ciro Menotti, and it went to some lengths to stay on good terms with the regency. Finally, on the evening of the 8th, Menotti's brother Celeste arrived with middle-class radicals from outlying districts and a new Provisional Government was created, with a local lawyer, Biagio Nardi, acting as Dictator. This was proclaimed and activated on Wednesday, 9 February, by which time Reggio, the second city of the Duchy, had also declared its independence and liberals were touring the apathetic countryside in attempts to whip up support for the new order.

Nardi's regime was to be tolerably active, but even so it can be seen as a move to prevent something more radical. Although it was to lower taxes, assist in the redemption of pawn pledges and, more unpopularly, offer some freedom to women, Jews and the University, it made no real reference to Menotti in its proclamations. Its main endeavour was to create a proper National Guard, including the old Ducal troops; but in this it did not get very far. All in all, it seems to have been a way for the middle classes to escape from the subordinate role they had endured under a regime which was both hostile to the well-to-do and financially incompetent. It did not therefore show a great deal of *Italianità* in its activities. However, a skirmish with the loyalists at San Venanzio on 15 February demonstrated the dangers of independence, and three days later Modena city united with Reggio dell'Emilia in a common government, chaired by Nardi, but with the ex-Napoleonic general Carlo Zucchi as its military commander. There was little time for constitutional initiatives; time only to set up a makeshift administration and to begin military organisation. Unfortunately, this went badly since 200 volunteers disobeyed orders on 5 March and tangled with the Austrian advance guard at Novi di Modena. The ensuing rout persuaded the government to abandon the Duchy, to be followed on the 8th by Zucchi and his 1,200-strong force. Francesco was able to re-enter his capital on 9 March, and the repression – already foreshadowed by peasant resistance to the liberals – began at once.

In Parma there was even greater caution and much less desire for change, since the church and the local authorities were hostile and the lower classes fond of their Duchess, Maria Louisa, whose tolerance led Francesco of Modena to nickname her the 'President of the Parmesan Republic'. So the revolution was even more half-hearted and short-lived than in Modena. Although there had been some dissidence in the University during the winter, it was the troubles further east down the Po valley which led to agitation in Parma. Even then this at first meant only isolated use of Italian colours, and though the students and middle classes had their grievances against Maria Louisa's new and unpopular minister and confidant, Werklein – including changes in the administration and a refusal to allow the city elders free access to the Duchess – these were not generally shared. However, as pressure did develop, the elders were allowed to see Maria Louisa on 13 February. They tried to persuade her that order could only be preserved if troops were withdrawn and a Civic Guard created. Rather than concede, however, she preferred to leave the city, only to have the gates shut against her by an indignant crowd of loyalists. Eventually (on the night of 13–14 February), she was allowed to go, by which time her troops had been disarmed by students, revolutionary fly-sheets were circulating and the 'Marseillaise' was being sung. Even so, the elders begged her to leave some form of authority behind her. By 18 February she was in the garrison city of Piacenza, whose loyalty she confirmed by a judicious grant of privileges.

Back in Parma her powers had not been very clearly or publicly re-allocated and, in order to quieten what was, at last, almost real disorder, a provisional government was created by adding some nobles to the existing municipality. This government acted very conservatively and legalistically. But, after clashes with troops, the students on 17 February were able to add their own representatives to the government and to force it to consider making real changes. Even so, the Parmesan government did much less than the others. This reflected not only its innate conservatism, but also the threatening military situation. The new National Guard had to be used to create a *cordon sanitaire* between the capital and the many loyalist communes; while on 21–2 February the liberal forces suffered a signal defeat in a small skirmish with the Austrians at Firenzuola d'Arda. The government then renewed its efforts to negotiate a settlement with Maria Louisa until a proclamation from Piacenza on 26 February made it clear that there was no chance of this. Yet not until 5 March was the Italian flag formally flown; and taxes and municipal authority continued to be exercised in the Duchess's name for another week.

By then the Parmese also reluctantly agreed to form a joint military command with Zucchi, only to find that many local guardsmen disregarded his orders to fall back on St Ilario in face of the Austrian advance. And when some 700 volunteers did abandon the city anarchy broke out as the crowd demonstrated its annoyance at the loss of the Duchess and the creation of the new order. The National Guard was hastily reconstituted to restore calm, only for many of its members to be arrested when the Austrians reoccupied the town late on 13 March. Partly because they offered no resistance, the repression was to be much milder than in Modena.

This left Bologna and the Romagna. They were to be the main problem for the new Pope, a hard-line monk elected at Modenese and Austrian instance on 2 February, who took the name Gregory XVI. He and his Secretary of State, Bernetti, the former legate in Bologna, found they could rely on Rome – despite a further riot there on 10 February – because of the economic and emotional attachment of the populace to the pontiffs, something which occasionally spurred them to attacks on liberals. Things in the Legations were very different and, although the new authorities vetoed some radical suggestions like the seizure of church property, the Vatican found it was facing a real assault on the theoretical and practical bases of the Papal States as a whole.

Thus in Bologna the new leaders set about creating a military establishment and the foundations of a regular and lasting regime. They set up a military committee of experienced Napoleonic officers, searched diligently for arms, created a National Guard and also gave much thought to the possible organisation of a regular army. This last, however, was never to materialise. On the civilian front they were active in police matters, creating a new force and taking measures to restrain likely sources of opposition – something which shaded into an attempt to rationalise and reorganise the judicial system. A great deal of attention had, of course, to be given to finance, since they urgently needed money for all their projects and they had only inherited the large debts of the papal administration of the city. To tide them over they made an appeal for 'patriotic contributions' and followed this up by revising the hearth and land taxes and the stamp duty. In doing this they tried to protect the lower classes from the worst of the fiscal burden, which was a reflection of the continuing economic crisis. They also sought, for the same reasons, to persuade landowners to take on extra workers in the countryside, but they had neither the resources not the expertise to reverse the decline.

They showed themselves very concerned about civic rights. The church, the press and education were much in their thoughts; and, while the first was not directly attacked, they did what they could to regulate the affairs of all three in the name of freedom. Perhaps as a result, some leading churchmen preached the duty of obedience to the new regime, and a leading professor offered a set of theoretical justifications for their take-over. This, like the statement issued by the lawyer President of the new government, Giovanni Vicini, on 25 February to explain the ending of papal sovereignty, did not lean very far in the direction of democracy or of popular sovereignty. The former stressed checks and balances, while the latter – somewhat to the embarrassment of certain of his colleagues – justified their move by reference to the way they had been stripped of rights obtained in the Middle Ages.

Yet even Vicini, regarded by some as the epitome of soft-centred moderation, went on to stress the way that, contrary to the medieval situation, the proud cities of the region were moving into one state. This was a reflection of the fact that, as early as 8 February, a proposal for an offensive and defensive alliance among the liberated cities was circulating, and this proved to be a pointer to the way things developed. Such an alliance would obviously need a representative body to run it, and the nucleus of this was provided by the Bologna city provisional government, which again took advantage of an opportunity to maintain the momentum of change, first from the way that initial outbreaks led to the creation of new governments and then from the way liberation spread further south. In fact, within three weeks of the movement starting in Emilia, most major towns of the Romagna, Umbria and the Marche down to Assisi, Foligno and Todi had more or less spontaneously thrown off the papal yoke, although this was not the case with all towns and certainly not with the countryside. At best there was some sympathy in the Romagna and the northern Marche, often apathy and, at worst, hostility as in the southern Marche and, especially in Lazio and the southern extremity of the Papal States which remained untouched by the contagion.

Even where towns adhered to the new order this did not always mean anything very dramatic. Around Bologna and Ferrara it was quite common for the smaller towns to maintain their old officials and to treat the change of regime as a purely administrative act. And , once they had gone through the business of changing their flags and agreeing to set up a National Guard detachment, the movement could easily lapse, with neither men nor money coming forward. None the less, the revolution did spread – in a way which certainly frightened the Vatican – and efforts were made to combine these isolated outbreaks into something larger.

The initial impulse for union had been followed by an enthusiastic correspondence amongst the free towns. As a result, Bologna called delegates to a constitutive meeting on 26 February while, at the same time, sending out delegates to help spread and consolidate the revolution. The call resulted in the coming together of an Assembly of Notables, many of whom had had experience of public affairs in the Kingdom of Italy. Although they were sometimes a little suspicious of the predominance and moderation of Bologna, so that debates were often stormy, they still acted very quickly. They agreed to abandon papal sovereignty, to establish a new provisional government and to support a military attack on Rome. March 1 saw the official proclamation of the United Provinces of Italy. Pending properly organised elections for a Constituent Assembly, which it was hoped would take place on 31 March, a date later brought forward to 20 March, the Assembly entrusted legislative power to a temporary Consultà. This consisted of one member from each of the ten provinces making up the new state: Bologna, Ferrara, Ravenna, Forlì, Pesaro with Urbino, Fermo with Ascoli, Ancona, Perugia, Macerata with Camerino, and Spoleto. This was to elect and strictly control an executive consisting of a president and seven ministers. The new state was also to have a uniform system of taxation, tariffs and regional government – this last modelled largely on the French prefectorial system.

The Consultà got down to work soon after its proclamation on 5 March, but within four days it was dissolved because of the threatening military situation. The rump of the Assembly, which remained highly suspicious of the executive arm, then reluctantly agreed to transfer emergency powers to Vicini and the government. The latter remained in Bologna, actively trying to pursue the policies pioneered by the Bologna city government: protecting the church, lowering tariffs and trying to resolve the fiscal crisis. After much debate it was agreed to anticipate the land tax – a move which was likely to be resented by the already ill-disposed large-scale landowners, on whom it fell. However, before the matter could be tested, the military situation worsened. The people of the United Provinces had been carried along on a wave of rather naïve faith in Neapolitan revolution, Polish victories and, especially, the promise of French aid. The Austrian advance soon dispelled such hopes, and on 20 March the government evacuated its own capital, leaving behind a mass of unfinished business, all of which had been based on the assumption that the state being created was a regular one, destined to endure.

An attempt on 16 March to raise thousands of volunteers having failed, the United Provinces found that its only remaining hopes lay in its own Roman expedition or in the workings of international diplomacy. The march on Rome had its origins in the revolution in Pesaro on 9 February, when a former colonel in Napoleonic service, Giuseppe Sercognani, was offered the command of local guards and deserters from the papal army. Thanks to his success in taking the two remaining papal fortresses of San Leo on Montefeltro and Ancona, not to mention defeating a papal force at Osimo in mid-February, he attracted many students and other volunteers to what on 14 February he called 'the Vanguard of the National Army'. He was then able to send out flying columns in what Map 11 shows to be all directions, including to Spoleto, Terni and Narni and, later, to Ascoli and Fermo, setting up new revolutionary regimes as he did so. All the time he was negotiating with Bologna about a push over the Apennines to

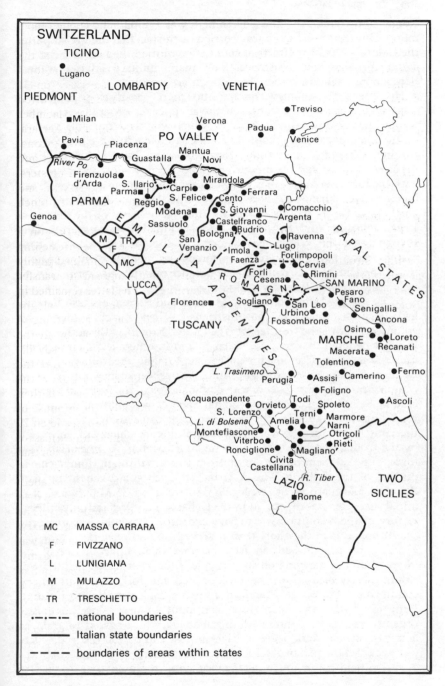

11 *Central Italy*

Rome; but, though the new government was sympathetic enough to let more volunteers join him, it was worried by the fact that the Vatican, after the failure of its own efforts at counter-revolution, had on 19 February asked for Austrian assistance. The main military adviser wanted Sercognani to dig in rather than launch an assault.

However, Sercognani, with some 3,000 men – mostly ex-papal soldiers – spread out over a wide front, chose to advance on 1 March all the same. Rather than go down the Tiber valley, which would have meant an assault on the main papal stronghold at Civita Castellana, he opted to go south through difficult country round Narni. Between 7 and 11 March he was repulsed at Rieti and his men fell back on Terni where, despite trouble with the local peasantry, they remained stationary for over a week. When inconclusive skirmishes were renewed the Vanguard achieved little, partly because its morale was badly affected by news of the defeats of Firenzuola and Novi. However, the demand made by the government in Bologna that the disobedient Sercognani should surrender his command seems to have revived his forces' enthusiasm. Unfortunately, this turned out to have come too late because of events elsewhere, and the very real threat to Rome was lifted.

In fact by 8 March not merely Modena and Parma, but also Ferrara, had been occupied by the Austrians. When Zucchi brought his volunteers across the frontier into the United Provinces the authorities in Bologna ordered that they be disarmed and interned, lest their presence undermine the United Provinces' diplomatic neutrality. Further Austrian advances led the government to reverse its strategy on 15 March, and to entrust Zucchi with command of all the forces in the area. Had he been willing, he might also have been given political authority as well. Thus it was that Zucchi's enlarged army came to cover the retreat of the United Provinces' government from Bologna, which was reoccupied by the troops that had taken Modena on 21 March. Another Habsburg force, of 8,000 men, pushed south from Ferrara through Commachio in pursuit of the Italians. The Austrian advance guard caught up with Zucchi's rearguard at St Arcangelo da Rimini on 25 March, and after initial successes was driven off by the Italians. This first and only military victory of the revolution was to have enormous symbolic importance in the future. But in the short term it served no real purpose.

The government had, in fact, become increasingly aware of the impossibility of carrying on the struggle. Indeed, it feared that to do so would merely bring down more bloodshed and suffering on its fellow-countrymen. So, on 26 March, it agreed a capitulation with Cardinal Benvenuti, who had been the government's 'guest' since coming to organise counter-revolution during February. He agreed to grant an amnesty, which would leave officials in post and permit the leaders free passage from the peninsula. In the event, these terms were rejected by the Austrian field-commander and the local papal representative, so that the revolution sacrificed itself for nothing. The soldiery wanted to carry on the struggle, but Sercognani ordered his men to lay down their arms in Spoleto, and Zucchi did the same in Ancona on 28 March, leaving the General and the leaders of the revolt to make an unsuccessful dash for freedom in a steam-ship called *Isotta*.

By the end of the month, then, the Italian revolution had failed. It had failed alone, for its other hope of diplomatic aid from France proved to be quite unfounded. The Italians had believed in what was known as the doctrine of non-intervention – the belief that, if their movement were peaceful and restricted to their own frontiers, it would be allowed to exist, since post-Revolutionary France would not allow Austria to resume the kind of intervention practised in the early 1820s. In reality the Austrians had no intention of heeding such a doctrine, and their ambassador in Rome had been empowered for months past to grant military aid if so requested by the Pope.

And, while the French may not have been responsible for the outbreak of the revolts as the Austrians believed, their agents and politicians in Italy and Paris had made encouraging noises. On 10 February a message was passed to Vicini which purported to be a guarantee of any new state against Austria. This was a forgery made up by extremists who wanted revolution, whether for its own sake or simply so that it could be the more easily crushed, but it served to cause Bologna to issue a formal declaration of non-intervention on 11 February. Later it encouraged Bologna to refrain from any co-operation with Modena and its men. However, all this delicacy was to no avail, especially as most of the Italian envoys could not even get out of the country; and, once the Vatican overcame its fears that the price of Austrian aid might be too high, the sad truth became all too clear to the unhappy central Italians.

The Austrian advance placed France in something of a quandary, for while the royal view of the revolution in Italy was less sympathetic than that found elsewhere in the political world, there was a problem of 'face' and a fear of getting dragged into an unwanted war with Austria. Metternich skilfully played on this fear by emphasising the dangers of all kinds of upheaval to settled crowns, especially when – as was briefly the case in Italy until the Bologna government put a stop to it – there were young princes from the family of Napoleon involved. So the French government tried to resolve its dilemma by arguing that there was a distinction between Modena and Parma, where the Habsburgs had a dynastic interest, and the Papal States, where they did not, hoping that this would persuade the Austrians to keep out of the latter. It did not, for Metternich replied that what counted was not rights, but invitations from legitimate rulers, and these he had.

Louis-Philippe decided to give in and, on 13 March, installed a new and conservative cabinet under Casimir Périer which reinterpreted non-intervention to mean that no French blood would be shed in a non-

French cause. Although he attempted to mitigate the blow by seizing on the idea of international talks about urging the Papacy to remedy its habitual maladministration and therefore avert such upheavals in the future, it left the United Provinces cruelly exposed as has been seen. Its leaders and supporters therefore came to blame the French for their defeat, and their resentment contributed both to a long polemic on the failure of the revolutions and to continuing dissent in the Papal States.

The revolution had dealt a terrible blow to the finances and economy of the states of the church, and so costly was it that the Vatican had to increase taxes to pay for it. This made it doubly difficult to do anything to rectify the basic grievances as some cardinals and the powers wanted. The latter met on 20 April and, after arranging for a rapid Austrian withdrawal from the Legations, went on to produce a Memorandum on 21 May which urged the Vatican to make changes in its institutional structure so as to allow elected laymen a large role throughout the system. This was rejected by Bernetti as endangering the very idea of the Papal States. All he would concede – on 30 June, just after the Austrian army had retired – was the formation of consultative bodies at a local level to which laymen might be indirectly elected. Even this was to be a temporary measure until a new volunteer and mercenary army could be raised to enforce the old system.

It took until 1832 to raise the new force and, during the intervening months, disgust over the lack of reform and fears aroused by the military proposals conspired to keep the liberals of the Romagna and of Bologna, in particular, in a constant state of effervescence. While the senior lay official, Count Grassi, tried to proceed gradually and sought change quietly, the liberals – many of whom had been involved in the Forty-Four Days and had not been disciplined because of the weakness of papal authority – opted for more extreme measures, using the newly created Civic Guard as their instrument for both civil and military pressure. Hence they sent delegations to Rome (inveighing against the June edict), sought for arms, created a regional committee to co-ordinate action and demanded a wide range of powers for it. When Bernetti insisted on disregarding them and imposed his own reforms they resorted to a legal strike and then called for the election of a regional guard assembly.

This was the last straw for Rome, and on 25 December the Pope appointed a hard-line cardinal as a special commissioner to run the four Legations. At the same time the new army was sent forward, and in mid-January some 5,000 men marched north up the Via Emilia. The Civic Guards flocked to meet them, only to be routed outside Cesena on 19 January. The triumphant papal army celebrated its victory by sacking Cesena and Forlì the next day. Although the Austrian army had then to return to protect the population against the new army, the Vatican was able to begin a purge in the region and to inflict the punishment for the first revolution from which it had previously been deterred. The hopes of the liberals were briefly raised when the French sent a task-force to Ancona in order to salvage something of their radical reputation and to balance the Austrian presence, but this proved to be a blunder. For, although it remained there until 1838, it gave little help to the opposition forces, who were steadily driven underground as the decade progressed.

Neither of the other centres of revolt suffered an equivalent aftermath, even though, in the case of Modena, Austrian troops remained in occupation until 1835. This was partly because of the violence of the Duke's repression, which led to a series of executions and trials that dragged on as late as 1837 in Reggio. One of Francesco's first and saddest victims was Ciro Menotti. The other Modenese leaders were luckier since they sailed with colleagues in *Isotta* and, after a period in the hands of the Austrians, were released to the places for which they had passports. Austrian subjects like Zucchi tended to suffer most. In Parma, on the other hand, the repression was a great deal milder, and a kind of reconciliation took place between Maria Louisa and her subjects by August 1831. This was due both to the implicit recognition that Werklein had been guilty of maladministration and to the advice of an Austrian observer. As in 1821, however, repression was extended to areas which had not been involved in the revolution, like the Trentino, Tuscany, Piedmont and even the Two Sicilies, where the amnesty proclaimed at the inauguration of the new reign was cancelled after a constitutionalist demonstration in Palermo on 1 September 1831. As in the Papal States, opposition had increasingly to take on a subversive form, and the great age of secret societies such as Mazzini's Young Italy and the more socially oriented Apofasimeni and True Italians really came after 1831 rather than before.

All this happened not only because the revolutions of 1831 failed, but also because no one in authority had been able to afford to regard them as responses to maladministration, whether strategically, in reaction to long-standing grievances, or tactically, as a result of mistakes made in the crisis of 1831 itself. The men of 1831 were thrust into a more politicised confrontation than they had imagined or could have hoped to sustain. For, while some critics claimed 'that a few thousand men, pikes in hand', would have been sufficient to sweep away the old order, the reality was that there was far too much opposition and too much inertia for any mass mobilisation to have succeeded. Thus to demean the leaders of 1831 as timorous incompetents is inaccurate and beside the point. The events in Bologna show that the liberals had regained their confidence sufficiently to seize such opportunities as came their way, and these were greater and more enduring than those elsewhere in the Po valley. What was lacking was not so much will as means. Because they had no aid from outside, they found themselves having to improvise in one movement what should really have been done in several stages. In other words, 1831 was a kind of

'Italia farà da se' revolution, which brought in people from many social groups, and not just the old élite of the Kingdom of Italy.

It was a revolution of participation which, as Emilia Morelli has said, was Janus-faced. It looked back to the rationalism of the eighteenth century, but also liberated the Roman moderation of later years. Because political activity had been virtually proscribed in the 1820s, reformist protests against maladministration had had to take on an impossible revolutionary form in 1831. And, once they did so, nobody stopped to look beyond form to content. The revolutionary carapace proved doubly self-defeating. Thereafter, reformism had to be rethought and to co-exist with enthusiastic, if unfounded, assumptions about the extent of national consciousness revealed in 1831.

12   The Dynamics of Change

The complicated point and counterpoint between revolution and political change which had marked the aftermath of revolution in the Papal Legations was an extreme form of the interrelationship visible in virtually all the countries affected by the crisis of 1830. Elsewhere, of course, the content was rarely so obscured by the form of revolution as was the case in Emilia-Romagna. That it was so different there is further evidence that, although the movements of 1830 both sprang from basically similar and interconnected causes and developed their own momentum on the European level, they also all had distinct personalities. For all that contemporary statesmen felt themselves facing a single challenge, this was not really so. The case-histories show that, while there was a diplomatic shape to the crisis on the European level, this is not a sufficient explanation of the way the revolutionary and political movements actually evolved. Their tempi and keys were ultimately determined by native factors in most cases. So when we come to look, as we now must, at the wherefores of the revolutions of 1830 this must be kept in mind.

The question which arises is whether the dissimilarities were so great that the underlying shape of the various outbreaks was completely different, rather than having the same kind of interrelationships as caused them in the first place. And now we have seen what happened in 1830, individually as well as generally, not to mention why it all happened, we are better placed to say what it all amounted to, who was involved in the movements and what effects they had. The last question will, of course, bring us back to the significance of the whole affair, the denial of which was one of the starting-points of our inquiry. To begin with, however, did similar forces keep the revolutions going and help them to develop their own momentums?

The question of whether there were underlying harmonies in the dynamics of the individual revolutions is a useful starting-point for an analysis of the shape of the revolutions of 1830 since the evolution of revolutions has all too often been ignored in favour of a preoccupation with their causes. In fact, the techniques and forces which helped to keep the revolutions going are vital to the success of the process of revolution and political change.

One thing that soon becomes clear, not merely about the how, but also about the who and the wherefore of the revolutions of 1830 is that they cannot easily be explained by such ready-made theories of revolution as Brinton's 'natural history' of revolution. These envisage revolutions as going through a series of stages such as a rule of the moderates, the rise of extremists, the Reign of Terror and a Thermidorian phase. For not only do the stages of revolution vary as between theorists, but they are also simply rationalisations from the very different circumstances of the first French revolution. Moreover, they do not really grapple with the way in which power was seized in so many countries at roughly the same time in 1830, as a result as much of government error as of revolutionary fervour. In any case, in 1830 there was neither time nor desire for any reign of terror or any Thermidorian reaction.

In fact, there is no one model of the revolutionary process which fits all the movements of 1830, even when southern and eastern Europe are left out of account. For, if all the revolutions were basically spontaneous, they were not all endogenous. There was, as we have seen, a definite exogenous or external dimension to the dynamic of 1830, with governments being more significant than any counter-revolutionary pressures. Nationalism was another complicating factor. Both process and participation in 1830 can only be understood as a triangular interaction between governments, social forces and political pressures. Very often it was governments which decided whether the crisis would issue in political change rather than in revolution.

The men of 1830 were to some extent revolutionaries in spite of themselves. They were aware of what had happened in 1789, and this helped to impose restraints on the dynamic of revolution, emphasising thereby the importance of these negative external factors. Hence we need to look at these factors and at the role of governments in developing the crises of 1830 before considering the limits to the organisation, euphoria and violence of the revolutionary process. However, for all these limitations, 1830 can only be understood as a year of real revolutions. The men of 1830 had hindsight where 1789 was concerned. They could not have been expected to foresee the subsequent events which caused supporters of change and theorists of revolution to offer such misleading models of revolutionary change.

So, although the dynamics of 1830 can be looked at in terms of a series of phases, this is less productive than an analysis of the forces and techniques which contributed to the evolution of the various movements. Thus it is obvious that the revolts of 1830 did not follow a single set pattern of phases. The idea of tension building up to a climax implicit in some versions of the 'natural history' model does not often apply. To begin with, whatever the underlying discontents and hostilities, these did not really take off outside of parts of Switzerland until after the July Days. Even afterwards the pattern of pressure for change inexorably building up to a massive explosion was not found everywhere. This kind of effervescence and mobilisation did sometimes take place: in Belgium in August and September, although the events of 25 August might be classed as something more than this; in Switzerland throughout the autumn and winter of 1830-1, the same time as in Hanover; and in Britain from the autumn of 1830 onwards. However, it is not a very helpful description of what happened in Poland and Hungry or even in France itself. There the confrontation with government remained latent until the actual seizure of power.

To all intents and purposes, the seizure of power was in fact part and parcel of the period of mobilisation. The two were really telescoped into one in both France and the first wave of German states to respond to the July Days. The initial step towards conflict turned out to be the last, at least at the centre. Even in Belgium the time which elapsed between the outbreak of disturbances in late August and the exclusion of the Dutch from the vast majority of Belgian territory was hardly two months, somewhat less than the time needed to shake the French establishment in the summer of 1789. In Poland the time-scale was much the same, while in many of the Swiss cantons the crisis did not issue in a seizure of power at all. Similarly, in Britain and Scandinavian countries the concept has even less application. And yet all these countries were gripped by the same crisis.

The classical model then talks of a honeymoon period in which the moderates ruled and a constitution was drafted to general applause. But, whereas it was the case that in many countries constitutions were drafted very rapidly after the seizure of power, it is not very useful to speak either of a honeymoon period or of the rule of the moderates. Even where power had been seized at the centre, whether this was in Paris, Basle or Warsaw, the new regime often faced a very difficult period as it sought to extend its control to the peripheries. The seizure of power in fact developed tension rather than released it. Thus in France the July Monarchy was faced with the outbreak of social disorder and the threats from left and right, while the liberals of Basle found that the rural population would not accept their solutions, and the Poles were unable to persuade the peasantry of Congress Poland let alone that of the other parts of the Old Commonwealth to rally behind the revolution.

Even in Belgium, where the revolution spread perhaps more rapidly than anywhere else, the diplomatic situation and the economic crisis meant that there was not much of a honeymoon there, either. And in central Italy there was certainly none at all. For, if in Bologna and elsewhere there was a fairly rapid rallying to the new order throughout the provinces, there is also evidence of some popular resistance, not to mention outside pressures. Something of this is also true of the German states. Only in some of the more flexible Swiss cantons can one really speak of such a thing as a honeymoon period.

Moreover, to talk of the rule of the moderates is only meaningful if there was a real extremist movement which eventually ousted the former and created its own, presumably violent, regime. In fact, although some people talk of the emergence of more radical elements outside Bologna in the case of the Papal Legations, and it is true that there were more extreme elements involved in both the Parisian and the Warsaw crises, none of these really came to power. Certainly none of them created a reign of terror. Even the Warsaw riots of August 1831 proved to be a flash in the pan, and the extremists failed both to develop a coherent alternative policy or to deflect the existing authorities from their chosen path. One could perhaps see the liberal movements of south-western Germany in this light, but to do so would be to overlook the fact that this was also the period of initial effervescence in those parts of the region.

Only Belgium really developed something which was recognisably a revolutionary movement in the sense in which this had been known in the 1790s, and it was never able to capture power. Like the left in France, it found itself forced to embark on a long-term campaign for influence. Similarly, if there was no reign of terror, then there was unlikely to be any Thermidorian phase, in the sense of a period in which exhaustion forced the revolution to go back on its tracks. There were countervailing pressures, but nearly everywhere the revolutionary movement was stopped in its tracks – whether by outside influences as in Italy, Poland and Spain, or by internal pressures as in France, some of the Swiss cantons and especially the German states – not forced to backtrack. Belgium seems to occupy a mid-point between the two.

In sum, models of revolution derived from longer and more complex events like 1789 and 1917 are not much help in understanding the process of revolution in 1830. The events were much more compressed in time, and there was little possibility of a revolution within the revolution such as has been hailed as one of the main dynamics of other movements. The revolutions of 1830 were anyway so much more diverse than those in France and Russia that no one model can really cover them all. If the crises were all very rapid, with old regimes crumbling at their first brush with oppositions encouraged by the July Days and yielding to makeshift regimes which in turn were scrambling to establish control in the face of resistance forces which had not, for instance, even existed in France in 1789, the ways they actually developed or were repressed varied considerably from country to country. Not the least of the failings of the models of explanation is that they posit revolutions which were much more self-contained than those of 1830.

If there was no single, neat model of revolution in 1830, what factors did cause the revolutions to develop as they did? To begin with, the external dimension needs to be borne in mind. Apart from the aid lent by the Lucerners to the revolution in Aarau, by the volunteers who went to Belgium, and the exiles from Poland and elsewhere who somewhat haltingly took up the cause of revolution in Frankfurt, Portugal and Savoy, there was no real parallel to the practical support given by France to other radical movements in the 1790s. The positive stimulus to revolution was symbolic and diplomatic. France did at one stage threaten to assist the Spanish patriots, but this was only as a negotiating ploy with Ferdinand, and the provision of open aid to the Pedristas came only after the crisis generally was dying down. The nervous reaction on the part of the powers to French involvement in Belgium serves to show how careful the French had to be in this respect. The example of Italy also proved that reliance on French aid was wholly misplaced. Yet the hope that aid would be forthcoming, even if only in diplomatic form, did much to shape and mute the Polish and Italian outbreaks. The legacy of 1789 thus proved as deceptive in practical terms as it seems to be in so far as theories of revolution are concerned.

Some movements in 1830 were almost wholly self-contained. This was the case in Switzerland, for instance, which was largely ignored by the powers. However, knowledge of what was happening in other cantons obviously spurred developments on elsewhere. This kind of knowledge was also a rather minor element in Britain, while sympathy for the Poles played a not insignificant role in promoting radicalism here and in France. Once the Dutch had been expelled from Belgium the whole process was intimately bound up with diplomatic pressures which, although the Belgians preferred to ignore the fact, helped to consolidate a free and independent state south of the Moerdyk. Resentment at the way the powers were allegedly abusing the rights of the revolutionary state helped to maintain tension there well into 1831. And, had the Vatican been more accommodating, diplomatic pressure might have helped Italian liberalism a great deal more, too. On the other hand, the hostility evinced by Britain and Hanover towards Karl of Brunswick helped to smooth the way for the acceptance by the German Federation of the new constitutional regime under William of Brunswick-Oels. Similarly, Austria refused to support Quadri.

Yet, for the most part, diplomatic and other external considerations more often served to restrain the cause of revolution than to advance it. Thus even the Poles felt that they had to press the Belgians to moderate their own fervour and intransigence towards the powers, in the hope that a diplomatic settlement there would make it easier for the diplomatic community to take up the Polish case. The interests of one revolution here worked to mitigate the extremism of another. But the Polish initiative failed to produce any diplomatic advantage. The eastern powers, and particularly Prussia, continued to underwrite the Russian campaign. In Spain, of course, there was no need for any diplomatic or military aid. The combined forces of Spanish government and conservatism were quite enough to snuff out the invasions on their own. They were also able to provide Don Miguel in Portugal with considerable support, both moral and material. However, even when this was reinforced by aid from French and other ultras, it was so misused that the liberal forces were able to win a famous victory thanks to their own external allies. French influence was thus more effective there than it was in Italy, where the French totally failed to stop the Austrians repressing the United Provinces. Such hostile pressures did not always take a military form. The concern felt by the diplomatic community about the sudden change of regime in France was more than sufficient to extinguish any thoughts Louis-Philippe may have had of embarking on rash ventures beyond his borders.

Such diplomatic pressures may have militated more against revolution than in its favour, but they were far from being the only kind of influence which governments exerted on the fortunes of the movements of 1830. The evolution of the latter owed almost as much to the doings of rulers as had their outbreak. This was true not only in the cases of inept crisis-management – such as the refusal of Charles X and Polignac to make any concessions to the opposition until there was no chance that these could succeed – but also in the case of more strategic policies – such as those of Karl of Brunswick and William of Hesse. The way in which the former tried both to organise an invasion of his own country and to outbid the new regime by offering wide political concessions to the populace served to consolidate the new regime at home and in the mind of the Bund. It convinced the Federation that anything was better than Karl, even if brought about through violence. Similarly, the attempt of the Elector of Hesse to reinstate his mistress, the Countess of Reichenbach, during the early months of 1831 gave a new and ultimately self-defeating stimulus to popular anger there. The continuing refusal of the Tsar to make any concession beyond the possibility of an amnesty to the Poles undermined the attempts of moderate elements to direct the revolution into harmless channels and left the initiative in the hands of extremists.

Above all, there was the example of the double-dealing of William I of the Joint Kingdom of the Netherlands. He had first, somewhat half-heartedly, tried to coerce the Belgians by using force and then, equally half-heartedly, he tried to use his eldest son as the stalking-horse for his continuing ambitions on his southern provinces. All this did a great deal to reinforce the ferment in Belgium, not to mention turning the great powers against him. Such government intransigence also served to fuel the liberal fires for a considerable time in such countries as Switzerland and the Papal States. Of course, it was not only the old governments which often helped to keep the revolutionary pot boiling by their failure to adapt in the way certain northern sovereigns did. The hesitations of the new governments in France and Belgium were to do just as much to antagonise radical forces. Hence, as in the run up to revolution, the way that governments handled the crisis once it was upon them counted for a great deal in moulding its shape.

The obduracy and hamfistedness of rulers caused an immense amount of resentment and, as was particularly the case in Poland, curtailed chances of peaceful evolution towards political change. The protests which resulted were often directed against particular personalities who symbolised the existing authority, such as Werklein in Parma and the journalist Libry-Bagnano in Brussels. Attacks were less likely to be mounted against specific institutions of government with one particular exception. This was, of course, the security forces, whose strengths and weaknesses played a considerable part in the unrolling of the events of 1830. On the one hand, their brutality and officiousness provoked popular action, notably in Saxony; on the other, their basic insufficiencies had a cramping effect on governments' attempts to resolve the crises.

Outside Britain, and perhaps France, police forces as we now know them hardly existed. The police of the time were few in number and different in character from what they have since become. Policing was largely a judicial function, with magistrates possessing wide legal powers to maintain order, but lacking concrete means to enforce them, particularly in a preventative way. In Switzerland, indeed, many cantons had no police force at all and relied solely on the authority of the Justice of the Peace. Even the oppressive Francesco of Modena had no alternative to using his personal guard to deal with Ciro Menotti's threat. France, which had a more developed system than did most, with police commissaires in the towns and brigades of gendarmes in the country, still could not rival the provision represented by the Metropolitan Police in London which, from 1831, was reinforced by the Special Constabulary. Everything we know about Continental police forces points to the fact that they could not deal with civil disorders on their own and needed the support of regular troops. Recourse to the latter, however, tended to politicise and exacerbate conflict since the sight of, say, the uniforms of the Swiss Guard in Paris, or – to be fair – those of Scots' regiments around Merthyr Tydfil, made the opposition yet more angry and inclined to question an order of things which could turn the army on them. It may well have been these basic shortcomings of police forces which encouraged governments to attempt such immediate and heavy-handed repression as they often did.

The trouble was that not only was this seen as the virtual equivalent of declaring war on the capital city and its population, but also the armies were not even very effective. Their use therefore worsened the problems facing governments. Armies, too, could be psychologically unprepared for thus initiating civil war. Certainly they were often not sufficiently numerous for the task, and this deficiency was rendered more critical by failures to mobilise all those who could be called into action. Those that were employed were often poorly trained and equipped – another deficiency which told when they were also to be badly led and used. All this gave revolutionary movements a crucial advantage in places like Berne and Bologna where military confrontation never actually materialised. It also provided little stimulus for the supporters of the *status quo* to rally to the defence of threatened regimes.

Of course, dealing with civil disorder, especially in the teeming cities of the time, was never likely to have been easy. Troops would obviously have disliked the prospect, especially if taken unawares by a crisis which compelled them to fire on fellow-citizens or, as in Belgium, fellow-countrymen. In the case of France some regiments appear to have had a more positive predilection for opposition causes. This may have been a factor which contributed to the acute fears later aroused by French military intervention in Belgium. However, the most important fact was that the the number of troops available to governments was often so small. Switzerland may have been unique in having no central standing army, and having to raise a force from the cantons whenever the Federal Diet decided to take military action to maintain internal order, but other countries were not a great deal better placed. The papal army and *carabinieri* were not numerous, let alone effective and reliable. The two Duchies of Parma and Modena, furthermore, could only muster about 1,500 men each to control a population of several hundred thousand.

Again, although the nominal strength of some armies was impressive, they were unable to mobilise all their effectives when the crunch came. The paper strength of the army in the Netherlands was about 90,000, but the practice of releasing one fifth and recruiting another fifth every year helped to produce a situation in which no more than 25,000 men might actually be under arms at a particular time. This, indeed, was the situation in September 1830. Similarly, the flower of the French army was campaigning in Algeria during the summer of that year, while sizeable detachments were also operating in Normandy in an effort to control the wave of arson there. Even the Austrians could never afford to maintain the numbers they believed necessary to control Italy. This explains the slowness and reluctance of Frimont's response to the call for assistance from Modena in early February 1831. So, while there were one or two cases, notably Hanover and Russia, where forces were adequate, generally speaking the authorities were not well provided with the most basic means of coercion left to them, in the absence of real police forces.

Moreover, in very few cases did governments mobilise such men as they had, or even place them on special alert after the July Days. This happened in Russia and Prussia, but most regimes seem to have contented themselves with increased but discreet surveillance, so that when the crises actually broke they had to scrabble around to get enough men to deal with the problems. Polignac never even called in the men from the camps nearest to the capital, while the Bernese had to try to recruit former Swiss Guards in French service on their return home following disbandment by the July Monarchy. Grand Duke Constantine refused to use the Russian troops available to him in Warsaw. He may well have been wiser in this than his critics allow, since the too rapid deployment of troops in both Brunswick and Belgium did seem to exacerbate matters. Again, even when enough men were gathered there were few provisions or plans for them. In Brussels Prince Frederick found that he did not have the small-calibre cannon necessary for street fighting. In Paris there were only contingency plans for containing mild disturbances, not for a major confrontation. In any case, the troops had an uneasy commander and a grave shortage of ammunition and food.

Marmont, of course, was not the only commander to have reservations about the task entrusted to him. This was true also of Constantine and General von Herzberg, the officer in charge of the Brunswick garrison. Similarly, Prince Frederick's advisers in Brussels opposed a direct infantry attack, but the Prince's enthusiastic response to the promises of Delescaille that hundreds of armed burghers would rally to the merest demonstration of force led him to stumble into just this kind of offensive, rather than isolationg or bombarding the town. Political leaders were often just as disastrously hesitant over the use of the troops at their disposal. This was the case of Karl of Brunswick, Parraciani-Clarelli and the governing élites of Fribourg and other Swiss cantons, not to mention the Duke of Wellington and the High Tory leadership in England. A final point was that most of the armies involved in the crises of 1830 had not been trained for an urban security role. Parade-ground drill made up the bulk of the training of the troops stationed in Warsaw, while in Brussels a goodly number of those involved in the attack on the capital were actually raw recruits with little or no training of any sort.

Yet despite all these defects they could fight bravely. There was, for instance, little desertion from the ranks of the Dutch army trapped in the park. What ultimately led to the defeat of the royal forces in Paris was inadequate leadership and supply. Marmont's assault on the centre of the city played right into the hands of the opposition. Street fighting in towns which were still virtually medieval in construction demanded more sophistication than this. Few armies had the intelligence of leadership ultimately given to the Russians by Paskievitch or the readiness of those employed in southern England or Spain. As a result of these weaknesses and mistakes by such crucial elements in the struggle, the possibilities open to the opposition were much greater than they might have been.

A related factor is that 1830 did not generate the kind of counter-revolutionary movements found in some other revolutions. It was already present in Iberia, and certainly restrained opposition there, but nothwards and eastwards things were very different. The siezure of power was often so rapid that there was little chance for counter-revolution to develop, especially when, despite all their bluster, people like the ultras faded away when the crunch came. The Vatican had hopes of creating such a movement in the Romagna, but gave it up when the arrest of Cardinal Benvenuti deprived it of its intended leader. The recalcitrance of the peasantry, especially south-west of the Apennines, did not really fill the vacuum, although this combined with fear of the 'Germans' (as the Austrians were often called) to worry the supporters of the United Provinces. There were somewhat similar problems in Parma and Poland, but in neither case did rural hostility undermine the revolution. That was left to foreign armies.

It was in the later phases of the crises that countervailing forces and fear of them played their most significant part, although even then they never really amounted to a great deal. Thus although radical opinion in France was incensed by royalist demonstrations in Paris and the abortive landing of the Duchess of Berri in 1832, there is no evidence that either posed any real threat to the new order. Similarly, while Orangism was a bogey guaranteed to frighten many Belgians into continuing excitement, it does not seem that there was sufficient grass-roots support for the cause to do anything more than create a good deal of noise. In fact the activities of the High Tories in England and the conservative forces of Switzerland were probably a greater threat to liberalism. Even so, the Prussian authorities in Neuchâtel tried to distance themselves from the spontaneous royalist military mobilisation during the first attempted *coup* in September 1831.

The role of government in maintaining the momentum of revolution in 1830 was significant, even though the performance of government was often ineffective both militarily and in terms of rallying popular support. The fact that the threat from the establishment was so much less than it had been in the era of the first French revolution, at least outside Poland, perhaps helps to explain why the opposition in 1830 never really developed fully fledged revolutionary parties or organised movements. Thus, for all the talk of secret societies as causes of the revolution, there were hardly any references to them in the actual events of 1830, let alone any evidence of their activity. 'Are there really secret societies?' Flaubert makes a moustachioed young man ask in one of his novels. The answer: 'No, it's an old joke of the government, to scare the pants off the middle classes.' Thus the cadets faded from view in Warsaw, and the eclipse of Menotti's allies in Modena was even more complete. The only quasi-conspiratorial body which played a real part in revolution seems to have been the republicans in Neuchâtel.

There were only two real parallels to the Jacobin clubs of the 1790s. One was the Réunion Centrale club in Brussels, which was established in September 1830, but only survived for a few months and never succeeded in creating widespread or continuing influence on government. The other was the Patriotic Society in Warsaw, which helped to push the country into military confrontation, but also checked early on and reduced to somewhat carping criticism and despairing outbreaks of violence, simply because it was so marginal. Revolutionary clubs in Saxony and elsewhere were even paler reflections of revolutionary parties, and had much less influence than the more straightforwardly political pressure-groups like the political unions in Britain. These were partly modelled on the Catholic Association, which was one of a number of ways in which Ireland encouraged political action in Europe. Later on, of course, we can see the creation of more overtly nationalistic and radical groups like the Associations Nationales and Associations Patriotiques in France and Belgium. Similarly, social radicals like the Saint-Simonians sought to propagandise the working class. However, the new regime acted to curb such activities, while it was to be a long time before real lower-class political organisations were to develop outside of Britain and France.

For the most part, the principal aim of those involved in 1830 was to create legitimate and orthodox regimes, not revolutionary ones in the Jacobin or Bolshevik sense. Thus, while the Belgians did experiment with 'revolutionary institutions' they soon dispensed with them. This was true even of Menotti and his consorts. Violence was a way of seizing power from a corrupt and arbitrary regime, not a means of maintaining a new authority. So, although virtually every country created a National Guard of some kind, these turned out to be either inert or moderate, more concerned to repress popular disturbance than to carry the revolution further. As events in both the Po valley and in northern Belgium during the Ten Days War illustrate, the military potential of such bodies was, in any case, questionable. National Guard units in fact served as much as mobilising agencies for political activity as for anything else. New regimes seem not to have wanted to delay the establishment of regular constitutional government and, outside of Belgium prior to the meeting of the Congress, eschewed the use of transitional or exceptional institutions.

As a result, revolutionary euphoria of the old style was fairly rare. It appeared briefly in Poland and the Papal States when the old yoke was thrown off, and intermittently in the Réunion Centrale and its successors in Belgium, but basically enthusiasm for change was more controlled and cautious. The notable examples of 'boundless exultation' came from places where national feeling was involved. This was sometimes the case in Italy, where the poet Berchet could call: 'To arms, sons of Italy! Now dawns the day! We've done with kings that are traitors, for aye. We are brethren all – from the Alps to the sea!' It was certainly present in Poland with even greater fervour. And in Belgium the apparently unprovoked assault by the Dutch had an electrifying effect, creating a patriotic consciousness.

Thus Isidore Gillain, a brewer from Namur, who was in the capital during the crisis, wrote home to his parents on 24 September of 'Thursday, a day forever memorable, on which the Belgians became immortals. I escaped the greatest dangers with only a slight wound, truly very slight. It was nothing and did not stop me acting and fighting. I decided to die rather than give in to these cowardly Dutch. We will over-come! Reinforcements are reaching us from all quarters and perhaps today we shall master all the legions we have to fight. We have seen a great number of brave souls die to defend their liberty. But in revenge we have massacred the mad men who wished to enslave us. Perhaps, too, by tonight we shall be masters of the park. My courage will not tire and, if I die, console yourselves by saying that your son has fallen for liberty. Farewell, I flee to arms!' Because of the nature of the fighting in Brussels, feelings obviously ran very high. A similar trend can be seen in Switzerland, south-west Germany, and even France, where the radical Cavaignac declared, with more than a little exaggeration, that it would have been easier to make the crowds march on the Rhine than on St Cloud.

In Britain, Germany and Switzerland the main feeling at work seems to have been a passionate desire for change and reform: to see the old order swept away. This was not just imitative, because it was rooted in such obvious local grievances. However, it was not enough to encourage people to shed blood. The Belgian reaction to the shedding of blood by the Dutch in fact reinforces the impression of a reluctance to engage in out-and-out conflict. The revolution of 1830 was a spontaneous but controlled movement for participation and procedure which was turned into a crisis of legitimacy by the errors of government and the effects of social distress. Where this process could not manifest itself, as was the case in the south-east of Europe, one of the main elements of dynamism was removed. But in countries like Switzerland and Belgium social questions helped to produce mass mobilisation which underwrote the political and patriotic protests, so that they became irresistible.

As time went on, of course, social protest was to become less evident and central, though it always remained latent. The events in France, Belgium and Poland had initially intensified the economic malaise which had helped to start the process, and made the lower classes either more agitated – as in France, where we can see the growth of working-class consciousness and new forms of organisation and protest – or more hostile to the whole opposition venture. The latter was most obviously the case in Poland. Food troubles continued to unsettle Germany even though early and successful palliative measures were taken in the cities where changes had started. But generally, when the apocalyptic hopes generated by the July Days and the subsequent popular explosion did not prove justified and the uncertainties merely worsened the situation, social protest began to wane and to give way to apathy.

Neither the fact that the popular element faded nor the placement of limitations on political fervour and experiment should lead us to think that the events of 1830 were bereft of violence. There was violence in virtually all the movements of 1830, whether reformist or revolutionary. Only in Scandinavia was violence absent. But violence was usually employed as a means to an end, and was subordinate to political campaigning. In Switzerland and Britain violence thus occurred at critical stages of a search for political change which also used all the other available political channels and techniques. The first response of the Belgian notables in September was to negotiate and argue their case in the States-General. Violence was used as a means of pressurising regimes into conceding concrete political demands. Only amongst the cadets, the Modenese conspirators, Bourquin and the republicans in Neuchâtel, and especially the Spanish liberals was there a predisposition to use violence deliberately from the outset.

Violence, then, despite its symbiotic relationship to demands for political change, was essentially spontaneous. Even in Warsaw the popular upsurge that saved the cadets was unplanned and unexpected. And while Menotti and his colleagues placed much faith in Bologna as a centre for revolution, it is unlikely that they had thought of the factious porters of the town in this context. Yet, for all that it was spontaneous, the violence was not of the same type or intensity. In Brussels in August, as in Bologna, Kassel, Dresden and Leipzig, the violence was partly a demonstration against armed forces which did not stay to argue, and partly an expression of social dissent directed against the police as well as against economic conditions. Where there were large bodies of regulars who did fight, the presence of social unease often tipped the scales against the former: where it was not present, as in Modena city, the regulars tended to win.

In Belgium in September the social protest tended to become subsumed in the nationalist upsurge that followed the Four Days, whereas in the Papal States, Spain and especially Poland this was not the case. Indeed, in the latter the war of liberation was very largely fought by regular troops. Elsewhere, although regulars did go over to the rebels, civilian volunteers played the largest part. In nearly all cases, however, the conflicts took on what we might call a regular form. The opposition tried to create an army or a militia of its own which then sought to measure its strength against the established forces in open battle. Guerilla warfare seems to have passed 1830 by, despite the use made of it in Greece. It was only after the revolutions that Italian and Polish radicals, amongst others, started talking of the possibility of carrying on the struggle in this way, the next time around.

As a result of these factors, the violence of 1830 was rarely terroristic or nihilistic. There were instances of this – in the attacks on peers in England and the orgies of destruction in Bristol and Derby, not forgetting Louvain, Paris and Warsaw – but generally the violence was controlled. Even where fear of internal opposition incited people to violence – as with the recapture of Argenta in the Po valley, the revival of Orangism in Belgium, and the activities of Duke Karl of Brunswick – there were no atrocities. Indeed, in Switzerland violence was often limited or implicit. In the Ticino there were merely a few scuffles; in the Vaud an occupation and a menacing gathering; and elsewhere a series of marches which usually brough governments to their senses. In Fribourg this only happened in the nick of time, but generally it did happen, and it was only in Basle and Neuchâtel that things got out of hand. Such examples were also, of course, amongst the least violent of all in 1830. Sorokin rates the Belgian revolt as the most extensive in this respect. In terms of the numbers involved, this may have been so, but in duration and scale of fighting Poland took the prize. On either count France probably rates third, followed by Italy and the central German states. And, of course, the violence in Iberia and in the Reform movement in Britain cannot be ignored.

Thus outside of Poland the element of popular violence in 1830, although omnipresent, was as muted as was the intervention of government forces and government policy. The dynamic of revolution was very different from that of the first French revolution, and not very similar to that in 1848. What was the process of revolution actually like, then? Charles Tilly has suggested that, while the 'natural history' of revolution does not apply to 1830, there was none the less a distinctive shape to the process of revolution in France at that time. He and Rule locate the roots of revolution in the normal processes of the polity, in which contenders for power form a coalition, attract public support and help fragment the polity. Then, if the government cannot or will not suppress this alternative power-base, control passes to it, and its problems then begin, since not merely does the level of violence tend to rise as the new regime seeks to extend its control from the centre to the extremities of the state, but also the decisions this implies tend to split the coalition, on tactical rather than ideological lines. Hence there is a good deal of unease and division until the polity is eventually reconstituted round the new regime. The first stages of this process, it is probably true to say, were at least latent in many countries of Europe prior to 1830; but outside places with a relatively advanced and accepted political life – like Britain, Belgium and France – the terms they use are a little inflated as a description of what was possible. The theory also fails to cope adequately with the rapidity and unexpected nature of the transfer of power, and particularly with the outside connections involved in this in 1830.

However, when it comes to the subsequent stages of the revolutionary process, with which we are concerned here, the idea does have something more to offer. For, although in places like Poland, and to a lesser extent in the German states, the attitudes of the rulers involved tended to prevent or threaten consolidation, and talk of the break up of coalitions (especially in the short term) and the reconstruction of the polity can be somewhat otiose in the relatively simple circumstances of 1830, the stress on the way that difficulties increased *after* the seizure of power rather than *before* it – as the 'natural history' model implies – does seem to work. The problems, however, did not really have their origin in tactical disagreements about the process of consolidation. Often the problems were external pressures rather than internal disagreements.

In France the annoyance of dissatisfied workers, republicans, proto-socialists and even some liberal supporters of the new order over the limits to the changes that followed the July Days did mean that the revolution encountered more difficulties and violence than had the regime of Charles X. And, if this problem was less visible in Belgium, the unease produced by Orangism produced challenges there, with violence continuing round the major fortresses of Antwerp, Luxembourg and Maastricht and then exploding in the Ten Days War. Similarly, in Italy the switch to the new regime was smooth enough in the Romagna, and the real difficulties came later, with the Austrians and the papal resistance. Again, in Switzerland the wave of constitutional change in 1830–1 was to be the prelude to further troubles, as new areas like the Lower Valais and Neuchâtel sought to join the movement and new issues arose out of the reform and integrity of the existing confederation. In the course of these disputes the coalition which had brought about the initial Regeneration did break up, just as it had in Belgium and, to a lesser extent, in France, where the coalition had never been a reality. So that, although the polity was reconstituted in certain cases, this was to prove merely the prelude to continuing and sometimes deepening disagreement and dissent as the issues implicit in 1830 were more systematically debated than they had been during the hand-to-mouth crises of the transfer of power.

However, if the theory reminds us of the fact that the dynamic of revolution in 1830 continued for longer than some historians have been inclined to think, it does not provide a fully coherent or convincing explanation of the process of revolution. Indeed, it is doubtful whether there could be any such simple model of the process of revolution. The 1830 revolutions were often too short to display the characteristics of other revolutionary eras, or even those found in the most advanced polities of continental Europe at the time. The variety of confining conditions in each separate area and the external complications mean that models deriving from the internal affairs of single countries – and particularly from France, which departed more from the norm than people tend to think – do not really enable us to cope with the strange mixture of endogenous and exogenous factors that gave 1830 its particular character.

The revolutions of 1830 were basically spontaneous protests designed to secure the political goals of greater participation and recongnition, carried along by a wave of social protest which for a while saw in the vague idea of change a solution to a wider range of problems. Taken by themselves they might have been easily forgotten or absorbed, but coming together as they did they created a whole which was larger than the parts. For, although each separate country did tend to go its own way, the very fact that it did so was a matter of much wider significance, to both supporters and opponents of change. This counterpoint of internal and external dynamics is essential to 1830. To study the former without the latter is to miss the point. Internally the dynamic of revolution may not have run as deeply or as intensely as in other eras, depending as it did as much on the external complications and the doings of government for its shape as it did on the appeal to force. And, of course, 1830 is not a terribly good advertisement for the kingship of the time. If, as Tolkien says, 'a king is he that can hold his own, or else his title is in vain', the rulers of the time ended up by convincing nobody of their effectiveness.

The normal attitude to limited revolutions is to ignore or sneer at their lack of bite. Yet it is only the symbolic appeal of revolutions which causes both revolutionaries and pacific historians condescendingly to dismiss the events of 1830 because of the lack of blood, toil, tears, and sweat. In reality, the fact that the political and social protests never fully came together outside Belgium and possible Switzerland, and that revolutions were often led by the press rather than by conspiratorial parties, should deprive them of neither their significance nor their revolutionary status. Whether they wanted to or not, people in 1830 did resort to force when they were unable to obtain the political reforms they wanted in other ways, and the attempt to attain these ends involved a large number of people from a wide range of social strata, as will shortly be seen. In extent and in popular understanding, the events of 1830 were real and dynamic processes of revolution. It is the use of models which originate from different and previous events which tends to obscure the nature and significance of the revolts of 1830.

13 Contenders for Power: Social Participation in the Events of 1830

If governments and their security forces were major factors in the crises of 1830, they were not the only ones. There were at least two other groups contending for power on the other side. It is important to ask exactly who they were and why they participated in the revolutionary movements of those years. Participation, of course, can mean at least two things, for there is an obvious difference between active leadership on the one hand, and some more passive form of popular support on the other. To a large extent, the people who took these respective roles in 1830 came from different social groups, but the identification of the middle classes with the leaders and the lower classes with the led is not exact. In any case, it is in the interrelationships of the two that the potency of the movements of 1830 is really to be found. Furthermore, classes as such did not act in 1830, and even less did people act from self-conscious class motivations. Social concerns and interests helped to fuel political and other forms of protest, but other motives also had their part to play. People did not always participate in revolution with clearly defined expectations of what might result. Participants were not all to be rewarded. Opposition contention for power in 1830 cannot be understood in simple and anachronistic economic terms.

Indeed, exploring participation in 1830 is anything but easy. The sources are poor and often give little indication of who was involved. Interpreting such evidence as there is also has its problems, for not merely did social structures and problems differ from country to country, but very often insufficient research has been done on social stratification to enable us accurately to place such contenders or to interpret their motives. Social historians of France and especially of Britain are in an immensely privileged position in this respect compared to students of Switzerland and Italy. None the less, the broad indications which emerge about the forces of leadership and popular participation do show something more of the social dynamic of the events of 1830, and therefore of their character and significance.

What we find is that the contenders for power in 1830 came from a broad range of the social spectrum. Though 1830 was not a mass revolution in a classic sense, it was far from being as limited and narrowly based as that of 1820-1 had been. Leadership in 1830 was offered by people from throughout the middle and upper reaches of society; and, while the peasant masses played only a minor role in the popular protests, especially when compared to that played by pre-industrial artisans, they cannot be overlooked completely. So, after further considering what being a participant or a contender in 1830 actually involved, we can examine the various groups and individuals who did take part in the two main forms of revolutionary action in 1830. This will provide more insight into the nature of the revolutions. And, just as there is no one model to the dynamic of revolution, so the contenders cannot be too easily categorised.

Perhaps the first thing to be noted about participation in the events of 1830 is that, with only a very few exceptions, all of it was spontaneous. The revolutions were made despite would-be revolutionaries. Only amongst the Spanish and Italian exiles in France, the cadets in Warsaw, the Menotti group in Modena and the republicans in Neuchâtel were there conscious intentions to overthrow existing regimes by force. Virtually all these failed. At most, as in Bologna and Warsaw, they helped to stimulate a wider rising in which they were soon lost from view. Moreover, although such groups had some kind of ideological commitment, they also had very precise material interests of their own: the desire to pursue proper military careers in the Polish case, or redressment of the fiscal grievances of the lower Modenese in the Italian one. This served further to lessen their impact. Hence spontaneous participation was doubly important.

Spontaneous participation should not be taken to mean self-conscious membership of a formal political organisation. As has been pointed out of resistance in the Second World War, participation could range from simply listening to the BBC to fighting in the Maquis. Similarly, in 1830 it could involve, at one extreme membership of a new government and at the other merely wearing revolutionary colours on the odd occasion. In between there were a number of other roles like service in the new militia, membership of local government bodies, participation in street demonstrations, or exercising one's electoral rights. At the time, of course, such distinctions often seemed nugatory. A list of crimes committed by patriots in Parma showed no discrimination and thus accused the largest number of being agitators or rabble-rousers, and almost as many of having taken part in the disarming of the Ducal guard on 13 February. The next largest category were those indicted for alleged membership of a secret society during earlier troubles in 1823, and there were more of these than there were people actually accused of taking up arms in 1831. Others were prosecuted for being extremists, for holding office under the new authorities, or for wearing the tricolour. Only about one in ten was specifically accused of planning troubles or engaging in the subversive activities of secret societies. A few had been in the National Guard, some were merely suspected and the names of others were just mentioned in the course of investigations, while a handful were convicted for being vaguely sympathetic to the new regime. The Ducal regime thus regarded any kind of political activity as subversive. Intention was as dangerous as implementation.

Not merely were important and insignificant roles mixed together; so, too, were active and passive ones. Thus crowds and militia could parade or, as they did in Paris and Rimini, actually confront the security forces. A lot depended on where things happened. Any kind of action was often significant in capital cities. Outside, where the revolutions seem to have made less impression and, as in the Bolognese revolution, could be carried out by existing authorities as a mere administrative act, it took a good deal of effort to make an impact. Wearing National Guard uniform or a tricolour scarf did not greatly advance the cause of revolution, even though it greatly worried the authorities. As a blanket term, then, 'participation' is not a very helpful one.

Even dividing participation into two broad categories is a considerable simplification. Not all those who played a leading role would have joined in a new government. Some would have sat in parliamentary bodies, others in local government, and some would have held military office. And this assumes that all those appointed to such posts actually took them up and used the powers available to them, which was not always the case. Holders of official posts could be much less active than unofficial leaders. None the less, they deserve separate investigation.

It was the opinion of both Metternich and some modern historians like Langer that all such active roles were filled by academics and other members of the intelligentsia. This judgement is far too sweeping. Elements from the whole range of the social élite can be found at the head of the revolutions, including the aristocracy. The provisional governments of Bologna, Modena and Parma were well provided with nobles: four of the eight initial members of the first being aristocrats. And, although as the revolution spread more commoners, particularly lawyers, came to direct the movement, the nobility remained a significant minority. Often they could be amongst the most active and radical, as was the case with Count Carlo Pepoli and Count Terenzio Mamiani delle Rovere from Pesaro.

This phenomenon of a liberal aristocracy can also be seen in much of northern Europe as well. The July Monarchy maintained a Chamber of Peers, even though these were no longer hereditary, and also relied heavily on the services of nobles such as Broglie, Louis and Molé. Pinkney, indeed, suggests that five of the twelve men most influential in bringing about Louis-Philippes's succession were nobles – an insight which has to be set against the more common stress on the purge of the old aristocracy from the prefectorial corps after the July Days. In Belgium the liberal aristocracy also played its part in the revolution, and turned out to be one of the main gainers from the new order. The Dutch regime had recognised the nobility as a corporate order and had given it large representation in provincial and national assemblies, but there had still been friction, especially over the lack of concern shown for landowning and agriculture on which the southern nobles depended. So many nobles seized the chance offered by the new regime and, like Baron Emmanuel van der Linden d'Hoogvoorst, played a major part in creating a new military and civilian order in August and September, or took their place amongst the quarter of the Congress which came from the nobility. Seventy per cent of the members of the new kingdom's Senate were, perhaps more significantly, to be nobles and a fifth of the Lower House as well. Local government also had its fair share. There were, of course, nobles who remained true to Orangism, but aristocrats of new, foreign or Napoleonic creation secured an influential place in the new regime they had helped to establish.

The division of opinion amongst the Belgian aristocracy sprang partly from economic roots, with landowners being more likely to turn against the Dutch connection. Much the same has been claimed for England. David Moore has argued that it was the country gentlemen who really brought about the Reform Bill because of their dissatisfaction with the economic and political policies of the Tory parliamentary managers. Although this view has not won universal assent, it is certainly the case that the Whig grandees played a large part in the Reform movement, and remained well represented in the new House of Commons. Some echoes of this phenomenon can also be seen in Saxony, where the younger nobles were prominent in the opposition to King Anton's absolutism before the revolution, and in Brunswick, where the Freiherr von Cramm was the symbol of resistance to the Duke and a committee of nobles was responsible for switching the succession to his brother. Even in Hesse it is likely that the Elector's preference for an ignoble mistress failed to endear him to his nobles.

When we turn to Poland it is obvious that the whole rising would have been impossible without the gentry. As Kieniewicz says, what distinguishes revolutions in Poland and the east of Europe is the dominance of what Lenin termed the 'revolutionary nobility'. Not merely did magnates like Prince Adam George Czartorywski preside over the government of Free Poland, but the *szlachta* also provided the bulk of the rank and file of the patriotic movement. The Sejm retained the form given it by the Russians, so that it was dominated by the middle *szlachta*, the people who had led the opposition to Russia in the 1820s. They both happily voted to depose Nicholas and steadfastly refused to make necessary concessions to the peasantry. The ranks of the administration and the officer corps, furthermore, swarmed with members of the petty gentry, often landless and heavily dependent on such employment for their livelihood. They could be amongst the most radical elements in the revolutionary ranks. Yet the role of the gentry went far beyond this. Only 6 per cent of the known, and presumably most prominent, members of the Patriotic Society and 14 per cent of the military cadets were commoners, so that with this dominance of the lowest ranks of the leadership of the revolution it is hardly surprising that just one bourgeois joined the assault on the Belvedere. As the Decembrists had shown, in a society so polarised no political movement could survive without noble support at all levels.

None of this means, of course, that the nobility as a whole was always in favour of revolution, let alone always participated in it. There were cases in some of the Swiss cantons, and especially in Hanover, where the nobles were one of the main targets of the opposition. Elsewhere the nobility was often divided, and sometimes it was not even in contention at all, as in Scandinavia. And, of course, the nobility did not always participate as a distinct social class. In a society which was basically rural, landowners were an essential element in the social élite, and nobles were usually landowning, even if they did not always have the monopoly enjoyed by the *szlachta*. Thus in central Italy *possidenti* were as active in 1831 as they had been in the Carbonari earlier, while the Swiss farmer – who was admittedly a somewhat different kind of person – was the backbone of the whole protest movement there. Landowning was also far from irrelevant in both Britain and France. In the former farmers were known to use the Swing riots to push their own case against tithes, and in the latter fears about the émigrés' milliard ensured that many landowners were only too happy to rally to the new order, just as they also did in Belgium.

Another group of notables who sometimes played a part in leading the revolution were the clergy. Thus, while the Vatican was dead set against any kind of revolution, Flemish clerics of all ranks were ill-disposed towards the Protestant Netherlands and went on to occupy a significant number of seats in the Congress. In Poland there are similar cases of priestly activity in support of the revolution, and even Italy boasted one or two. However, there, as in England and Switzerland, the influence of the established churches was usually cast against change, although pastors like Thomas Bornhauser could be influential in the liberal movement, just as they were in Scandinavia. Finally, we should not forget Saxony, where the weight of the Lutheran Church was firmly behind change because of the Catholic persuasions and policies of the royal family.

Despite the fact that the revolutions of 1830 have often been seen as an onslaught on such social élites, in truth they played a major part in the leadership of nearly all the movements in question, and in Poland, Switzerland and perhaps Belgium as well they were also fundamental to the broader mass movement. Around Rimini the opposition to the Papacy would have been non-existent had it not been for the *possidenti*. In relatively undeveloped societies people with skills and education were less numerous than they have since become and were therefore called on to play a correspondingly more active role, especially in the small towns of the time. As a result, it is probably the case that, although they were often seen as belonging to lower social strata, the intelligentsia ought also to be included in the élite. Els Witte has suggested that in Belgium there was an upper level of artists and authors who played just this sort of role, but it is not clear that this was the case elsewhere. In Poland, of course, most of the intelligentsia had emerged from the gentry anyway.

Certainly the leadership of many revolutions would have been very limp without such university figures as Guizot in France, Jourdan in south-west Germany, Lelewel in Warsaw and Monnard in Lausanne. Academic liberals were also prominent in countries as diverse as Norway and Spain. Perhaps only in Britain was there no professional academic intelligentsia of this kind. However, journalists and writers were as vital here as anywhere else. Students in Britain were also much less likely to take part in radical movements than were students in Continental countries. In Hanover the Göttingen National Guard thus had 500 student members as against 200 artisans. In Bologna the students formed their own military units. Given their participation as inspirers, decision makers and simple militants, it is not surprising that they gained much from the new order. Indeed, in Belgium intellectuals seem to have gained more than any other group. They were thus to provide 43 per cent of the Congress and 20 per cent of the electorate of the new state.

Significantly, the elements of the middle classes which seemed to have exercised most influence on the revolution were those related to the intelligentsia. Thus, the Warsaw Patriotic Society contained, as well as forty officers and twenty-one landowners, thirty civil servants, fifteen magistrates, thirteen journalists, eleven men of letters, six professors or teachers, six doctors, six priests, six students and only six people in trade. Equally significantly, there were only three artisans, despite the contribution of the latter to the November rising. Generally speaking, professional men were heavily over-represented in revolutionary leadership in comparison to their proportions in the population as a whole.

In central Italy as in Iberia lawyers were particularly visible, although, of course, a legal training was a form of general education as much as a professional initiation. Lawyers made up a third of the Congress in Belgium, while in Germany young lawyers like Bernhard Nossdorf, who founded the revolutionary club in Dresden, were at the centre of nearly all the liberal movements. Doctors, officials and employees were also significant. Many countries had large numbers of civil servants – whether senior magistrates like Bode the Burgermaster of Brunswick or the more lowly French clerks who served on the barricades in Paris – who staffed the revolutionary movements and often, where they were able to operate a purge, succeeded in advancing their careers as well. Teachers, engineers, chemists and the like, on the other hand, were few and far between both in society and in the ranks of the revolutionary leadership.

All this is not to say that there was no participation from the commercial middle classes; only that they were less evident and less significant. Very few factory owners seem to have figured in the revolutions save as targets. Such men were usually opposed to any tampering with the *status quo*, and so in Belgium the industrialists of Wallonia and the large wholesalers of Antwerp, Brussels, Ghent and Liège were usually opposed to the break-up of the new Netherlandish joint kingdom. However, the fact that the rupture was consummated led them to play a more active role politically after 1830 than might otherwise have been the case. Bankers, on the other hand, seem to have been quite sympathetic to the idea of change, notably in France where they were more than prominent in the counsels of Louis-Philippe. However, given the state of economic development at the time, there were not all that many large-scale industrialists and businessmen in the first place. Of the 1,818 richest men in Belgium at the start of the Joint Kingdom, there were almost 500 landowners, over 300 officials and 260 *rentiers*, compared with a total of just over 300 traders and industrialists. Bankers could only muster six representatives in these serried ranks.

The scale of economic organisation being so much smaller than today, merchants, shopkeepers and the like tended to be rather local in interest and outlook. As a result, they were not likely to be available to play leadership roles. Very often they are hard to distinguish from the popular *milieux* of the towns who participated in mass action. However, they did gain from the revolutions in the sense that electoral qualifications were often revised to take more account of non-landed property and business qualifications. They also benefited from the change of attitudes and the reformed structures ushered in by events in which they had not played a major part at any level.

Generally speaking, then, the professional middle classes and the traditional landed and other notables provided leadership for the revolutions and political movements, where government, administration, the military sector and ideology are concerned. It was they who gave the revolutions their structure and shape. Very often the same sort of people, albeit of a less distinguished stamp, tended to provide, too, the middle management of the movements. Sometimes they figured also in the mass activities that sustained the movements, although usually participation at the sharp end of revolution was left to those lower down the social scale. Few nobles and social leaders were found dead on the barricaades. The bulk of the revolutionary crowds came from the lower-middle and lower classes, or, to be more precise, from that somewhat indeterminate social zone which made up so much of the population of pre-industrial towns and is best known as the *sans-culottes*. Although their political consciousness and organisation were much less than had been the case in the 1790s, their social origins and motives remained virtually the same.

In other words, popular participation in mass action was not a matter of a rabble from the dregs of the population seeking to enjoy itself through mindless violence but, rather, of solid working and business people responding to provocation and seeking remedies to their political ills, not to mention trying to realise their political dreams. Spontaneously, master craftsmen, shopkeepers, journeymen, clerks, and small merchants took revolutionary action in 1830. In Belgium the nickname given to such people, 'Gaspard', was extended to all in the popular movement in August and September, and the workers' blue blouse became their symbolic uniform, rather as the Chinese wear the Mao Tse-Tung style of tunic. Yet, simply because we often know something of these people when they died, or were arrested, for their militancy, it does not follow that all mass action was the same. In capital cities like Paris, Brussels and Warsaw revolutionary action and armed confrontation with regular troops might have been almost synonymous, but elsewhere things were different. In smaller and provincial towns violence was more symbolic and latent, often more demonstrative than anything else.

Again, many ordinary people did participate in straightforwardly political action, notably in central Italy and Germany. In Poland, too, of the total membership of the Warsaw Patriotic Society of 486, some seventy are reputed to have been commoners, showing that ordinary people did have a role to play in political matters. Of course, not all popular action was purely political. Much of it, as has been seen, was social in nature, as artisans sought to protest against their worsening conditions. But, if most social protest was urban in nature and location, it was not wholly absent from the country. All these forms of protest led many of those involved to finish up in police hands or records, which is why we know something about them. What we do not always know is precisely what part they actually played. Some must have been leaders, others followers, and there is a certain amount of overlap with the kinds of particiption we have already noted.

Obviously in the events of Paris and Brussels there seem to have been hardly any leaders at all, resistance to the royal armies emerging spontaneously and simultaneously at a variety of points. In Paris the majority of those killed, or who sought official recognition and reward for their efforts, were artisans. One sample suggests that almost exactly half belonged to this category, with carpenters, stonemasons, shoemakers, locksmiths and jewellery craftsmen being among the most frequently found. After such artisans came domestic servants, with 15.7 per cent, and employees, with 7.2 per cent. There were also a few people described simply as poor, together with as many members of the liberal professions. In Belgium many historians believe that the August troubles, with their attacks on machines and factory owners, were the responsibility of impoverished and unskilled workers, attracted by the possibilities of destruction and looting. Such people, however, were firmly dealt with by the new authorities, and it seems as though those who resisted the Dutch in September were also sober and serious artisans, resentful of both the Dutch and their own lack of prospects, and hoping to obtain the bread and employment jeopardised by the crisis unleashed in August. Neither political nor economic motives alone adequately explain their action.

Although the evidence is scanty and has never been satisfactorily analysed, it seems that the vast majority of those who died or requested recognition of their role were workers of one sort or another. As in Paris, few landowners, *rentiers*, merchants or manufacturers were involved: no more than sixty out of some 1,700. On the other hand, there were numerous small tradesmen, shopkeepers, students and legal clerks, together with a few foreigners, usually English and from the leisured classes able to indulge in tourism. Yet without the workers the Dutch would never have been resisted, let alone defeated.

Many of those involved lived in Brussels itself or had come in from Brabant, often quite recently. Their average age was about 30 and they were more likely to have been single than married, although married men actually figured more amongst the dead. Some 60 per cent of them were Flemish-speaking, driven into the capital by the decline in the textile industry in the hinterland. What kind of workers they were is hard to say. Two samples, totalling 116, where precise trades are mentioned show thirty-one day-labourers – presumably unskilled – nine joiners, eight people in domestic service, seven textile workers, as many involved in various fine arts, five each of firemen, woodworkers, metal workers, stone cutters, building tradesmen and clothing workers, four blacksmiths, four general workers, four printers, four soldiers, three masons, two people from the food trades, one *rentier* and one manufacturer. Such people, then, acted out of a mixture of patriotic anger and economic resentment, although machine-breaking and looting were nowhere near as visible as in August.

Political motives were more evident in smaller towns where violence was less common and extreme. Hence, all kinds of people were reported as reacting to the news from Paris in the French provinces, including skilled workers such as the tapestry-workers of Aubusson in the Creuse, the typographers of Blois and the paper makers of Voiron in the Isère, along with many textile workers throughout the country. Middle-class participation and leadership were even more evident in the Belgian provinces. Commercial travellers, lawyers, wine merchants, students and ex-soldiers were reported much more frequently than in Brussels. Amongst the stories of arms workers in Liège and miners from there and further south, there were also cases where a quarry owner in Rebecq-Rognon and a master plasterer in Antwerp led all their employees to the capital. And, given that the Belgians were responding to the news that the Dutch were attacking their fellow-countrymen, it was to be expected that the social spectrum would be wider.

In Italy the situation was similar. Thus amongst those arrested as Carbonari in the 1820s had been landowners, lawyers, soldiers, nobles, doctors, civil servants, merchants, students, priests and even some policemen. Things were, however, slightly different in the Papal States. There 1,634 have been recorded as being involved in the revolutionary movement. Of these 27.3 per cent came from the liberal professions, 19.5 per cent from the artisanate, 17.9 per cent were landowners, 8.3 per cent tradesmen, 5.9 per cent students and teachers, 5.7 per cent soldiers, 5.5 per cent employees, 4.7 per cent from the service trades, 3.2 per cent were officials, and the rest were either nobles and clergy or poor and others.

Where the liberal professions were concerned, the largest group was, not surprisingly, made up of lawyers. However, there were also a number of people from rather lower-status professions such as painters, barber-surgeons and thespians. The artisans included a large body of shoemakers, joiners, tailors, cabinet makers, hatters, printers and the like, on the one hand, and people like bricklayers, wool carders, hemp workers and general labourers amongst whom craft skills were less prominent on the other. The tradesmen were almost equally divided between merchants and shopkeepers, the latter including booksellers, jewellers, innkeepers, butchers and haberdashers.

Finally, making up what was much more of a fair cross-section of the population of Bologna and its region were the barbers, domestic servants, carriers and launderers who made up some of the large body of service personnel in the town. The latter provided almost the same percentage of the conspirators as they did of the population as a whole, rather like the artisans, whereas professional people were greatly over-represented (especially when we remember that the conspirators came from a wide area and the statistics from Bologna alone). Landowners and tradesmen were slightly under-represented, and children, servants and especially the poor greatly so. In the neighbouring towns, although workers played a part – the two people who were killed in Forlì being a tailor and a legal employee – the evidence suggests that graduates, landowners and sometimes even some sharecroppers played a larger role. Obviously many of the first two groups would have played leading parts, but the cross-class pattern of participation suggests that much of the community was involved in grass-roots opposition to the authorities.

Farther up the Po valley the popular element in the troubles was usually less marked. Thus in Modena the revolutionary government was wholly made up of nobles and lawyers, and even in the lower Modenese where fiscal grievances counted for a good deal in mobilising support for Menotti it was advocates, doctors, chemists and employees who rallied to him. However, in the capital there was also a crowd of masons, joiners and some rural wage earners which helped to make the activities of the former possible. In Reggio d'Emilia artisans were singularly prominent among those arrested for complicity in the troubles, along with peasants, tradesmen and the expected members of the middle class. In Parma, however, the popular element was a great deal less prominent and one list of 415 suspects was dominated by officials, nobles and landowners, with only six artisans, although there were also stories of cobblers and tailors waving tricolour flags at times.

There was a good deal of violence latent even in the more pacific Italian protests. None the less, in places where there was only political action, similar patterns can be seen. Along with the lawyers and officials who dominated the Pressverein in south-west Germany there were thousands of artisans and even a few manufacturers. In the Vaud the Casino Club committee which led the efforts of the radicals in December 1830 was made up of two lawyers, a bookseller and a legal agent, while the crowds certainly included artisans and small tradesmen along with the majority of farmers. Alphonse Bourquin, after all, was himself a wine grower. Generally the Swiss movement included peasants, tradesmen, discontented artisans and professional people.

The evidence suggests that the republican movements which developed in France and Belgium after 1830 were very often composed largely of people from the middle classes, but this does not mean that the lower classes dropped out of politics. Recent investigation shows that movements like that in Lyons in 1834 and throughout the 1830s in Paris became increasingly autonomous as French artisans found that the purely political approach of republicanism did not offer as convincing a solution to their problems as did the ascent of mutual-aid societies, unions and socialist thinking. Hence, whereas in July 1830 young casual workers new to the capital have been seen as the most receptive to political influences, especially during the economic depression which affected the building trades, by the mid 1830s they were embarking on a different path. Something of the same can also be observed in the way British artisans and radicals – silk-ribbon makers in Coventry, shoemakers and others in London and handloom weavers in Preston, for instance – began to break away from the more established reformism of the political unions during the crises of the early 1830s. Whatever the limitations to their political consciousness, there is no denying that the artisans of the time were not motivated purely and simply by mindless opposition to their economic situation.

On the other hand, there was a strong element of social protest which underlay virtually all the movements of the time, whether urban or rural. In the towns the news of the July Days did appear as a chance of liberation from the pressures of population growth, capitalist organisation and, sometimes, mechanisation. So not merely were artisans active on the barricades in Paris and Brussels, but they can be seen both joining in troubles in other places – as did the hand and farm workers of the Hanau area of central Germany and craftsmen and service workers of Dresden and Leipzig – and mounting their own protests over their own conditions – as happened amongst the Belgian-based textile workers of Aix-la-Chapelle and the silk makers of Krefeldt, not to mention the more organised workers of London and Paris.

The reason why artisans were so prominent in all forms of protest was that the conditions of their working life made corporate action both necessary and easy. To begin with, artisans were not merely proletarian wage-slaves. Most worked in small units consisting of a master, two or three journeymen and some apprentices. In theory the apprentice could eventually rise through the hierarchy to become an independent master himself, so that the normal division of capital and labour was not really applicable, and it was only a little later on that, as Sewell shows, the journeymen began to separate from their patrons and arrogated to themselves the traditional rhetoric of the guilds. In 1830 there was still a good deal of solidarity amongst the artisan community which lent itself to corporate action, especially where the old guilds or *compagnonnages* had survived. This, coupled with the fact that they were highly skilled and usually sold their own produce – rather than leaving this to retailers – meant that they were in contact with the general public and had a marked sense of dignity, status and tradition. In some cases the last characteristic could often take a violent form, as it did amongst the sabre-bearing tailors of Warsaw. They believed they had a place in the world and they were easily upset by changes to established ways of doing things, to what Thompson has called the moral economy. Given that they were likely to have had a higher-than-average rate of literacy, it is not surprising either that they responded to liberal stimulae (especially when these suggested a chance of gaining political recognition) or that they blamed economic and social problems on government.

There was, of course, a second and economic reason for their behaviour. As we have seen the late 1820s and early 1830s were a period of considerable strain for them, with rising food-prices and increasing competition, whether from new provincial or foreign centres of production or from the new capitalist organisation of labour. Thus, skilled tailors and cabinet makers found themselves facing the competition of much less skilled operatives, each producing one element of a saleable product – for example, the drawers for a commode – on behalf of an entrepreneur who, by paying low piece-work rates, could undercut workshops capable of producing all kinds of suits and furniture. Since the guilds were on the decline and union organisation was but poorly developed, such craftsmen had little protection. Not surprisingly, they took violent action when they had the chance, sometimes against machines, as with the stocking knitters, but more often against the tools and work-places of the new-style mode of production. This was noticeable amongst Parisian hatters, for example, whose action was maintained after the initial explosion as the continuing political unease further depressed the market, especially for luxury goods.

Since such workers traditionally did not believe in competition they were incensed by the situation, and demanded that the liberty offered by the July Days should be shown in the reduction of hours, the raising of wages and the destruction of unfair competition. And all this they expected governments to do for them. The failure of regimes both new and old to oblige helped to spin out the malaise until the artisans lost heart or the government built up enough courage to curb their activities. Basically, it was such skilled and thoughtful workers who made possible much of the political changes of the early 1830s. It has been claimed, however, that in Brussels in August 1830, and more generally in Paris, it was the younger, less skilled workers employed in fetching, carrying and handling materials, notably in the building trades, who were most active and politically conscious. Such is probably true of Belgium, but the case for Paris is less convincing. Unfortunately, the sources do not allow us to resolve the question.

In any case, the situation of the urban worker, whatever his precise status, made him much more likely to take political and other action than the peasant majority of Europe's population. The peasantry, however, were not as uninterested in public affairs as is sometimes assumed. Malia's argument that peasants are only capable of mindless outbursts and cannot, save in a few Alpine valleys, sustain a state is far too patronising a view. It ignores, for a start, the dependence of Scandinavian democracy on peasant farmers, as well as the protests against feudal dues, internal tolls and taxes in Brunswick, Hesse-Kassel and Hanover. There was, too, a distinct correlation between the small-farm districts of south-west Germany and the success of liberal ideas there. There are even some indications that the *braccianti*, or wage labourers, of the Po valley may not have been totally apathetic, especially if encouraged by their landlords. Admittedly, the peasantry were often conservative and fearful of big cities and their ideas, but the political message of 1830 was not wholly lost on them, at least in the heartland zone. Further east and south the picture was indeed one of inertia at best and often, as in western Russia, downright hostility to revolutionaries and their message.

None the less, the rural community was essential to the wave of social protest which initiated the whole revolutionary crisis in 1830. Rural violence in England, France and the Rhineland was the most obvious example, but we should also remember that some peasants were involved in the August riots in Brussels, as well as providing considerable support for political reform in central Germany by their attacks on noble landlords, tax offices and customs barriers. Such actions involved a variety of country dwellers. In Brunswick and Hanover, landless peasants seem to have been most active, whereas in England the Swing riots were the work of younger but relatively skilled and well-paid specialists; reapers, mowers, ploughmen and craftsmen generally. In Switzerland the owners of medium-to-large farms seem to have contributed most to the Regeneration, although this was not uniformly the case, as the Vaud shows. Finally, in France the whole rural community seems to have taken part, including, as in England, the many artisans who lived and worked there: carters, wheelwrights and innkeepers. In Issodun, for example, those arrested included two tanners, a weaver, a roofer, a shoemaker, a cabinet maker and six *vignerons*. The last seem to have been particularly active both in the south-west – for instance, in the Aude and the Dordogne – and in central and eastern departments like the Cher, the Doubs, the Indre and the Yonne. As with the forest dwellers, each kind of farming seems to have contributed its share to the general social disorder and, through this, to the general dynamism of 1830.

Hence, while the governments may have been the major contenders for power, the other side needed to make a revolution was also present. If revolutions are a change in a wide variety of social activities brought about from below by violence, then the events of 1830 certainly qualify for the title. They may not have been mass revolts in the sense in which the more nationalistic twentieth century has come to understand them, but they involved a goodly element of the population, drawn from right across the social spectrum. For all that the leaders and real gainers came from the middle and upper classes, the analysis of participation in the events of 1830 makes it clear that they were not the only popular force contending for power. The special problems of the artisanate led to their being extremely well represented, and not only in social protest. They, like many more of the participants, also had political aims and interests. Indeed, there was a fusion both of motives and of roles in popular participation in 1830. Thus the gentry in Poland provided not only the rank and file, but also the leaders of the war of liberation; a war the success of which was severely handicapped by the primacy they gave to their own economic interests.

One of the key dynamics of the revolutions of 1830 was, then, the interrelationship between the political aspirations of the professional middle classes and other élites – who necessarily had to play a leading role in what was still a very poorly educated society – and the lower classes. Where the grievances of the latter took on a political colouring of their own – as happened, for example, in Paris, Brussels and, to some extent, Warsaw – the combination was hard to resist. Outside of such capital cities, however, the two strands did not often coalesce into a single powerful revolutionary movement of the type seen in the 1790s in France. None the less, their relationships always formed a complicated pattern in which the roles played by the two often overlapped and sometimes were almost reversed. As a consequence, the authorities had to face a far from negligible challenge from what must often have seemed like a real revolutionary party.

Yet, if the roles played by the two groups overlapped, the gains they made certainly did not. The lower classes benefited to only a marginal degree from the constitutional and other changes brought about by the events of 1830. The major gains went, as the analysis of élite participation would lead us to expect, not to any industrial bourgeoisie, but to the new notables; landlords, officials, lawyers, intellectuals and the like. As were the artisans who helped to make their successes possible, these were the products of a transitional society in which modern class divisions had not yet fully crystallised and in which not merely did questions of age, occupation and ethnicity play a role, but in which social motives were distinctly secondary to political ones. Thus there was an element of a generation gap in the struggle between liberalism and the establishment. Similarly, much more than social class, it was membership of élite groups like armies which often counted. However, neither the young nor the soldiery were as significant as they had been in 1820. As with the development of national impulses, 1830 represents a movement towards revolutions with a wider base in the community.

At the time, however, the major fissure was over political questions. Even the nobility could be deeply divided by them, as has become clear. This was no doubt the consequence of the growing awareness of political issues which had manifested itself since 1820, when it became clear that the Restoration was not going to live up to its promises. Arlettaz has gone as far as to argue that, in these early stages at least, liberalism had no social base but was a set of political issues and sympathies around which a diverse group of opposition interests could coalesce. Only later did it develop a class basis. There is something to be said for this view, although, while political questions were paramount in 1830, people were unconsciously contending for social power as well, and the social aftermath of 1830 was to be as significant as the more immediate and obvious political changes.

14   The Revolutions and Their Effects

In the long run one of the major effects of the events of 1830 was to be the intensification of new and bitter social divisions. This was not apparent at the time, particularly to the statesmen of Europe. Nor, one suspects, would they have been terribly impressed with the idea that in the main the revolutions of 1830 were limited ones, caused by the inept dealings of governments with a complicated mixture of politically frustrated members of the professional middle classes and generally aggrieved artisans. Statesmen tended to be obsessed by the whole phenomenon and did not see that, although both groups were necessary for revolution and political change, they did not gain from it equally. The political effects with which they were, understandably enough, concerned seemed rather more threatening and widespread than some historians came to think in retrospect. Hence one dyspeptic English observer remarked that 'the *chemin de fer* is one of the very few, if indeed it be not the only, advantage derived to Belgium from the events of 1830'. All the rest in his view was disadvantage, not to say disaster.

Historians, on the other hand, have tended to play down the effects of 1830 because with the passage of time, bringing with it both the events of 1848 and the dramatic restructuring of Europe which took place between 1859 and 1878, their limited nature became more apparent. Yet, just as the events of 1830 were real revolutions in their own fashion, so they did leave a significant legacy to Europe, even though this was not always comprehended by the heirs, whether these came from the establishment or the opposition. To try to rectify this, and to develop the analysis of the wherefores of the revolutions of 1830, we must look at the effects of the revolts at three levels: the local, the national and the international. And in each case, in the short term, it was indeed the political implications of the events which were the most immediate and the most striking, although as has already been suggested they were not always fully understood by contemporaries.

At the local level there were often quite noticeable regional differences in the way the effects of the revolutions were experienced. For example, the east of France was particularly sensitive to the diplomatic situation which resulted from the change of regime. Many people there, notably officials, understandably saw themselves as being in the firing-line of any invasion and sought to persuade the government to adopt more vigorous foreign and defence policies by joining the Associations Nationales in large numbers until they were warned off by the government of Casimir

Périer. In Belgium a similar phenomenon can be seen in Limburg and Luxembourg, the long-term future of which remained unsettled because of the refusal of William I to accept the London Conference settlement. Different parts of the Old Polish Commonwealth, under varying foreign control, also reacted differently to the promptings and probings of both Russians and Polish émigrés, so that it was in Austrian Galicia that trouble was to develop in the 1830s and 1840s. Even where there were no such military and nationalist pressures, localities experienced the effects of revolution in different ways. Thus it was the south-west of Germany, which had not been really involved in the initial troubles, which was to lead the fight to consolidate and extend constitutional government throughout the Bund. And, in France, Lyons was to play an absolutely crucial part in the development of social feeling and organisation after 1830 because of the problems and militancy of its silk weavers. Similarly, in England the nature of the Chartist response to the failure of the Reform Bill to carry political liberalisation very far has been shown to have varied from town to town according to the structure of the local economy.

Generally speaking, the towns were to be the major centres of concern and debate after 1830, although their prominence in the cases of Lausanne and Bologna could lead lesser towns and country areas to resist their lead and to try to prevent their exploiting the political gains of 1830 to the detriment of other parties. Outside the towns the effect of the revolutions could be to stimulate conservatism and to encourage the peasantry to turn against the liberals. Thus in places as dissimilar as the Grand Duchy of Luxembourg, Poland and the Vendée there were many examples of rural violence. In the first the Tornaco band of brigands operated for a time with some success against the Belgian authorities, while in Poland the peasants went even farther and helped the Russian occupation forces to coerce nationalist landlords. In the last example, on the other hand, the local peasantry were not willing to turn their sympathy for the Duchess of Berri into concrete action. However, perhaps we should not exaggerate the extent of such local diversity and dissidence, because the trend generally after 1830 was for localism to give way to more national issues and action, partly because of the way the rather disparate outbursts of 1830 had failed to do more than gnaw away at the strength of the Restoration establishment. Only in Germany, as Wallenberger has argued, was the stress on development through the emancipation of the individual princedoms – the so-called *kleinstaaterei* approach to inification – to remain important. Amongst Italian liberals and Polish exiles broader ambitions began to make themselves felt. No doubt such things as the Mazzinian movement caused statesmen a concern which was not mitigated by evidence of agrarian conservatism or the divorce between the various types of social radicalism.

In other words, though one of the effects of the events of 1830 was to intensify political and, to a lesser extent, social debate and conflict locally, the shape of the impact of 1830 cannot really be appreciated until we turn to the national level. In political terms the events of 1830 had a reasonably positive effect. A good number of states were able to maintain and develop the constitutional gains which were so prominent a feature of the crisis. Thus, not merely was the French Charter of 1814 somewhat liberalised, and hesitant steps in the same direction taken in parts of Germany, but in Switzerland and Belgium major and influential changes were also made. Although the attempt to revise the Swiss federal constitution of 1815 petered out, the cantonal reforms opened the way to a far more active parliamentary and constitutional life than before, and ultimately this was to help bring about revision at the federal level. Thus in the Ticino the constitution of 1830 is still spoken of as 'the first love of the Ticinese people'. Even more significantly, the Belgian constitution of 1831 created one of the most advanced political systems (with the most genuinely limited monarchy) outside Britain, and this was to have a considerable influence on a good many countries when, in succeeding years, they came to draft their own new constitutions. And, obviously, the passage of the Reform Bill in Britain and the establishment of provincial assemblies in Denmark did much to advance the cause of genuine parliamentary government in northern Europe.

Even in countries which might have been expected to see the extinction of the very idea of constitutional government, the events of 1830 often saw continuing gains. Thus, while the Russians effectively annulled constitutional life in Poland, despite the pretence of the 1832 Statute, they did maintain the Organic Regulations in Moldavia and Wallachia, while at the same time rewarding the Finns for their loyalty with more flexible and sympathetic administration. The Polish Organic Statute did, moreover, represent at least a token admission that rule by mere fiat or unstructured diktat was no longer as acceptable as it had been. Similarly, while Cardinal Bernetti rejected the suggestions of the powers, his July Edict showed some recognition that political life had to be tolerated and structured. Finally, despite a vast amount of resistance in Iberia, the early 1830s were to see both countries embark on the path of constitutional monarchy. So, even if such gains were often limited and sometimes short-lived, they still made pure absolutism harder to sustain. Even conservatives began to see that their cause could benefit from involving people in its political defence.

Along with such changes in the basic rules of the game came new institutions and political practices. Where institutions are concerned, the revolutions gave a boost to civic militias, for example, which were restored in France, expanded in Belgium and, for a while tolerated in the Papal States. Legal procedures were also revised in a number of countries, with changes in the penal codes, greater stress on juries and more acceptance of the realities of the idea of equality before the law. The revolutions also made an impact on the church, education and administration. In Switzerland and Italy the established churches managed to come through the crisis relatively unscathed, despite the fact that the threats to their position had become much more obvious. Hence, despite the role which it had played in liberating Belgium, liberal Catholicism came under considerable pressure from Rome in the 1830s.

Yet, all in all, the church had to be more active in politics because of the events of 1830. It could no longer survive on its traditional assumption of superiority, particularly as another institutional effect of 1830 was to encourage education, notably in Belgium, Switzerland and France – through the Guizot Law of 1833 – as well as in the countries of south-eastern Europe. Finally, some people saw the revolutions as producing a gadarene rush for office in bureaucracies which began to expand greatly after 1830. Certainly there were purges in both the prefectorial corps and the ministerial staffs in France, with people like the son of Marshal Bourmont, the royalist commander in Algeria and Portugal, being ousted from the Ministry of War in Paris and some heroes of the barricades finding their way into office. And, locally, failure to obtain office could lead disappointed liberals to join the radical movement, as happened in the Allier in France, or even the forces of conservatism, as sometimes happened in Belgium.

Besides gently encouraging parliamentary government and reforming institutions, not to mention sustaining a few progressive rulers, 1830 also stimulated informal and grass-roots political life. In the most advanced countries – like Belgium, Britain and Switzerland – real political parties and movements began to emerge, whether built round the religious issue as in the first, or on attitudes to the extent of liberalisation as in the other two states. The 1830s saw the development not merely of Whigs and Conservatives in Britain, but also of the Chartist movement and the radical Protestant party in Switzerland. Amongst many people the revolutions of 1830 stimulated desires for a much more radical restructuring of politics, with direct democracy and universal suffrage animating an assertive and populist nationalism. Sometimes such desires went even farther, so that there was a great boost amongst intellectuals and workers to socialist thinking, which began to diverge from mere republicanism in France. Amongst the Polish exiles the emergence of quasi-communistic ideas in the ranks of the former soldiers in the Polish Democratic Society who formed the Polish People Group in Portsmouth was notable. Such political activity often had to revert to subversive forms since it was regarded as being as much of a threat by new regimes as it had been by the old ones, and in some cases, notably Spain, it could take on a notably reactionary character.

Yet perhaps equally important as the impetus that 1830 gave to radicalism because of the limited changes it brought about was the stimulus it offered to the development of political life, organisation and solutions to problems. The invention of politics, which began in the first

French revolution, was certainly speeded up by 1830. As Alan Sked has said, 'political awareness in Europe increased dramatically in the period after 1815', so that even crowds were aware of what was happening in other countries and supported particular political ideas, as they had begun to do in the crises of 1830 themselves. This was uncomfortably evident to the statesmen of the time.

According to Malia, indeed, not merely did 1830 renew the positive political effects of 1789 in Germany, but it also began the calling into question of established constitutional monarchy because of the social conflicts it initiated. In his view, Marx's language was really the language that became necessary and current with the July Monarchy, the period marking the beginnings of the rule of finance capital. As Balzac once remarked, 1830 led to the three orders being replaced by two classes; or, to put it more ideologically, 'it marked the definitive defeat of aristocratic by bourgeois power', leaving the latter to face up to the challenge of the emerging proletariat in Hobsbawm's formulation. In fact, this is to anticipate a great deal. It is also somewhat extreme as a description of French society at the time, and even more so when applied to other countries in Europe. In fact neither in social nor in economic terms was there any major change after 1830, and such changes as there were did not really compare with changes in the political sphere.

Thus it is true that the aristocracy generally lost ground as a result of 1830. In Switzerland they vanished from view; in France they lost their access to a hereditary Chamber of Peers and their places in the prefectorial and other corps; and in Britain they lost control of some of their pocket boroughs. Yet they did not cease to exist, and the revolutions, as in Belgium, could even bring new elements of the aristocracy into power, whether because of their efforts in the actual events or because of new creations such as those by the liberal leadership in Portugal or the Orleanist monarchy. And, had Wellington not given way in 1832, there could have been a whole new generation of peers in Britain. Even in Poland, although the revolt was unsuccessful, the *szlachta* remained in control of their lands, and to some extent strengthened their position by turning their backs on the patriotic movement in Galicia and elsewhere. So, while the effect of 1830 may have been to trim and change the power of the aristocracy, it did not seriously undermine its general standing. It was to take many generations before the aristocracy was really defeated and demoted.

Similarly, although the revolutions were to open up new channels of social mobility and change, it was not the case that the industrial or financial bourgeoisie were the sole gainers. The revolutions usually meant greater provision of and access to things like education, administration and politics, which could of course benefit the middle classes; and governments were also to do more for economic development after 1830 than they had before. Even the Russians and the Vatican felt it necessary to create investment banks. Yet the evidence does not suggest that the industrial middle class won most advantage from the new opportunities. In Belgium it took them a long time to adjust to the new regime, and even in Britain it has been reckoned that there were no more businessmen in the reformed House of Commons than there had been in the old one. Much the same was true of the French Chamber of Deputies, which turned out to be increasingly dominated by officials and landowners. Similarly, journalists and other professionals and intellectuals were to be prominent not merely there, but also in parts of Switzerland, Germany, Italy and Belgium. Bankers there were, and even some factory owners, but basically it was the middle classes of the *ancien régime* who made and benefited from the changes of 1830, not a new industrialist class.

Admittedly, further down the social scale it is hard to see many gainers, or even a great deal of change. In the towns the numbers of artisans continued to grow, and their position deteriorated as a result; and nowhere did they gain sufficient political power after 1830 to do much about this. Yet very few of them moved immediately into the factory-based working class. As late as 1847 in France there were still 3.7 million artisans to 1.3 million factory workers, and the average size of production unit amongst the latter was still only ten. Elsewhere on the Continent, save in parts of Wallonia and eastern Switzerland, the situation was even more traditional than this. And even in Britain the role of artisans in the Chartist movement has often been noted.

On the land, the revolutions certainly helped peasant emancipation, politically in Switzerland and legally in Germany, where the serfs were freed in Hesse-Kassel, Saxe-Altenburg, Hanover, Saxony and Brunswick between November 1831 and October 1832. But there is no evidence that their economic position improved greatly. The problems of English labourers and Irish cottars continued to deteriorate despite their violent protests in the early 1830s. Structures and problems remained much the same on the land as they did in the towns, and the apocalyptic protests proved to be a considerable deception, perhaps even counter-productive. Indeed, where the economy as a whole is concerned, the major effects of the revolutions in the short term may have been to intensify difficulties. The upheavals, threats of war and, in the case of Belgium, the disruption of an integrated economy caused a marked period of crisis. This was particularly the case in Iberia, where civil war tended to extinguish the faint signs of economic recovery which had been visible in the late 1820s.

Elsewhere, and nobably in Britain, this was much less of a problem and growth soon resumed, or, as in Italy, remained as noticeable by its absence as it had always been. Especially where the revolutions brought to power regimes more sympathetic to the idea of economic develpment, the improvement could be marked. Thus, in Switzerland, although the Regeneration did not bring the complete economic unification which some had looked for, there was a period of consolidation and concentration. The burning of the main cotton-weaving factory in Uster in Zurich in 1832 shows both the extent of mechanisation and rationalisation there as well as resistance to it. Watch production in the Neuchâtelois Jura, moreover, was to double between 1827 and 1846. Perhaps the most spectacular changes, however, were to be achieved in Belgium, where in 1834 the new government, endeavouring to reverse the precipitate slump caused by the loss of access to the Dutch market, committed itself to a carefully planned programme of railway development designed to make cross-continental trade-patterns run through the country. Thanks to this and the development of investment banking, large-scale manufacturing began to increase dramatically so that by 1840 the country was second only to Britain in coal production, volume of steam-power and mileage of railways. And it was also running a close third to Britain and Switzerland in cotton-processing and the use of pig iron. Moreover, growth in both Belgium and Switzerland helped to stimulate develpment in neighbouring parts of the heartland, including north-east France, western Germany and northern Italy.

Yet all this was to take a good deal of time, and throughout the 1830s and 1840s continental Europe remained primarily agrarian, and even such industrial development as there was remained highly traditional, as was shown by the continuing predominance of charcoal over coke furnaces in France and Belgium. Not until 1839 and 1841 were Factory Acts called for in Prussia and France; whereas a number of German states actually strengthened their guild systems as a result of the revolutions. This reflected the continuing pressure on the artisans, who were eventually to rise in Silesia in 1844. Their problems, like those of the peasantry, were aggravated both by the continuing increase in Europe's population, which rose from 230 million in 1830 to 274 million by 1850, despite the beginnings of emigration, and by the gradual expansion of the scale of commercial operations, symbolised by the creation of the Zollverein. In other words, although the rate of change continued to increase after the brief hiccup in 1830, the European economy was far from being transformed overnight, and the pressures which had helped to bring about the revolutions remained unassuaged.

Furthermore, many of the changes which did take place were imperceptible ones, lost to sight amidst the flames of social protest and political upheaval. Hobsbawm, for instance, has also claimed that the events of 1830 produced fundamental change in all aspects of life, including shattering once and for all the settlement of 1815 and the idea of intervention by congresses to prevent change. As Map 12 makes clear, there were no wholesale changes and the major alteration was the creation of the new kingdom of Belgium, and even then its existence along with that of the Grand Duchy of Luxembourg was not to be clarified for some time. Developments in the south-east of Europe, of course, had led to the

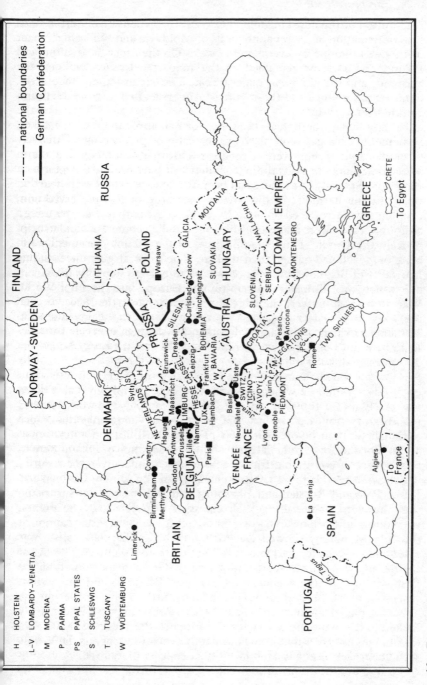

12 *Europe, about 1835*

national boundaries
German Confederation

H   HOLSTEIN
L-V LOMBARDY-VENETIA
M   MODENA
P   PARMA
PS PAPAL STATES
S   SCHLESWIG
T   TUSCANY
W   WURTEMBURG

NORWAY-SWEDEN

FINLAND

RUSSIA

LITHUANIA

POLAND
■ Warsaw

GALICIA

MOLDAVIA

WALLACHIA

SLOVAKIA

HUNGARY

SLOVENIA

CROATIA

SERBIA

MONTENEGRO

OTTOMAN EMPIRE

GREECE

CRETE

To Egypt

PRUSSIA

SILESIA

● Carlsbad ● Cracow
● Munchengratz

BOHEMIA
● Dresden
● Leipzig

Brunswick

AUSTRIA

● Frankfurt
W BAVARIA

HESSE-CASSEL
LIMBURG-CASSEL
Lille ●
Maastricht

Sylt(S)
H
DENMARK

NETHERLANDS
Hague ■
Antwerp ●
Brussels ●
London ●
Namur ●
LUX
Hambach ■

BELGIUM

Coventry ●
Birmingham ●
Merthyr ●

BRITAIN

Limerick ●

Paris ■

VENDÉE

FRANCE

Lyon ●
Grenoble ●

Basel ●
Neuchâtel ●
SWITZ
TICINO
Uster ●

SAVOY L-V
Turin ●
PIEDMONT

Pesaro ●
Ancona ●
LEGATIONS
PS

● Rome
TWO SICILIES

Algiers ●
To France

La Granja ●

SPAIN

PORTUGAL

R. Tagus

recognition of the new kingdom of Greece, the expansion of Serbia, and the confirmation of the separate status of Moldavia and Wallachia. None of this was undone by events in the west. On the other hand, although Poland and Cracow remained on the map, the former had no real existence and the latter was under threat. The expansion of Modena by dynastic inheritance and the seizure of Algiers and Crete from the Porte counted for very little.

In any case, there had been no formal abrogation of the 1815 settlement. Changes took place in the realm of practice rather than of principle. And, if there were no congresses to organise intervention, there were conferences to assist the independence of Belgium and the reform of the Papal States, just as there had been for Greece. There were fears of war, but the harmony of the powers was more or less preserved and problems were resolved as often by diplomacy as they were by force, although troops were made available to the Italian conference and to help restrain the Dutch. Thus, the principles of the Vienna settlement were bent or developed rather than broken. The general guarantee of the neutrality of Belgium, for instance, was an important step forward, albeit one which was ultimately to help plunge Europe into the First World War. Relationships were therefore less strained than in the 1820s, despite the way the eastern *entente* was renewed by the Convention of Münchengratz in 1833, and a Quadruple Alliance emerged between Britain, France and the two Iberian states. In fact the eastern question did more to disturb the peace.

So, while the relationships of the European powers remained relatively civilised, it would be wrong to think they were terribly cordial. France was rarely if ever fully trusted, and Palmerston tended to work with her mainly to restrain her. In fact 1830 produced a Continent rather more nationalistic than before, with new or latent hostilities in a number of areas. The failure to remodel Italy and the absorption of Poland were to be a source of continuing friction and unrest; while, given the rivalries which were revealed in 1830 between Belgian and Dutch, German and Dane, Pole and Russian and Habsburg and Italian, it is not surprising that the word 'nationalism' itself emerged in the 1830s. The French tricolour might still be used as a symbol, but the self-interested caution of the July Monarchy showed that Mazzini's belief that nationalism was essentially a force for harmony was doomed from the outset. The end of the decade was thus to see the first Franco-German confrontation, the first stirrings of the language issue inside Belgium, and the earliest responses to the Magyar revival in the Habsburg Empire. So, despite the hopes of pan-Scandinavianists and of the Polish émigrés who naïvely looked to Germans and Romanians for support, the impact of 1830 was to encourage the forces that would ultimately destroy not merely the Vienna settlement, but also any kind of rational concert of Europe.

To sum up, the events of 1830 helped to overthrow absolute monarchy in Portugal and to undermine it in Spain, although this was to be the work not of the valiant but foolhardy invaders of 1830 but of civil war. In France a slightly liberalised constitutional monarchy under a new ruler was catapulted to power by the July Days, but it remained isolated not just abroad because of acts like the occupation of Ancona but also at home because of the resentment its caution aroused amongst those who had helped to overthrow the old monarchy or who had been excited by the hopes it generated. In somewhat similar manner Britain's reformed Parliament found itself faced by Chartism and Switzerland's Regenerated cantonal goverments by more radical (and more conservative) forces, as well as seeing a good deal of more positive political development. In Scandinavia the influence of absolutism was checked and the peasants began to make their presence felt in politics. For a while the German states had made similar gains; and, although these were to be partially reversed, such events were to encourage political aspirations at both the national and the particularist level. In Belgium a new state was carved out of what the Vienna settlement had regarded as a *cordon sanitaire*, creating a nation which was to inspire Europe both constitutionally and economically. In the south-east of Europe such changes as had been in the wind, like the emancipation of Serbia and Greece, were confirmed by 1830. And finally, although the revolts failed most signally in central Italy and the Congress Kingdom, the very failures were to have a long-term effect on the future of the two countries.

In such countries the events of 1830 were obviously highly significant and a starting-point for future thinking and activity. Again, if on the general or European level such changes were not as extensive or as deep as those of 1848, they were still sufficiently numerous and unsettling to worry the politicians of the time. Hence a few were moved to a greater awareness of the need for political flexibility. The majority, however, like the Austrians of the Vormarz, tended to ignore the obvious evidence that 1830 had produced of a wide desire for political rights. This kind of refusal to take 1830 seriously, together with the absence of dramatic and visible social and economic changes and the relative caution of the revolutionary leaders themselves, was to mean that 1830 was to be a beginning as well as an end. In other words, its very limitations were one of its most significant features, rather than being something to be deplored as many historians have done. It showed that the relatively facile idea, derived from 1789, that European problems could be solved simply through political means, was not sustainable. The failure of 1830 to knock out the main bastions of the establishment or to create a political system open to all forced many of the disfranchised and their allies to embark on a long period of debate and experiment to find better ways of bringing this about. Hence, as John Gillis has said, 1830 was another attempt to restart the engine of political growth, continuing the mobilisation begun in the French Revolutionary era and then held up by the Restoration. It was to open as many doors by its failures as by its successes.

And because the major reaction of statesmen and establishments, whether old or new, once the initial crisis had faded, was to turn their backs on the problem, the opposition began to look to the social dimension to achieve its aims. So, although Poles and Italians began to discuss the possibility of seeking liberation by guerilla warfare in the future, and Mazzini and Blanqui to seek more broadly based and better-organised *coups*, the most important strand in this debate was the insistence on bringing a social dimension into any future revolution, symbolised by the Belgian exile Louis de Potter's booklet *De la révolution à faire*. Whereas in 1830 the elements of political and social protest had never quite coalesced, this became an aim for the future. The continuance of the economic problems of the old society and the gradual emergence of industrialisation were to make this aim increasingly relevant. In a way, we can say that, although the revolutions of 1830 were not brought about by class rivalries, they none the less did make these more likely and bitter. Unfortunately, not everyone realised this; and just as statesmen wrote off peasant and artisan unruliness as a regrettable but passing environmental distraction, so professional revolutionaries ignored in their search for technical improvements both the inherent national divisions of the opposition and the limits to support for really wholehearted revolutionary action. Like their opponents, they were largely blind to the extent to which governments had the solution in their own hands. Both sides had hoped or feared something much worse in 1830 than actually developed and failed to see that, although the revolutions were in line with what the leadership then wanted, they were still ultimately explosive.

15 Conclusions: The Significance of 1830

The fact that relatively few people recognised 1830 as a turning-point in European history does not make the crisis of that year any less significant. Although Kieniewicz has reminded us that anniversaries alway make historians exaggerate the importance of the event they are studying, it remains true that 1830 was a dress rehearsal for the future, even if the critics preferred to sleep through it. The way it ended one revolutionary tradition and ushered in another was conveniently symbolised by the appearance of both the black flag of anarchy and the red flag of socialism in France in 1831–2. Had the events been as half-hearted as some critics claim, it is doubtful whether people would have protested as vigorously after 1830 as they did. In fact the outcomes of revolution in 1830 were in line with what many of its leaders wanted, and the process by which these ends were reached was certainly experienced as a real revolution, locally as well as centrally. Talk of the limited nature of the revolutions of 1830 thus rather misses the point. For 1830 was a serious revolution, and it was its basic nature, not its failure to meet more grandiose ends devised by outsiders, which gave it its historical significance.

To a considerable extent the revolutions did achieve the targets of their middle-class leaders, albeit only briefly in some cases. Their aims had been very general and hastily devised: a search for a return to normal participatory politics and for concrete domestic changes. They wanted things like a better distribution of power in Switzerland, the remedy of specific grievances in Belgium, and a minimal share in responsibility in the Papal States. Only when these were not conceded did they move on to more deliberate attempts at state-building. They objected to arbitrariness in all its forms, but by and large their aims were more a litany of things they did not like than a finished programme for the millennium.

Even radicals like the cadets had no precise vision of the free Poland they sought to establish, while those of the Café Lointier group in Paris were willing to leave everything to a referendum or to the kind of constituent assembly called in Belgium and the Swiss cantons, thereby creating a political vacuum which more pragmatic politicians could fill. Hence the latter seem to have owed more to the rationalism of the Enlightenment than to the new enthusiasms of the Romantic era, except where national feelings were concerned. Even then few of them were deliberate revisionists in so far as the Vienna settlement was concerned. Nor did their social aims go very far. So the kind of constitutional and political outcomes we have already seen were really very close to what people seem to have wanted.

Moreover, getting that far did involve a process of change which was experienced by society as a real revolution. Although in lesser towns this might mean no more than a few proclamations, a nominal decision to create a national guard, and the flying of a new flag – once paid for by a ten-franc piece from a harassed mayor in Chaumont in an attempt to divert an angry crowd – there was real turmoil in many centres. The revolution did not just come from the capital with the stagecoach. The example of a provincial town like Namur shows that the whole gamut of violence and political mobilisation could be found there, too. And from Namur the impulse went out to smaller towns and villages in the surrounding area. Hence people throughout Europe saw change achieved by revolutionary upheaval.

If this was not wholly understood at the time, it has also been misconstrued by historians. Thus at least one strand in the conventional view of 1830 is erroneous. There are others. The revolutions of 1830 were not namby-pamby splutterings. They were serious revolutionary experiences. In other words, when considering the wherefores of 1830 we must look not only at its immediate historical impact, but also at its significance in terms of historiography. The conventional picture is indeed flawed by virtue of its inadequate appreciation not merely of the meaning of what happened in 1830, but also of the actual happenings of the time. By now it has become clear that 1830 was not as pallid and simplistic as has been claimed. It was not limited – as is often implied – to a few capital cities; it was not brought about by secret societies nor by some mechanical response to the July Days devoid of real roots in local problems; it did not operate only on the diplomatic stage; and it did not lead to the enthronement of the new industrial bourgeoisie.

To begin with, the truth is that the revolutions did not happen in merely a few capital cities nor even – as the franco-centrism of much Anglo-Saxon writing on European history leads us to suspect – just in France. It affected the whole of the European heartland. Indeed, the larger dimension of the crisis showed that in some ways Europe was a real community at the time. For not merely did the great powers agree to act moderately, but they also devised new diplomatic means of resolving the problems caused by the crisis. Furthermore, the social élite was not alone in its consciousness of the crisis, but shared it with the lower classes of town and country, who often responded as well to the news from Paris and elsewhere, showing that there was a growing awareness of politics on a European scale. Without this general involvement political change would have been much less likely to have been conceded inside individual countries. Perhaps this was not integration as we now understand it, but none the less it was a system of interrelationships. So, too, was the crisis far more than a momentary explosion in July, August and September 1830; but a general crisis in all phases of which the Continent was intimately involved. So 1830 was a crisis not merely broader in scope than often is admitted but also a good deal more threatening and enduring.

A second point where the received version falls down is that this upheaval was too deep to have been caused by either conspirators or French agents. In fact it was the result of a long-standing political malaise with which Europe had been pregnant since the Revolutionary era. The actual upheaval was induced by the social crisis at the end of the decade and delivered by the symbolic effects of the July Days. The events of Paris did not produce the complaints and constraints which ultimately were responsible for revolution, but they greatly affected the way that oppositions – and especially governments – dealt with them. Political change, though teetering on the brink of violence in some cases, could be carried through without disturbance if properly handled. Not surprisingly, Charles White, a contemporary observer of the Belgian scene, quoted Bacon's dictum that 'the surest way to prevent sedition (if the times do bear it) is to take away the matter of them: for if there be fuel prepared, it is hard to tell whence the spark shall come that shall set it on fire'.

The inflammable situation, of course, was not a purely transnational phenomenon. As well as family resemblances, there were marked individual characteristics in the various countries. Situations varied as much as did government responses. Both the national and the transnational dimensions were essential to the making of the crisis, although the conventional image tends to exaggerate either the one or the other. Thus, while all shared in the general crisis, the movements in Switzerland were concerned above everything else to secure the honouring of existing political commitments; those in France were a combination of social protest and political miscalculation on both sides; the Belgians were pitchforked into creating a nation when they could not obtain the practical concessions they sought; whereas the Poles were swept along by romantic nationalism. In Italy and northern Europe cautious hopes for better government were transformed into more drastic changes by the differing government responses. Only in the south-east was there insufficient domestic pressure to produce change, showing that the external side of the crisis was of itself inadequate to produce the kinds of political change people in 1830 wanted. For, although there was no single model of revolution in 1830, the existence of domestic crisis was essential for any kind of response to the July Days.

A fourth point where the conventional image can be faulted is that, although the events of 1830 were basically political, their political nature was not, as is even now still asserted, restricted to diplomatic means and ends. For, if the revolutions of 1830 were endogenous as well as exogenous, it follows that domestic political processes must have been essential to the crisis, even if they have been overlooked by some historians. Throughout Europe there were crises of participation and politicisation which governments could, and sometimes did, turn into revolutions of legitimacy. The role of government was as crucial in the dynamic of revolution as it had been in its causes. Political activity may have been somewhat restricted, and certainly no real revolutionary movements like those of the French Revolutionary era emerged; the time-span of certain individual crises being still too brief and the events too spontaneous for more than the rudiments of an ideology beyond the desire to be citizens rather than subjects to evolve amongst radical participants. None the less, 1789, was obviously not the last revolution in which political matters predominated over social ones. This is also true of 1830.

Yet the dynamic of 1830 also owed a great deal to the spontaneous unleashing of the kinds of social protest endemic in traditional society. These were intensified, first, by the demographic and economic pressures of the time, and then by the effects of the revolutions themselves. The way this vital aspect has been played down in favour of an erroneous stress on the supposed relationship of the revolutions to the Industrial Revolution is the final point which illustrates the inadequacy of the conventional image. For 1830 was not the first revolution 'for capitalism, in capitalism' as has been said. It was much broader and more old-fashioned than this. The revolutions were carried forward by the joint efforts of the old middle class and the artisans, and the latter acted for political reasons as well as for social ones. If the alliance so dramatically portrayed by Delacroix was to be ruptured because of the revolutions, it was still essential to the events themselves. In any case, the middle classes who led the movements did not always wish to oust the old élites, or even to rule directly themselves. There was more continuity beween the old and the new élite across 1830 than has been admitted. Not till much later did the nature of middle-class participation really change.

The revolutions of 1830, in sum, were not revolutions of a new kind, whether social or national. They were mixed revolutions somewhat like those of 1789: a series of interrelated yet also highly individual revolts which, if not truly mass movements, certainly had a broad base in society. They were far from being fortuitous, having deep roots in the normal political and social processes of the Restoration era. They were not the work of a few democratic dons, let alone of aggressive factory-owners, but of a wide if diffuse coalition, not so much struggling against the ruling class of the *ancien régime* as reacting somewhat involuntarily to insecure and unreliable governments. That there was revolution rather than peaceful political change was more often than not the fault of the establishment itself. Its fears and errors combined to conjure up the very demon it had sought to exorcise. With such a turning-point sprung on both sides in the way it was, it is not surprising that 1830 evolved in the moderate way it did. Had it been the kind of revolution which critics have imagined it to be, the subsequent development of Europe would have been very different.

Such a view of the nature and significance of 1830, which sees its limitations as essential to its place in European history rather than as a lamentable error, obviously clashes with what the Eldar still remember among the histories of the kings. No doubt that, in so far as the wherefores of 1830 are concerned, there is still a lot of argument to come, and the somewhat tentative ideas advanced here may not survive unscathed. If the image and interpretation change, so be it as long as 1830 is for once remembered and further investigated. The materials are there. Previously their use has been rendered particularly difficult because the whole geography of the period has been shrouded in obscurity. If the present work manages at least to delineate the frontiers of 1830 more clearly, by showing why there were revolts throughout Europe and especially what took place in them, then it will have served its purpose, even if the interpretation finally comes to differ from that advanced here. Just as the revolutions of 1830 stood at the end of one phase of political modernisation and left the way open for another, so this study may end the prehistory of 1830 and leave the way free for something better.

For a work such as this can only be a prolegomena to a better understanding of 1830. No one book, particularly one written on the basis of restricted primary research, could hope to provide a definitive portrait of 1830, especially bearing in mind the problems inherent in the documentation presently available. All we can hope is that the snapshots offered here will both provide students of 1830 with something to go on as well as conveying something of the delight there is in investigating such obscure provinces. For to test and refine the ideas advanced here much more work will be needed. Such work, however, must treat Europe in its entirety if it is to be successful. No partial studies will really avoid both the Scylla of mononationalist historiography and the Charybdis of assumed uniformity.

Whether models of revolution, especially those borrowed uncritically from the French experience, will help in such an endeavour remains unproven. It is probably that the events of 1830 were too diverse to fit into one pattern, despite their family relationships. There may be more to be gained by using the insights of normal social science to help explicate the many things which still remain unclear about the process of change in 1830 than by treating 1830 as a kind of separate category of revolutionary super-event, which it definitely was not. It was part of real life and is best understood as such. Only when the events of 1830 are a great deal better known than they are now will they be able to make the contribution they should to the theory of revolution.

Admittedly the past experience of the historiography of 1830 does not encourage us to think that the conventional image will change dramatically. Just as Delacroix has been over-used and misunderstood, so no doubt the Doom of 1830 is to be ignored and misconceived. Yet the story of how the men of 1830 felt compelled to seek to change the political conditions under which they lived is an honourable one which does deserve a proper place in the histories of the peoples of old. The events of that time were significant both for Europe itself and for its historiography. They deserve to be judged as they were and not as others require them to have been. This should now be possible. Whether it will be so is another matter altogether.

Bibliographical Essay

Since so much of the voluminous material relating to 1830 is only available in a foreign language, and abroad at that, or is flawed in some other way, as far as present-day British undergraduates are concerned there is little point in trying to provide anything in the way of a comprehensive bibliography or list of references. Indeed, as was suggested in the Introduction, the nature of the enterprise makes the use of notes rather gratuitous as well. As a consequence, what follows is a rigorously selective bibliography, divided into two parts. The first is a critical review of the best books in English which undergraduates may expect to find available in this country. The second part provides some indication of the range of sources on which the book is really based, for the guidance of anyone who wishes to take their study of 1830 further.

I A Basic Bibliography

As far as general discussions go perhaps the best is still that by F.B.Artz, *Reaction and Revolution* (New York: Harper & Row, 1963), even though it actually dates from the period of the centennial. W. Langer's volume in the same series, *Political and Social Upheaval* (New York: Harper & Row, 1969), though longer and more recent, is not always reliable and, in any case, does not deal with all the outbreaks of 1830 because of its anglo-centric starting-date. David Thomson's *Europe since Napoleon* (London: Longman, 1962) still has a lot to commend it as a broad textbook coverage, as indeed have even older works like A. W. Ward *et al.* (eds), *Cambridge Modern History*, Vol. X, *The Restoration* (Cambridge: Cambridge University Press, 1907), and W. Alison Philips, *Modern Europe 1815–1899* (Rivington, 1924). Much background infomation on a country-by-country basis can be found in Jean Sigmann's *1848* (London: Allen & Unwin, 1973), while Eric Hobsbawm's *The Age of Revolution* (London: Weidenfeld & Nicolson, 1962) sees things both more generally and from a vigorously left-wing point of view.

Some particular aspects are elucidated by S. Pollard, *Peaceful Conquest: The Industrialisation of Europe*(Oxford: Clarendon Press, 1981), and A. Sked (ed.), *Europe's Balance of Power, 1815–48* (London: Macmillan, 1979), along with a series of articles on diplomatic history by R. Billinger on Metternich, Germany and the war-scare – in *Central European History*, vol. IX, no. 3 (1976), pp. 203–19, and *Consortium on Revolutionary and Napoleonic Europe. Proceedings: 1978* (Athens, University of Georgia Press, 1980), pp. 174–85 – and A. Reinermann on Metternich, Italy and the crisis in *Central European History*, vol. X, no. 3 (1977), pp. 206-19. Finally, some insight into the historiography of the period is provided by the writer's 'Forgotten Revolutions' in *European Studies Review*, vol.VII, no.1 (1977), pp. 95–106, and G. Rudé, *Debate on Europe, 1815–48* (New York; Harper & Row, 1972), although the latter is not free from error where 1830 is concerned.

Turning to individual countries, the best *History of Portugal* is now that by A. Oliviera Marques (New York: Columbia University Press, 1976), although S.G. Payne, *A History of Spain and Portugal* (Madison, Wis.: University of Wisconsin

Press, 1973), has a few chapters on Portugal, along with more detailed treatment of Spain. Neither, however, provides a fully developed study of the Portuguese civil war or of the invasions of 1830. The literature on France in English, on the other hand, is immense and wide-ranging. The indispensable starting-point is D. H. Pinkney's *The French Revolution of 1830* (Princeton, NJ: Princeton University Press, 1972), but a number of aspects are usefully examined in J.H. Merriman (ed.), *1830 in France* (New York: Franklin Watts, 1976). Amongst the large periodical literature it is worth mentioning especially R. Price, 'Popular disturbances in the French provinces', *European Studies Review*, vol. I, no. 4 (1971), pp. 323–50, and E. L. Newman, 'The blouse and the frock coat', *Journal of Modern History*, vol. 46, no. 1 (1974), pp. 26–59, which throw new light on popular involvement in the Revolution as, from another point of view, does W. Sewell, *Work and Revolution in France* (Cambridge: Cambridge University Press, 1980).

On Belgium, E. H. Kossman, *The Low Countries* (Oxford: Clarendon Press, 1978), is fundamental for background, although its account of the actual rising is a trifle general. The diplomatic side of the revolt is covered well enough, thanks to J. A. Betley, *Belgium and Poland in International Relations* (The Hague: Mouton, 1960), and J. A. Helmreich, *Belgium and Europe* (The Hague: Mouton, 1976), but there is still an obvious domestic gap. The best account of the British Reform movement is that by M. Brock, *The Great Reform Act* (London: Hutchinson, 1973), while the rural protest is brilliantly analysed by G. Rudé and E. Hobsbawm in *Captain Swing* (Harmondsworth: Penguin, 1973); where the other nations of the British Isles are concerned, G. O'Tuathaigh, *Ireland before the Famine* (Dublin: Gill & Macmillan, 1972), provides a balanced and well-informed introduction which is not really matched for Scotland and Wales. However, W. Ferguson, *Scotland: 1689 to the Present* (Edinburgh: Oliver & Boyd, 1968), has something to offer on the former, and G. A. Williams, *The Merthyr Rising* (London: Croom Helm, 1978), is a *tour de force*, dealing with one incident in the latter.

For Germany the best introduction is provided by H. A. Schmitt, 'Revolution and revolts in the Germanies', *Consortium on Revolutionary Europe, 1977* (Athens, Ga: University of Georgia Press, 1978), pp. 54–66. A. Ramm, *Germany 1789–1919* (London: Methuen, 1967), offers an evocative if imprecise account, while H. Holborn, *A History of Modern Germany*, Vol. II (London: Eyre & Spottiswoode, 1969), is more detailed and stronger on the economic side. A good case-history is W. Carr's *Schleswig-Holstein* (Manchester: Manchester University Press, 1963), while the most recent contribution on the Nordic countries more generally is one of the best, in T. K. Derry, *Scandinavia* (London: Allen & Unwin, 1979). Where Poland is concerned, the fundamental account is that by R. F. Leslie, *Polish Politics and the Revolution of November 1830*, which has happily been reprinted recently (Westport, Conn.: Greenwood Press, 1969). With this and the equally impressive but more general surverys of P. S. Wandycz, *The Lands of Partitioned Poland* (Seattle, Wash: University of Washington Press, 1974), and N. Davies' *God's playground. A History of Poland*, Vol. II, *Since 1975* (Oxford: Clarendon Press, 1981), Poland is relatively well catered for. Another excellent book in the same series as Wandycz offers a convenient introduction to the Balkans: B. and C. Jelavich, *The Establishment of the Balkan National States 1804–1920* (Seattle, Wash.: University of Washington Press, 1977). Unfortunately, the Habsburg domains are not so well served, as C. A. Macartney's otherwise exhaustive study, *The Habsburg Empire* (London: Weidenfeld & Nicolson, 1971); has nothing to say about the imapct of 1830, so that reference must be made to the articles already mentioned or to histories of the various national groups. The important case of Greece is well covered by R. Clogg, *A Short History of Modern Greece* (Cambridge: Cambridge University Press, 1979). The best introduction to the Regeneration remains that by E. Bonjour, G. Potter and H. S. Offler, *A Short History of Switzerland,* which, although published by the Clarendon Press in 1952, is as new as some apparently more up-to-date studies, and has remained in print until quite recently. It is also more sophisticated than at first appears. A good deal of background information can also be winkled out of C. Hughes, *Switzerland* (London: Benn, 1976), but overall the coverage in English of Swiss history remains unsatisfactory for the moment. Nor are things much better where Italy in 1830 is concerned. G. F. H. Berkeley, *Italy in the Making,* Vol. I (Cambridge: Cambridge University Press, 1968), provides a brief account of events in the Papal States, although a rather dated one. And, while S. Woolf's *History of Italy, 1700–1860* (London: Methuen, 1979) is much fuller and more attuned to social questions, it is also much affected by the traditional nationalist stereotypes of 1831, as a comparison with M. S. Miller, 'Rivoluzioni Mancate – Italian revolutionary patterns', in *Consortium on Revolutionary Europe, 1977* (Athens, GA: University of Georgia Press, 1978), pp. 67–82, shows.

II Taking Things Further

The fact that so many general books are thus essential to such basic readings on 1830 is another reminder of the weaknesses of the historiography of the period. Not merely are most recent textbooks short on 1830, but only for France and Poland are there easily available monographs which deal with the actual risings. If one wants to take things further, then recourse must be had to foreign-language materials. Unfortunately, the archival sources are not always very rich, or very easy of access. Thus work on Belgium really demands that one uses the deposits in The Hague since, because an independent Belgian state did not emerge until after 1830, there cannot be much material on the revolt itself. The decentralised nature of the Italian, Swiss and German polities also multiplies the number of archives to be consulted, and, of course, some material on the last must be sought in East Germany, just as that for Poland will partially be found in Russia. No attempt was made to work systematically through such archival collections in the writing of the book, nor was much use made of the diplomatic correspondence of the time, although this obviously had much to say on the events of 1830. One hopes that, in the future, research will draw on these sources once the outlines of 1830 have become clearer.

However, soundings were made in the archives of the three main countries investigated in depth. Thus in Belgium some use was made of the Archives Générales du Royaume, the Archives de Etat à Namur and especially the Archives de la Ville de Bruxelles, where much use was made of the neglected papers on 'Evénements de police, 1829-32' and the 'Listes des étrangers arrivant à Bruxelles'. In Italy similar sampling took place in the Archivio di Stato in Parma,

Modena and Bologna where the 'Atti riservati di polizia' and similar deposits were consulted, along with the 'Manifesti Bolognese' in the Museo Civico in Bologna. In Switzerland the Bundesarchiv in Berne yielded interesting material – in the Vaticano series, for instance – although there was very little to be found in the Archivio Cantonale Ticinese. Things are much better for the Vaud, since not merely does the Bibliothèque Cantonale et Universitaire have a number of interesting manuscript memoirs, but also the Archives Cantonales Vaudoises is rich in government papers in its series K, notably K III 10 which contains the secret register of the Conseil d'Etat. Finally in France, where Pinkney has largely exhausted the possibilities of the Parisian archives where 1830 is concerned, some use was made of police papers in such departmental archives as the Indre, the Nièvre, the Oise and especially the Haute Marne, e.g. 61 M 14–16.

To a large extent, however, such archival research was mainly a means of supplementing the findings of printed and secondary sources. For the former, there are no worthwhile general collections of documents covering Europe as a whole, but the three test-case countries can show a reasonable range of such publications. In Belgium by far the most important is the extracts from Dutch government papers edited by H. T. Colenbrander as series X of *Gedenkstukken der Algemeene Geschiedenis Van Nederland*, Vols 1–4 ('S Gravenhaage: Nijhoff, 1919–21). Then C. Buffin's two volumes, *Documents inédits sur la Révolution Belge* (Brussels: Commission Royale d'Histoire, 1910) and *Mémoires et documents* (Brussels: Commission Royale d'Histoire, 1912), have a goodly number of personal reminiscences and insights into the revolutionary movement. The most recent general collection of material was provided by C. Terlinden, 'Documents inédits sur la révolution de 1830 à Bruxelles', *Bulletin de la Commission Royale d'Histoire*, vol. CXXV (1959), pp. 226–85, but such personal accounts of the fighting as Juan van Halen's *Les Quatre Journées* (Brussels, 1831) are still essential to an understanding of the Brussels events.

In the case of Italy, there is one absolutely essential collection of documents: L. Pasztor and P. Pirri (eds), *L'Archivio dei Governi Provisori* (Vatican: Biblioteca Apostolica Vaticana, 1956). This is not merely a history of the Bolognese revolution through government pronouncements, but the only source which enables us to understand the actual course of events in early February. It can be supplemented by the parliamentary reports from Bologna and Modena in G. Montalcini (ed.), *Le Assemblee del Risorgimento*, Vol. I (Rome: Tipografia della Camera dei Deputati, 1911), for official acts. The social and military side can be seen in the *Monitore Bolognese* (and similar publications elsewhere), the *Diari* of Carlo Rossi, ed. G. Canevazzi (Modena: Società Tipografia Modenese, 1932), and especially *La Cronaca de Francesco Rangone*, ed. G. Natali (Rome: Istituto per la storia del Risorgimento Italiano, 1936.) There are also some useful police sources, notably A. Sorbelli (ed.), *Libro dei Compromessi Politici* (Rome: Istituto per la storia del Risorgimento Italiano, 1935).

Materials for Switzerland obviously tend to be cantonal rather than federal in focus at this time. Probably the most significant source for the Ticino is the new edition of the *Epistolario Dalberti-Usteri* by G. Martinola (Bellinzona: Edizioni dello Stato, 1975), which provides a commentary from inside the government on the evolution of the crisis. However, Franscini's *Della Riforma della Costituzione Ticinese* is still needed to spell out the reformers' case, as the newspaper record is very incomplete thanks to the way the crisis evolved there. In the Vaud, on the other hand, the records of *La Gazette de Lausanne* and especially the more radical *Le Nouvellist Vaudois* are full and indispensable. One remarkably fresh insight into the crisis has recently been published by M. Steiner and A. Laserre in the shape of *La Correspondence de Henri Druey* (Lausanne: Bibliothèque Historique Vaudoise, 1974), although the many pamphlets published during the polemic on the alleged violence of the events of December, such as the anonymous *Causes immédiates des événements* (Lausanne, 1831), are still very useful, too. Finally, where France is concerned there are a number of collections of documents which can be consulted with advantage. Perhaps the best is B. de Sauvigny (ed.), *La Révolution de 1830* (Paris: Colin, 1970). And, of course, the number of memoirs and accounts of the risings published at the time is legion.

Even with such printed sources at our disposal there are still many gaps which can only be filled by reference to secondary works. There are so many of these, particularly in the local studies and periodicals in which the Continent happily abounds, like the *Bolletino Storica della Svizzera Italiana*, that there is no possibility of listing more than a fraction here. What follows, therefore, is a highly selective list of those works which have been most helpful in the writing of the book, whether through the provision of basic information or in suggesting lines of interpretation. It makes no claim whatsoever to be either an exhaustive or a definitive guide to what are the best books on the subject, or even to all those which helped in the writing of this study. It is just an indicative guide. Even so, it is fairly long and includes a number of items which are not easily accessible, notably the unpublished papers which were presented at conferences to celebrate the 150th anniversary of the revolutions in Bucharest, Leipzig and Warsaw, only the second of which may ever now be published though all deserve to be better known.

Amongst general studies there is a good deal of information in G. C. Gervinus, *Histoire du dix-neuvième siècle* (Paris, 1864–74), a classic work of German liberal historiography. The Société d'Histoire Moderne's centennial volume of essays is rather more disparate; *Etudes sur les mouvements libéraux et nationaux de 1830* (Paris: Rieder, 1932). The diplomatic and social sides of the events are helpfully explained by V. de Guichen, *La Révolution de Juillet et l'Europe* (Paris: Emile-Paul Fréres, 1917), and John Breuilly, 'Artisan economy, artisan values, artisan politics', an unpublished paper of June 1980. Finally, a quite detailed interpretation of the revolutions from a Marxist point of view – which, ironically, leaves Italy out of account – is provided by S. Soldani, 'Il 1830 in Europa: Dinamica e articolazioni di una crisi generale', *Studi Storici*, Vol. XIII, nos 1–2 (1972), pp. 34–92 and 338–72.

The literature available on Portugal and Spain is limited. The writings of H. Livermore, for instance *A New History of Portugal* (Cambridge: Cambridge University Press, 1966), helped a little for the former, while for the latter G. Hubbard, *Histoire contemporaine de l'Espagne*, Vol. I (Paris, 1869), and M. Nunez de Arenas, 'La Expedicion de Vera en 1830', in R. Marrast (ed.) *L'Espagne des lumières au romanticisme* (Paris: Centre de recherches de L'Institut d'Etudes Hispaniques, 1963), pp. 243–91, provided much needed detail. For France a good deal of help in understanding social protest came from A. Faure, 'Mouvements populaires et mouvements ouvriers', in *Le Mouvement social*, vol. 88 (1974), pp. 51–92, and from J. Tulard, *Paris et son administration* (Ville de Paris: Commission des Travaux Historiques, 1976), who documents the failure of the police to comprehend the changing pattern of working men's politics. The economic background is set out in P. Gonnet, 'Esquisse de la crise économique en France', *Revue d'histoire économique et sociale*, vol. XXXIII, no. 3 (1955), pp. 249–91. The best recent general survey is A. Jardin and A. J. Tudesq, *La France des notables* (Paris: Seuil, 1973); while amongst the many older ones that by L. Riballier, *1830* (Nouvelle Librarie Nationale, 1911), has proved most sane and stimulating.

When we turn to Belgium the field is dominated by Robert Demoulin both through his thesis, *Les Journées de Septembre* (Brussels: Université de Liège, 1938), and the shorter *tour d'horizon, La Révolution de 1830* (Brussels: La Renaissance du Livre, 1950). Unfortunately, he tends to stop the story short once the country had rallied to the capital in October 1830. The gap can partly be filled by much earlier works like A. de Wargny, *Esquisses historiques* (Brussels, 1830–1), C. White, *The Belgic Revolution* (London, 1835), and T. Juste, *La Révolution Belge* (The Hague, 1872). The question of social participation is examined vigorously from a Walloon socialist point of view by M. Bologne in writings beginning with the controversial *La Révolution prolétarienne de 1830* (Brussels: L'Eglantine, 1929) and, strangely imprecisely, by J. Rooney, 'The Brussels street fighter', in *Consortium on Revolutionary Europe, 1978* (Athens, Ga: University of George Press, 1980). Conversely, two papers – derived from Dutch originals – presented to the Bucharest conference of 1980– by Jean Gilissen on 'Les premières formes de gouvernement et d'administration de l'Etat Belge' (published in *Revue Belge d'histoire contemporaine*, vol. XII, no. 3 (1981), pp. 609–40) and Els Witte on 'Changes in the Belgian élite (published in *Acta Historiae Neerlandicae*, vol. XIII (1980), pp. 90–113) – a provisional study', were a revelation which brought a whole new dimension to the understanding of the revolutionary movement in Belgium and its social import. Much would be gained if more Dutch-language works were accessible to foreign readers, as is E. R. Hoffman, *Noord Brabant en de opstand van 1830* (Tilburg: Contact, 1974), pp. 255–8.

For Switzerland as a whole, C. Somerlatt, *Histoire des troubles qui ont agité la Suisse* (Zurich, 1834), and J. Dirauer, *Histoire de la Suisse*, Vol. V (Lausanne: Payot, 1919), are a mine of information, especially on German-speaking cantons, although this aspect can be developed by works such as W. Wettstein, *Die Regeneration des Kanton Zürich* (Zurich: Schulthess, 1906). The social background of the Regeneration has been analysed by the writer in 'Switzerland and the problem of the European revolutions', *Moriaie*, vol. 2 (Belfast: Ulster Polytechnic, 1977), pp.74–87. The federal level also shares attention with the most recent, if slightly traditional, account of Ticinese history, in C. Calgari and M. Agliati, *Storia della Svizzera* (Lugano: Ticino Nostra 1969). The details of the constitutional changes there are scrupulously detailed by B. Sauter, *Herkfunt und Entstehung der Tessiner Kantonsverfassung* (Zurich: Schulthess, 1972), and much light is thrown on the peculiar cultural and historiographical problems of the canton in a special number of *Scrinium*, ed. G. Cheda and A. Gaggioni (Locarno, 1976), but the detailed history of the events there is still being written. For French-speaking Switzerland the most convenient overall view is '1830 in the "Suisse Romande"', a paper submitted to the Bucharest conference by the writer. When it comes to the Vaud, although there has for long been no good general history, everything else has been even more put in the shade by the appearance of G. Arlettaz' magisterial *Libéralisme et société dans la Canton de Vaud, 1815–45* (Lausanne: Bibliothèque Historique Vaudoise, 1980). The same author's *Les*

Tendences libérales en Valais (Fribourg: Université de Fribourg, 1969) is equally full of insights on the nature of liberalism in general. Turning to northern Europe, the best accounts of the German revolts are in M. K. Wallenberger, 'German nationalism and the revolutions of 1830', an unpublished PhD thesis, Radcliffe College, Cambridge, Mass. (1964), and the nationalistic H. Treitschke, *History of Germany in the Nineteenth Century*, Vol. V (1919). Two recent East German texts, K. Obermann, *Deutschland 1815–49* (East Berlin: NEB Deutscher Verlag der Wissenschaften, 1976), and H. Bock, *Die Illusion der Freiheit* (East Berlin: Dietz, 1980), offer slightly contrasting Marxist views, the latter in a comparative framework which includes France. Scandinavia is much less well served, although B. Hovde, *The Scandinavian Countries, 1720–1865* (Ithaca, NY: Cornell University Press, 1948), does document the social basis of democracy there. On Britain, N. Gash, 'English Reform and French Revolution', in R. Pares and A. J. P. Taylor (eds), *Essays Presented to Sir Lewis Namier* (London: Macmillan, 1956), pp. 258–88, is the classic demonstration that news from France did not influence the elections of 1830, while A. Silver, 'Social and ideological bases of British élite reactions to domestic crisis', *Politics and Society*, vol. I, no. 3 (1971), pp. 179–201, and, more controversially, D. C. Moore in a series of articles including 'Concession or cure', *Historical Journal*, vol. IX, no. I (1966), pp. 39–59, offer two differing views of the nature of the politicians' response to the crisis. The possibility of revolution is canvassed by M. I. Thomis and P. Holt, *Threats of Revolution in Britain* (London: Macmillan, 1977).

Further east an interesting article which takes its claims to the limits is 0. Orlik, 'La Révolution française de 1830 dans la presse russe', *Revue d'histoire moderne et contemporaine*, vol. XVI, no.3 (1969), pp. 401–13. On Poland, W. Zajewski (ed.), *Powstanie Listopadowe* (Polish Academy of Sciences, 1981), is a detailed and thoughtful collective celebration for the 150th anniversary of the November Rising. One of its essential motors is analysed by S. Kieniewicz, 'The revolutionary nobleman', in J. Pelenski (ed.), *The American and European Revolutions 1776–1848* (Iowa City; University of Iowa Press, 1980),pp. 268–86. A somewhat slighter but still helpful account of the revolt as a whole can be found in T. Lepkowski, *Powstanie Listopadowe* (Warsaw: Wiezdz Powszeckna, 1955). Of early writings, that by the radical Senator R. Soltyk, *La Pologne* (Pagnerre, 1833), was particularly helpful. The classic modern work on Serbia at this time is M. Petrovich, *A History of Modern Serbia* (New York: Harcourt, Brace, Jovanovich, 1976), while something on two other fairly central countries is provided by M. Constanescu *et al.*, *Histoire de la Roumanie* (Toulouse: Privat, 1970), and I. Barta *et al.*, *Histoire de l'Hongroie* (Roanne: Horvath, 1974). Further detail on Greece in the period can be found in D. Dakin, *The Greek Struggle for Independence* (London: Batsford, 1973). For the rest of the region, S. J. and E. K. Shaw, *Reform, Revolution and Republic: the Rise of Modern Turkey* (Cambridge University Press, 1977), and V. L. Tapié *Monarchie et peuples de Danube* (Paris:, Fayard, 1969), are a good start to an understanding of the multinational empires there.

The literature on Italy is as large as anywhere else, probably even more so. Of many modern general histories that by C. Spellanzan, *Storia del Risorgimento e dell'unità d'Italia*, Vol. II (Milan: Rizzoli, 1936),is indispensable for its detail at least. More convincing interpretations can be found in E. Morelli, *Note sul*

Biennio 1831–2 (Florence: Sansoni, 1958), and an unpublished paper presented to the Bucharest conference by M. S. Miller: 'The revolutions of 1831 in Italy, a re-examination'. For Parma, O. Masnovo's many writings including *I Moti del 31 a Parma* (Turin: Società Editrice Internazionale, 1925), and C. Pecorella, *I Governi Provisorii Parmense* (Parma: Battei, 1959), are sound runners in a small field. For Modena the entry is much greater, including many nineteenth-century works, often of somewhat dubious value. More recently, P. Trivia *et al.*, *Aspetti e Problema del Risorgimento a Modena* (Modena: Mucchi, 1963), have provided useful background, and P. Bernadelle, 'Gli inizi dei moti del 1831 a Modena,' *Rassegna Storica del Risorgimento*, vol. LV, no. 4 (1968), pp. 419–38, has widened the debate on the Menotti *coup* attempt. For Bologna, D. Lanciotti, *Il Governo delle Provincie Unite Italiane* (Rome: Guanella, 1940), is a scholarly and unjustly neglected study of the civilian side of the revolution there, rather as P. Zama, *La Marcia su Roma* (Faenza: Fratelli Lega, 1976), in a slightly vaguer way, is for the military side. L. Dal Pane's *Economia e Società a Bologna* (Bologna: Zanichelli, 1969) is a fundamental source for the social roots of the risings.

Finally, a series of books on the nature of revolution has helped to throw the very diverse events described in the foregoing chapters into new contexts. This is true of C. Brinton, *The Anatomy of Revolution* (London: Cape, 1953), G. Kelly and C. W. Brown (eds), *Struggles in the State* (New York: Wiley, 1970), M. Malia, *Comprendre la Révolution Russe* (Paris: Seuil, 1980), and J. R. Gillis, 'Political decay and the European revolutions, 1789–1848', *World Politics*, vol. XXII, no. 3 (1970), pp. 344–70. Yet while a study like that of L. Stone, *The Causes of the English Revolution* (London: Routledge, 1972), helps to define causations, and – turning more specifically to 1830 – those by E. Labrousse, 'Comment naissent les révolutions', in R. Fawtier *et al.*, *Congrès historique du Centenaire de 1848* (Paris: PUF, 1949), pp. 1–29, and J. Rule and Charles Tilly, 'The revolution of 1830 and the unnatural history of revolution', *Journal of Social Issues*, vol. XXXVIII, no. I (1972), pp. 49–76 (a version of which also appears in Merriman, cited above) have much to say on causation and process, it is not clear that using models of revolution can take us much further, even if we do not accept all the criticisms listed in J. Mears *et al.*, 'Multi-disciplinary approaches to the study of revolution', *Consortium on Revolutionary Europe, 1975* (Athens, Ga: University of Georgia Press, 1978), pp. 149–70, as the writer has argued in an as yet unpublished paper on 'Models of revolutions and the European revolutions of 1830' presented to a colloquium held in the University of Leipzig in 1980. We may be better advised simply to deepen our understanding by avoiding such attempts to create a stasiology and using both the insights of the social sciences in general, as has been done by R. Grew (ed.), *Crises of Political Development in Europe and the United States* (Princeton, NJ: Princeton University Press, 1978), and by further research, into the many materials which it has not been possible to indicate here.

Index

DATE DUE